Learning with Artificial Worlds

Learning with Artificial Worlds
Computer-based Modelling in the Curriculum

Edited by

Harvey Mellar
Joan Bliss
Richard Boohan
Jon Ogborn
Chris Tompsett

 The Falmer Press

(A member of the Taylor & Francis Group)
London • Washington, D.C.

UK   The Falmer Press, 4 John Street, London WC1N 2ET
USA   The Falmer Press, Taylor & Francis Inc., 1900 Frost Road, Suite 101,
        Bristol, PA 19007

© H. Mellar, J. Bliss, R. Boohan, J. Ogborn, and C. Tompsett, 1994

First published in 1994

A catalogue record for this book is available from the British Library

Library of Congress Cataloging-in-Publication Data are available on request

ISBN 0 7507 0312 1 (cased)
ISBN 0 7507 0313 X (paper)

Jacket design by Caroline Archer

Typeset in 10/12pt Caledonia and printed by
Graphicraft Typesetters Ltd., Hong Kong.

Contents

Contents

Acknowledgments

The contributors whose work was part of the Tools for Exploratory Learning Programme wish to acknowledge the support of the ESRC, and of Professor Bob Lewis as Coordinator of the ESRC Information Technology in Education Initiative of which this programme was a part.

The contributors whose work was part of the Computer Based Modelling across the Curriculum Project wish to acknowledge the support of the TVEI UNIT within the Employment Department.

The contributors whose work arises from the Modus Project wish to acknowledge the dedicated support of British Gas, Longman Group, Research Machines and The National Council for Educational Technology; and their own institutions King's College London and Hertfordshire County Council.

The contributors whose work arises from the Worldmaker project wish to acknowledge the support of the Software Development Partnership Scheme (DES/ National Council for Educational Technology).

All contributors wish to acknowledge the great debt they owe to the many LEAs, schools, teachers and children with whom they have worked in preparing the work reported here.

Lastly, we would like to acknowledge the support of the whole of the London Mental Models Group who have been responsible for helping us to refine and clarify our ideas over the years.

Chapter 1

Introduction: Modelling and Education

Harvey Mellar and Joan Bliss

Modelling and Education

This book is about modelling in education. It is about providing children with computer tools to enable them to create their own worlds, to express their own representations of their world, and also to explore other people's representations. It is about learning with artificial worlds.

The use of modelling in education always keeps in the forefront of our attention the humanly (both individually and socially) constructed nature of our ideas about the world. It tries to give children as much freedom as possible to manipulate those ideas, both in order to help them understand the world better, but also in order to lead them to an understanding of the nature of the task of theory building itself.

The majority of the contributors to this book are members of the London Mental Models Group (see below for a fuller description of this group). Between the years 1989 and 1992 this group was engaged in a major research programme, the Tools for Exploratory Learning Programme, examining the nature of children's reasoning when they are working with modelling tools, and it is this research that forms the basis for this book. Other members of the London Mental Models Group, and other friends outside the group, were simultaneously working on aspects of modelling within education. In this book we have put together contributions from these colleagues working within their own projects around a structure derived from the research design of the Tools for Exploratory Learning Programme. This book therefore reports on some five years of very exciting and diverse research activities, and aims to begin to create some form of synthesis of this work.

In the course of the book we will examine a large number of issues about bringing computer-based modelling into education. The book does not constitute an elementary introduction to the area, for that the reader should turn to materials such as the *Modelling Pack* (Computer Based Modelling across the Curriculum, 1992). Rather this book attempts to take consideration of computer-based modelling a step further. The book has much to say to the classroom teacher who has used some modelling, and now wishes to seriously consider the role of modelling within their curriculum. It also has important messages for software

1

designers about the kinds of software that children can use to express their ideas, and it has much to say to psychologists and cognitive scientists about the kinds of reasoning children can use when working with symbolic systems embedded within a computer.

The focus of this book is therefore quite deliberately forward-looking; it is about where we should be going with modelling in education. But the book is not just of theoretical interest, it is not simply about where we should be going, but where we know we can actually go over the next five years. It reports on experimental studies, on software development, on classroom implementations, and curriculum development, and reports on the problems we have found as well as the exciting opportunities we have discovered.

The remainder of this present chapter describes the London Mental Models Group, provides an overview of the Tools for Exploratory Learning Programme and finally outlines the structure of the remainder of the book.

The London Mental Models Group

The London Mental Models Group was established in the Spring of 1986 by Joan Bliss. The group is multidisciplinary: its members are drawn from the fields of science, mathematics and history education, linguistics, cognitive psychology, educational computing, expert systems and artificial intelligence. The group is also multi-institutional, with members from a number of institutions: King's College, Institute of Education, Imperial College, Kingston University and the University of Surrey. The membership of the group has generally been between twenty and thirty people.

Our area of common concern is that of modelling cognition, with mental models as one approach to this theme. Within this specific research focus there is a more general direction concerned with the educational issues of learning and teaching in an information-technology setting. The group's purpose is to examine how ideas from a range of disciplines such as cognitive psychology, linguistics, expert systems and artificial intelligence can inform these issues. The twice-termly meetings of the London Mental Models' Group provide a forum for discussion and exchange of ideas.

The group as a whole has been awarded a number of grants (independent of those awarded to individuals as part of their respective institutions):

- Tools for Exploratory Learning Programme within the ESRC's Research Initiative on Information Technology in Education.
- An award from the EEC for the Basic Research Actions ESPRIT Programme for a Working Group together with partners in Paris at University of Paris Sud, Orsay and the Institute of Informatics, Royal Danish School of Education Studies. The underlying theme of this work was the nature and form of children and teachers' explanations and the gap between how we understand these and how machines can represent them.

- In collaboration with a number of other centres the group has recently been awarded funding to organize an ESRC seminar series entitled 'Internal and External Forms of Representation', aimed at generating research and publications in this area.

The Tools for Exploratory Learning Programme

The Tools for Exploratory Learning Programme set out to investigate how pupils (aged 11 to 14) reasoned with computational modelling tools. We posed two underlying questions about modelling:

- can working with modelling tools which contain models of a domain facilitate pupils' reasoning in that domain?
- are learners helped to reason about a domain by using modelling tools to express their own ideas about that domain?

The programme made two major innovatory distinctions: (i) the distinction between two different types of learning activities: expressive and exploratory; (ii) the distinction between three different types of reasoning with modelling, quantitative, qualitative and semi-quantitative. Whilst quantitative and qualitative modelling were already well established, semi-quantitative modelling was a novel concept (for a full discussion of semi-quantitative modelling see Chapter 14).

Exploratory and Expressive Modes of Learning Activity

In our research we set out to look at two different types of possible learning activities:

- exploratory learning activities which involve the learner in exploring ideas about a topic presented by someone else (teacher or expert), where these ideas may often be quite different from the learner's ideas.
- expressive learning activities which involve learners in expressing their own ideas.

This is a more general distinction than the distinction that is often drawn between tools designed to allow learners to explore a given model (this includes many simulations and some microworlds), and tools designed to permit learners to construct their own models (examples of which include LOGO and simplified versions of PROLOG together with spreadsheets, and modelling systems). We feel that this distinction between tools is too limited and that many tools can be used in both modes of learning activity.

Tools used in the expressive mode enable pupils to externalize some aspects of their ideas. Once they can formulate these ideas into a model they can experiment with, and reflect on, these ideas and on how well the model represents them. The exploratory mode is powerful in different ways. Taking a basic model and exploring it, can produce startling and unexpected results and so learners are led to confront another's view of a problem. In the former mode learners are modelling their own assumptions while in the latter they are interacting with models based on the assumptions of others, but bringing their own ideas to interact with those provided in the model. Thus exploratory and expressive modes are different and complementary ways of using a given tool, not differences in kind between tools.

Reasoning with Modelling Tools

We aimed to investigate three kinds of modelling, and so of reasoning:

- quantitative;
- qualitative;
- semi-quantitative.

Quantitative modelling is familiar from science and mathematics. Qualitative modelling uses qualitative rules or structures, as in decision games, expert systems or models of grammars. The idea of semi-quantitative modelling is new: it involves thinking about systems in terms of rough and ready sizes of things and directions of change. When we began the research no suitable practical semi-quantitative tool existed and so a tool (*IQON*) was developed for making models through direct manipulation in which no mathematics is needed to create the relationships between variables. This program is described further in Chapter 15.

For quantitative reasoning tasks we developed a prototype tool *Q-MOD* which allows models to be built using simple algebraic relations between variables. This is further described in Chapter 8. Finally for qualitative reasoning tasks we designed the tool *Explore your options* which provides for building a tree-like structure out of situations and actions. The structure is drawn graphically on the screen and the system both maintains the structure of situations and actions, and displays situations and actions as they are selected. More details of this are given in Chapter 17.

In order better to compare expressive and exploratory activity we chose to use the same tool in both modes rather than to use different kinds of tool for each mode. For the exploratory mode this meant filling the tools with suitable models and providing suitable problems and activities to go with them, and for the expressive mode it meant giving pupils the empty tool together with materials and tasks challenging them to construct models. In both cases we were primarily concerned with similarities and differences in the kinds of thinking these task–tool combinations evoked in the two modes.

Topics

We selected three cross-curricular topics: (i) fitness and diet; (ii) shops and profits; (iii) traffic and congestion. It was thought that pupils would be familiar with these

Chapter 2

Overview: The Nature of Modelling

Jon Ogborn

What Is Modelling?

In the fashion industry, a model is a person who is used to wear clothes so that others who might buy the clothes can imagine themselves wearing them. Models are selected as possessing some idealized human characteristics; these characteristics change from time to time but are always ideals, such as slimness, height, skin colour, insouciance, etc. Also, fashion models and modelling themselves become an artificial world of their own with which some of us become fascinated on their own terms, perhaps celebrating the model who throws tantrums or who, 'Won't get out of bed for less than £10,000'.

All modelling activities have the first two aspects in common: using one thing (a model) in order to think about another, and choosing for the model something more or less idealized or simplified. Many of them share the third aspect, that the modelling resources exert their own fascination, and that modelling activity becomes something pursued for its own sake, acquiring its own history and social context.

Children naturally and spontaneously do a lot of modelling. We adults provide them with toys, like dolls, toy cars and trains, which give them ways of thinking about activities in the grown-up world. Whether we give them toys or not, they exploit the materials around them — sticks, stones, mud and sand, water, and our adult cast-offs such as old boxes, worn-out clothes, and broken furnishings, to play out imitation dramas of adult life which at the same time are activities played out for their own sake. Play, of course, is not 'mere play'. Through play the child (and the adult) can learn about what can and cannot be done, about how things could work, and about how to use playful tools for thinking.

Many games, from chess to Monopoly, look like highly simplified idealized versions of real-world (that is, the 'not-playtime' world) activities, carried out mainly for their own sake rather than being used to think about those real-world activities. Play has taken over from representation, and becomes something to be taken seriously as a 'real world' activity, though we tend to treat (say) chess as more serious than Monopoly, with (say) poker falling somewhere in between. Other physical games, from football and tennis to horse racing, fall into the same pattern: activities which look like idealized and artificial mirrors of certain non-game-like activities (including wars), which themselves have become things to be done on their own terms.

All these modelling activities share the same three features mentioned before:

- one thing used in place of another;
- idealization and simplification of modelling resources;
- a tendency to play with the modelling resources for their own sake.

This introduction to modelling may seem, so far, not to be wholly serious. What do the fashion industry, board games and babies playing in sand pits have to do with economists modelling the economy, doctors modelling epidemics or physicists modelling the evolution of the early Universe? What do they have to do with mathematicians studying geometry in N dimensions, studying the fractal forms of mountain ranges or coastlines, or investigating what can be proved from given logical axioms?

In fact, the parallels are substantial and wholly serious. The actual world in which we live is by no means easily predictable and understandable; we often know little of how things work or of what they can or will do. One human strategy to deal with this is to construct artificial worlds made of entities whose behaviour we do know because we decided what it should be. This does not at all mean that we know in advance everything which can happen in such an artificial world, even though we 'know everything' which went into it. Artificial worlds give us many surprises. Examples are many: new lines of attack or defence are continually being discovered in chess, even though the rules are fixed; new behaviours of simple equations such as fractals and chaos are found, even though the rules remain just those of simple arithmetic and algebra; models of particles moving and exerting forces on each other newly illuminate such things as the formation of galaxies in the Universe or the formation of crystals from a solution, even though all that goes into these models are well-known pushes and pulls between moving particles.

Pure mathematics can be understood as serious play with artificial worlds. Geometers make artificial worlds from idealized objects such as points, lines, triangles and circles, originally abstracted from the activity of measuring out land, and investigate what can be established about necessary relations between them, given the rules which fix their behaviour and nature. Surprises await, even in so 'obvious' a world, one being that one cannot prove that parallel lines never meet, and must instead assume that this is so (or dare not to, leading to the discovery of non-Euclidean geometry). Similar play with artificial worlds of logic designed to capture idealized aspects of what is involved in reasoning has led to proving that there must be truths which any one such system cannot capture (Gödel's theorem, Turing's theorem). Play with equations which specify absolutely deterministically how something will evolve with time, shows that some of them have solutions so sensitive to the initial starting point that the outcome is completely unpredictable more than a very few steps ahead, despite being fully determined.

It is sometimes complained that pure mathematicians care nothing for what their results may mean, that is to say, that they do not care what artificial worlds representing which aspects of the real world might be built using the resources with which they play. They are accused of merely playing games with meaning-less symbols. This very accusation is precisely what the pure mathematician is proudest of, namely that results will be valid no matter to what they are applied. And in this way deep connections between seemingly totally different kinds of things have been uncovered, for example between logical combinations of sen-tences and the behaviour of electric circuits containing switches, between the decoding of cryptograms and sources of complexity in computer programs, or between the onset of turbulent flow in a river and the sudden freezing of water when the temperature is low enough. Any one artificial world may be able to be used to model a very wide range of totally different kinds of phenomenon. An example is the cell automaton which allows games in which a cell in a large grid of cells changes state according only to the previous state of itself and its neighbours, a game format which has been used to model amongst many other things the growth of crystals, the flow of oil in cracked rocks, the growth of forest fires, the magnetism of materials, and the basis of self-replication. Thus pure mathematicians take idealized modelling resources, and treat them as pure objects of play, trying to find out what can or cannot be done within given rules of a given game.

All this leads to looking at modelling in the following way. We humans cannot understand many aspects of the world as it is, because even if we can carefully experiment on it (which we often cannot) we never quite know what else may be going on which we ought to have allowed for but about which we as yet know nothing. So we build simplified, idealized, stripped-down models in which we do know everything about the components of the model, simply because we decided what they were to be. Despite their artificiality, simplicity, and fully predetermined nature, such models have given us many surprises and have led to new and powerful insights. To make such models humans have invented a wide variety of resources, including logic, algebra and geometry, as well as a variety of simplified physical models ranging from architectural models to wind tunnels, and games ranging from dice throwing to war games. These artificial worlds and the resources used to build them have turned out to have a fascination all of their own, leading to 'pure' game playing with them which has itself turned up new resources and insights about what can and cannot be done with a given kind of artificial world. Modelling is thinking about one thing in terms of simpler artificial things; Mathematics is thinking about these simple artificial things, in-cluding inventing new ones.

Purpose of this Section

The aim of this section of the book 'The Nature of Modelling' is to establish a framework of different perspectives from which modelling needs to be understood. The chapters in it develop a number of perspectives, all rather different from one another, which contribute to this goal.

It is not the purpose of this section to give a definitive or complete picture of modelling. Rather, the idea is to look at modelling in a number of ways which complement one another. Other sections of the book take up and develop themes only touched on here, so this section may be seen as setting an agenda for the rest of the book, and as introducing ideas and terms which will be useful in reflecting about the other contributions to the book.

Contents of this Section

In Chapter 3 'Models, their Makers, Uses and Problems' Jon Ogborn and Harvey Mellar deliberately stay clear of the educational issues which suffuse the rest of the book. The chapter is concerned with modelling as it appears in the world away from education (which some are tempted to call the 'real' world), in order that later accounts of modelling in educational settings may be seen against a background in which models serve other purposes, which affect every citizen and every scientist.

As a way of appreciating the variety of kinds of modelling which exist, the chapter begins by describing a number of very different examples, beginning with weather forecasting. This leads to an analysis of some of the problems of making models, some of them very fundamental, to the point of casting doubt on the reasonableness of making models of some kinds of situation.

The chapter then turns to the ways in which models may be used, for good or ill, in the political, economic and social context in which they exist. The delight which making a model may give its maker is, sometimes, overshadowed by the inappropriate uses which its technical expertise may be called on to serve.

Chapter 4 by Joan Bliss, looks at modelling from the point of view of the psychology of the learner using a model or modelling program. Entitled 'From Mental Models to Modelling' it raises a number of matters of fundamental importance. It traces some of the subtle connections between models people may have in their minds, themselves sometimes the subject of computational models of cognitive processes, and computational models which they explore or which they may themselves create using some appropriate computational system.

Crucial to this chapter are the ideas of internalization and externalization. That people have some internalized models of the world which guide their thinking is hardly in dispute, even if describing them is difficult. How people internalize or construct these models, starting from infancy, is the subject of fundamental psychological argument. The complementary process of externalization concerns how people might express their ideas in some external medium, which may be a computer modelling system but may just as well be words or a picture, and in doing so partially work out what their ideas 'really were'. Thus the difficult issues of language and thought, and the role of others in helping us form our ideas, cannot be avoided.

As with economic forecasting, some important and interesting 'variables' are hard to quantify sensibly. How might 'school performance' be indicated? What, if anything, is a good measure of children's ability? The existence of a wide range of sophisticated statistical modelling tools increases the pressure to define and quantify, even when there are arguments that there is no sensible way of doing so.

Different statistical models naturally give different answers, and it may be a matter of judgment which to use. The arguments about which method to employ are often difficult and technical, further undermining ordinary people's faith in the value of the results. Statistical models necessarily have to model random error, judging the reality of seeming differences against the estimated size of such error, and in doing so it is easy to draw false conclusions.

Despite all this, statistics provides a body of theory and practice, and a wide range of sophisticated tools to use. Statistical models continue to contribute both to our understanding of the world and to our management of affairs, including trying to determine our genetic relationship to other species and telling manufacturers what kinds of goods various people prefer.

Engineering Models

The concept of engineering modelling is simple, but its practice is complex and very technical. The general idea is to predict the behaviour of material artefacts one is designing. Thus one might design a possible bridge structure, see how it would behave, modify the design as a result, and repeat until the predicted performance is satisfactory. For this process to work the model must correspond adequately with the real thing. But of course to get a model to correspond in this way may mean making it very complex.

In fact, the relation between artefact and model is a bit subtler than this. We do not know how to model just any engineering artefact anyone can propose, so the pressure is on the designer to choose a design which can already be modelled. The Sydney Opera House was built only when the consulting engineers found a way to modify the shapes of the roof shells drawn by the architect to ones that were amenable to models for stress calculation. They — but not the architect — thought they had not departed too far from the roof's intended aesthetic form. We make what we can model, not model what we fancy making. A good reason for designers to use standard designs is that these classes of design have previously been exhaustively modelled and tested.

Another subtlety is the influence of modelling on how near the limits of possibility people will go. Traditional designs, built using experience and intuition, normally have very large safety factors built in. Old stone bridges built to carry people and horses now carry cars and lorries safely. But the wish to do something new continually drives people nearer the limits of the possible. The development of the gothic cathedral is an example, building large, impressive, airy structures with large glass windows and slender pillars. Flying buttresses were invented as a solution to keeping the walls from falling outwards, but many a cathedral collapsed while these experiments were tried.

In aircraft guidance systems, modelling has been used to stretch the limits of the possible. A computational model is used to calculate what the aircraft will do next, and take corrective action. Aircraft now land on automatic pilot in thick fog or cloud. More remarkably, the new generation of fighter aircraft are now actually designed to be impossible to fly 'by hand'. An aircraft with a normal tail-plane is inherently stable, in that a small change in direction generates forces opposing that change. But this makes such aircraft difficult to force into tight turns. The alternative is to put small wings at the nose. This is inherently unstable, since a small change in direction tends to amplify itself (try throwing a paper dart backwards). The small wings at the nose have to be continually and rapidly adjusted, and this is too demanding a task for a human pilot. Thus the existence of computer models for aircraft guidance has itself generated a new design of aircraft, which is much more manœuvrable but at the same time relies totally for its safety on the correctness of a model.

This makes the problem of what a model does in circumstances for which it was not designed or which were not foreseen much more problematic. In the very nature of a model, it is a restricted and simplified representation of reality, and so is necessarily always open to surprise. In the above example, a surprise can kill.

Models for Lack of Data

A 'standard story' about models is that a model should accurately reflect known data about some aspect of reality, and that if it does not, it should be modified until it does. But some uses of models are in areas where we have inadequate or even no data.

We have limited data about the interior of the Sun, and no chance of doing experiments on it. So solar astronomers use a computer model. This model predicts a rate of arrival at the Earth of particles called neutrinos which is about three times larger than current observations suggest. Nobody at the time of writing knows whether the model is wrong, whether the experiments are wrong, or whether neither are wrong and something else is going on. Of course such a model can be evaluated to some degree. It should correctly describe Nature's alternative Sun designs, in the form of other stars, getting for example the relation between their brightness and their mass correct. It should use processes which are known to occur in other experiments, not just invent them *ad hoc*.

An extreme example of modelling with very little data involves models of the evolution of the early Universe. Such models are built on theory much of which is speculative. Only very few such models can reproduce even simple large-scale features of the Universe, such as the degree of clumping of matter into galaxies or the very uniform distribution of background radiation. Thus these simple features set very narrow limits on any acceptable model. Models are here being used to cross-check one another, not to be compared in detail with data.

Models Make New Realities

It is not always the case that one starts with some aspect of reality and constructs a model to help understand it.

One type of model which has itself generated new ways of seeing reality is the cell automaton. Von Neumann's idea was an abstract one, of an array of small simple computing elements interacting with their neighbours. Given this concept, people began to think what they might model with it, rather than drawing on it to model what they already saw as problems. This led to the invention of the class of 'percolation' problems, in which mixtures of types of material are investigated to see if material of one kind is connected throughout or whether it exists as 'islands' in a 'sea' of the other types. The idea has been applied to the percolation of oil through rocks, and to the insulating properties of mixtures of conductor and insulator, as well as to electrical and other networks.

It turned out that cell automata are also related to problems to do with fractal shapes, that is, shapes all of whose parts are in some way the 'same' shape as the whole and as each other, just as a branch of a tree is much the same shape as the whole tree. This has led to ways of modelling what nobody had thought of modelling before, such as the form of natural landscapes. Computer-generated movies now often use such models.

Here then are cases where the existence of new kinds of model drew attention to aspects of reality, which although they had always been there, had not previously been thought of as things to be understood. The movement was from model to reality. And the models provided new concepts, such as 'fractal dimension', with which to make sense of reality.

Logical and Symbolic Models

Logical or symbolic models have been a concern of Artificial Intelligence (AI) since its earliest days, for example to create models of reasoning, initially about logical puzzles. To solve such puzzles, programs analysed goals and starting points, using rules for getting from one 'position' in a puzzle to another.

Production systems, used mainly in psychological research, model reasoning as taking place in a small 'working memory' which triggers knowledge in the form of 'if-then' rules stored in long-term semantic memory. By contrast, work on expert systems has concentrated on power and practicality. A considerable number of commercial expert system shells have been produced, and in the 1980s these were held to have great promise for commercial purposes, replacing expensive and scarce experts by systems which provided their expertise on tap. Amongst successes claimed are a system built by DEC for configuring their mainframe computers, together with medical diagnosis and ore prospecting systems widely and repeatedly cited in the literature.

Recently an alternative way of looking at the computation of logical or symbolic problems, namely connectionism, has gained popularity. Connectionist machines function as interconnected nets of artificial 'neurons', with their 'knowledge' being distributed across the weights of the 'synapses' linking 'neurons'. The 'solution' of a problem becomes the finding of a stable state of the net, with certain output 'neurons' firing. There is no program and no logical reasoning.

The above account does not reflect the passion with which the Artificial Intelligence effort to model or to surpass human cognition has been disputed. Supporters point out that when a machine achieves a cognitive task, it is unfairly declared not to count as cognition after all, since it is clearly mechanical and not human. They also argue that no alternative clear-cut account of cognition is on offer. What else, they ask, can the brain be but a symbol-processing machine?

Its detractors see AI as a de-humanizing activity which cannot in principle capture what is important about cognition. They also point to the unreasonableness of some of the very large claims made for the potential of AI. An example is full natural-language translation, promised in the early days as just around the corner, yet proving in practice to be extraordinarily difficult to achieve.

Morals About Modelling

Computational models are not all sophisticated things used for special and difficult purposes. Some, like spreadsheet business models are everyday bread-and-butter tools, no more remarkable than a word processor, which can and should be taken for granted as part of everyday life.

Much modelling is about predicting possible futures, to suggest actions we can take now to avoid undesirable outcomes and encourage desirable ones. They are what part of the human brain is for: namely, thinking ahead a bit.

Because the future often arrives sooner than we can imagine it, models help most when they predict quickly, that is, ahead of time. The power of the computer to compute rapidly is here of the essence. This is true for the businessman saving time and money by having a few hundred calculations done in a few seconds, but it is even more true of weather forecasting with perhaps billions of calculations being done in a few hours, or the aircraft guidance system working fast enough to correct an error before it happens.

If we are using a model to know better how to act so as to influence the future, we need to think especially clearly. Are we ourselves and our possible actions which may influence the future, needed as part of a model? In the economic sphere there is the special problem that the existence of a prediction may influence the very future the model is predicting. Given that such models are part of a system of power and influence, these aspects give special cause for concern.

Computational models can help us resolve some complex questions, but by no means all. Where data and relationships are clear cut, but are too extensive and complex for our minds to manage, they are at their best. Where complexity arises from an uncertainty as to how to analyse the problem at all, models may be at best suggestive. But computational models have also taught us that complexity itself is more complicated than we had thought. Very simple models can generate very complex and unpredictable behaviour. Simplicity is not the same as determinism.

A model may be more or less all we know about some aspects of reality. Where we cannot get at reality on any human scale of space or time, all that we may have is a model. That model should fit whatever else we know or believe. But by modelling reality in some particular way, it may point to new things to look for. Thus models guide new thinking as much as they solve old problems.

Thus models help construct reality as well as to dissect it. They may be the spectacles through which we look at reality. The fashionable modern examples are chaos and fractals, but we should not forget that when Newton and Leibniz invented the calculus they invented a whole new way of modelling the world which has dominated much of our vision ever since.

Models: Their Problems

The complex ways in which modelling enters into our everyday lives have begun to be expressed in popular culture. In P.D. James' crime novel *Devices and Desires* the discovery of the incorrectness of some of the assumptions made in generating a mathematical model associated with a nuclear power station becomes a cause for murder, as the murderer attempts to delay the publication of the discovery.

What then are the potential problems with modelling? There seem to be three broad sets of problems:

- modelling can be done more or less badly, so much so that it can become dangerous;
- the modelling of situations involving human choice raises all sort of difficulties that do not arise in modelling the behaviour of inanimate objects;
- models once created may be used in dubious ways.

It is worth reminding ourselves that there are situations in which modelling has been of no help or is just irrelevant. Arguments within geography about the place of modelling (see MacMillan, 1989) point this up. Geographers note that modelling has had successes in areas such as journey-to-work, spread of epidemics, and atmospheric dispersion of pollutants, but has failed to help in looking at the sudden explosion of Third-World debt in the 1970s, or at the rise of geopolitical tensions. Other geographers see their subject as to do with personal and aesthetic appreciation, a concentration on the idiosyncratic rather than the generalizable, an acceptance of a variety of perspectives, and an examination of values, conflicts and beliefs. For them, modelling is simply irrelevant.

Also, human purposes change over time. An example is in urban planning (Batty, 1989). Urban planning models such as those for transportation were developed in the boom years of the 1950s and 1960s in a specific social welfare policy context. By the late 1970s the whole policy context had changed and there was a widespread disillusion with large-scale planning (and hence modelling).

Strategic planning of growth gave way to the tactical management of decay; public interest gave way to private competition. The original function of the planning models became irrelevant.

Ill-founded Modelling

Modelling may be inadequately done because of restraints placed on the modeller. If a fixed short time is allocated to modelling (say) traffic flow, the resultant models may ignore crucial variables which it was judged too costly in time to incorporate.

More fundamentally, Boos-Bavnbek (Boos-Bavnbek, 1991; Boos-Bavnbek and Pate, 1989) argues that there are problems in the use of modelling that arise from a confusion between different types of models and the grounds we have for believing in them. While some models can be checked for consistency against a theory (e.g., Newtonian mechanics), many (for example economic models or risk analysis models) are based on purely *ad hoc* assumptions, the only check on them being against empirical observation. It is important that the two types of models be distinguished, since the 'mathematical respectability' of the one is often unwarrantedly transferred to the other.

Models based on good theory can compensate for lack of data, and models based on broad evidence can compensate for lack of theory, but models alone can hardly compensate for the lack of both. However we are now seeing an increasing use of models in highly complex situations where we have neither theory nor data (e.g., global military strategy).

Effective models can be constructed for situations which are ill-understood, for example heuristic models which improve the chances of finding underground water. These models reduce the number of wasted drillings, and the consequences of their (fairly frequent) failures are acceptable. But if the same model were used to identify safe underground depositories for toxic waste, then the consequences of failure could be catastrophic and need not show up until it is too late.

Modelling is often used in order to try to make increased technological risk acceptable, for example in industrial control systems. They enable working closer to the limits of the process, whereas human operators need to work further from critical values (we saw a similar example earlier when looking at aircraft guidance systems). However, once things go wrong in such a process the human operator is left alone to find the way out of a new and unexpected situation. Here modelling inherently increases risk. Sometimes that increased risk is acceptable (as it will be to a fighter pilot turning away from an enemy attack), sometimes it will not be acceptable (increased productivity of a manufacturing plant may not be sufficient reason for acceptance of increased risk to people living near the plant).

Extreme simplification is often a feature of the application of modelling to war. A guidance system that is adequate for controlling an unmanned tank's path across a battle field might be recognized as using an adequate model of navigation if, say, half the tanks get through. Using the same system for navigating lorrics in a large city with the same results would however hardly be recognized as adequate. Talking about the application of Artificial Intelligence models in the military, Boos-Bavnbek comments:

> In the military context of AI system use it is of relatively minor interest whether a system functions well or badly. The disaster is often complete when it is used at all.
>
> (Boos-Bavnbek and Pate, 1989, p. 17)

Modelling Human Actions

The modelling of situations involving human choice raises all sort of difficulties that do not arise in modelling the behaviour of inanimate objects. As we pointed out earlier, the very existence of an economic model can change the economic behaviour of the people whose behaviour it attempts to model.

The modelling of the behaviour of inanimate objects is done both in order to understand that behaviour but also often for the purposes of prediction and possibly control. Where modelling of human actions is undertaken for the purposes of greater understanding then it is open to the charge of detracting from a fully rounded picture of human behaviour; for example it may replace individual people by 'rational economic man'. Even more serious, however, are the implications when we turn to using models to control human behaviour.

Some authors see information technology starting from the punched card machines of the 1920s and 1930s as playing a crucial role in the control of our society. Beniger (1989) traces the origins of present-day information technology in the crisis of control introduced by the Industrial Revolution in manufacturing and transportation. The response to this crisis, he argues, amounts to a revolution in social control. Following Weber, Beniger identifies 'bureaucracy' and 'rationalization' as important control strategies. By 'rationalization' he means that control can be increased not only by increasing the capability to process information but also by decreasing the amount of information to be processed. For example, people can be more easily governed by reducing their representation to a few key variables. This view of the control technology of rationalization shares much in common with what we have called modelling.

How Are Models Actually Used in Decision-making?

A third approach to looking at the place of modelling in society is to ask about the role that models actually play in real decision-making. Dutton (1987) proposes four perspectives on the use of models in decision-making. These perspectives he calls: rational, partisan, technocratic, and consensual.

In the rational perspective models are seen as tools of 'scientific management' that provide better information for policy making. In the partisan perspective models are tools of propaganda and persuasion rather than information. Models are used to legitimate decisions made for other reasons. Dutton points to a number of empirical studies which suggest that computing is selectively used to serve the interests of those who control the organization rather than as an aid to rational decision-making.

Levy (1989) makes a similar argument in pointing out that economic spread-sheets are more often used to persuade than to explain, and in pointing to the manipulation of economic models in the early 1980s by Reagan's advisors in order to make his economic policies appear reasonable.

In the technocratic perspective modellers use information technology to baffle, to impress and to promote their own positions. Technocrats try to gain political power by the authority of their expertise. Models are just complicated representations of the modeller's personal theory and biases.

A somewhat similar view is expressed by Lyon (1991) who talks about the use of computer models in political (for example economic) debate, where they become an aspect of that 'technocratic reason' that hides crucial value judgments and the distribution of power in our society. Political debate is thus reduced to a purely technical level and the possibilities of meaningful participation are reduced.

Some of Dutton's empirical work supports a view of models as potential tools of interactive decision-making and negotiation; this he calls the consensual perspective. In this perspective modelling is also viewed as a political process but as one that can be useful for achieving consensus. Modelling then has an effect on the decision-making process by affecting the language in which negotiation is conducted.

To summarize, these four perspectives lie along two fundamental dimensions:

- Locus of control: who controls the modelling process? Some argue it is the modellers who do so by dominating the technical actions; others that it is political elites, for it is they who dominate model adoption.
- Interests served: whose interests are served by the process? Proponents of modelling suggest that the process is objective; critics of modelling often suggest that models serve partisan interests.

Chapter 4

From Mental Models to Modelling

Joan Bliss

Mental Modelling

Thinking is very varied: it includes working out sums, explaining events, solving problems, and making models. Some psychologists try to explain what is happening when people are thinking, while others are more concerned with how cognitive abilities develop. For example, Piaget gave an account of how cognition develops in children, assuming the last stage of his developmental theory to be the beginning of a description of adult thinking. Others, seeing thinking as the mental manipulation of imagined entities in the Mental Models tradition, have largely thought about the thinking and reasoning of adults, and have not been concerned with development. Despite these differences, there are some similarities in their work.

Piaget's formulation of how we think describes 'what you use to think with': the mental 'tools for thought', which he called 'operations' or more generally 'schemes'. They include mental classification schemes which allow children to differentiate between living and non-living things, or between objects which will sink or float. The thrust of Piaget's work is the description of how such schemes develop and allow us to adapt to the world around us.

The beginning of thought is action. The initial schemes of infants are just coordinated actions on the external world. Once children start to think about the world through the development of imitation, images and the use of language, they are no longer dependent on their action schemes. But this needs more powerful schemes, and between 4 and 6 years old they start to turn their actual actions on the world into mental actions, allowing them to imagine actions.

Work in the mental models tradition goes back to Craik's (1943) book *The Nature of Explanation*. Two strands of work developed: one known as qualitative or naive physics, and another concerned with mental models as more general tools for thought. In the first, 'mental models' are used to describe the 'content of thinking', that is, 'what you think' and not 'tools for thinking'. Gentner and Stevens (1983) argue that to study mental models it is necessary to choose domains for which there already exists some knowledge, leading to a focus on simple physical systems or devices: 'The reason why mental models research has focused on seemingly technical domains is precisely because those domains that have proved the most tractable to physical scientists are the ones for which there exist the best explicit normative models' (p. 2).

de Kleer and Brown (1983) follow this approach, constructing a theory of people's models of physical systems. They attempt to construct computer systems which 'reason naturally'. An example is working out what a device such as a pump might do, given a description of its parts. In describing a mental model de Kleer and Brown distinguish the construction of a model, envisioning what it could do, and testing it by running it.

The second approach to mental models is that of Johnson-Laird (1983). For him too the psychological core of understanding consists of having a 'working model' of the phenomenon in the mind, 'where a model has, in Craik's phrase, a similar "relation-structure" to the process it models, and hence can be useful explanatorily' (p. 4). But, unlike qualitative physics, Johnson-Laird is attempting to describe 'tools for thought' — as was Piaget — rather than the 'content of thought'. His aim of cognitive science is to understand the mind by constructing 'a "working model" of a device for constructing working models' (p. 8).

Johnson-Laird's account of mental models accords well with what Piaget described as concrete operational reasoning. Piaget sees the concrete operational child operating on entities representing the real world, thinking about the real world in terms of objects and events. The difference between them is that for Piaget formal reasoning is done through logic, while Johnson-Laird sees it not as done using any 'mental logic', but as done by building models with tokens, and searching for examples and counter-examples. There is a good case for saying that Piaget too much undervalued his account of concrete reasoning, seeing it only as a step towards formal reasoning. Unfortunately, Piaget rarely discusses the nature and content of concrete representations.

However, Piaget is concerned with development. We are not told how mental models account for the development, learning and acquisition of knowledge, rather than the solving of problems. What then are the processes of acquiring both the mental tools for thinking, and the knowledge which constitutes the content of mental models? How does the outside world (including our actions) get inside our thoughts? That is, what is the process of internalization? And how does our thinking get represented outside our minds — what is the process of externalization? How does externalizing thoughts help us to think?

Internalization of 'Tools for Thought'

Where Johnson-Laird takes mental models as tools for thought as given, Piaget wanted to understand how children's actions on the world could become internal mental schemes. He speculated that it happens through logico-mathematical activity, 'unconscious intellectual work' that permits an individual to abstract a general scheme from a set of coordinated actions on the world. For example, if a set of pebbles is rearranged in a variety of ways — a circle, a square, a line, etc. — and after each rearrangement the pebbles are counted, it is possible to abstract from these actions that the number of pebbles stays the same in spite of the different rearrangements. The pebbles themselves do not matter, it being the actions of rearranging and counting that matter for arriving at an idea of 'invariance of number'. Once abstracted and internalized, the scheme can be applied to different content. Such mental schemes derive from the most general types of actions, such as classifying and ordering.

Piaget is quite clear about the unconscious nature of mental operations or schemes, the individual being aware only of the results of operations and not of the structures that organize them: 'the "lived" or (conscious) can only have a very minor role in the construction of cognitive structures for these do not belong to the subject's consciousness but to his operational behaviour which is something quite different' (Piaget, 1968, p. 68).

Internalization is differently described from a Vygotskian point of view: 'the process of internalization is not the transferral of an external activity to a pre-existing internal "plane of consciousness"; it is the process in which this plane is formed' (Leont'ev, 1981, p. 51). Vygotsky differs from Piaget in taking into account (i) that internalization is concerned with social processes and not just with an individual's activities, and (ii) that language is one of the major mediators between the social and the individual. The building blocks for Vygotsky's description of schemes are external social activities, internalized through language to become internal mental processes.

Thus Piaget and Vygotsky both speculate, but differently, on how we acquire the mental tools which will help us, in turn, to acquire knowledge of the world. During a lifetime, we acquire a lot of knowledge, but without being equally aware of all of it. In eliciting knowledge for expert systems, experts are often found unable to make explicit much of the knowledge they have. Thus a distinction is drawn between surface and deep knowledge. Surface knowledge is easy to get; deep knowledge is tacit or not consciously articulated. Similarly others of us have hypothesized that people have a naive theory of motion, acquired so early in life that it is largely tacit (Ogborn and Bliss, 1990; Bliss and Ogborn, 1993).

We should distinguish between mental models acquired without explicit instruction, and those deriving from teaching. The first will often be tacit and not easily available to reflection; the second will often be conscious and possibly able to be consciously thought about.

Externalization of Thinking

The equation 'thought equals language' over-simplifies a difficult problem. We do not simply have prior thoughts which we then express well or badly. Nor however do we always have to speak to find out what we think. Vygotsky (1934 edited and translated 1962) gives a much subtler account of the transition from thought to speech:

> The relation of thought to word is not a thing but a process, a continual movement back and forth from thought to word and from word to thought. . . . Every thought tends to connect something with something

else, to establish a relationship between things. Every thought moves, grows and develops, fulfils a function, solves a problem. This flow of thought occurs as an inner movement through a series of planes. (p. 125)

Vygotsky argued that it would be a mistake to think that there was only one path from thought to external speech. The development could stop at any point on its complicated course: 'an infinite variety of movement to and fro, of ways still unknown to us, is possible'. He describes this movement as going, 'from the motive which engenders a thought to the shaping of the thought, first in inner speech then in meanings of words and finally in words' (p. 152). Each of these planes differs from the others and has its own characteristics.

Quite a lot of thinking happens without our being aware that it is happening. We manage to get to the corner shop without thinking about how we got there. We expertly cook and wash dishes without much thought, often chatting or listening to the radio meanwhile. Only when something goes wrong do we start to ask questions, and consciously work out what may have gone wrong. If asked how we knew what to do, we often have trouble explaining, since many of these and other cognitive activities are taken for granted or tacit. In general, in any given activity, we use a mix of conscious and tacit mental tools for thinking, and a mix of conscious and tacit knowledge of the world.

Externalizing our thoughts through actions and speech can help to shape our thoughts. Vygotsky pointed out that, 'thought is not merely expressed through words: it comes into existence through them'. But actions and speech are transient. An idea uttered soon gets blurred, muddled or forgotten if it is not written down. Action and speech can happen immediately, without time for reflection, deliberation or choice. Written language, drawing, painting, musical notation etc. are all some of our classic ways of externalizing thinking. They all have the virtue of some degree of permanency, so becoming available to be reflected on. We can then more easily think about our thoughts.

Modern technology, in going beyond the technologies of paper, pencil, ink and paint, has provided new means for externalizing thinking. Word processors can help thinking about writing by making it easier and less painful to construct, compare and combine different drafts. Computer modelling may be able, at least in some specific if modest ways, to help students to think.

Modelling as a Means of Externalizing Thought

Earlier in this book (see Chapter 1) the distinction was made between two types of learning activity in modelling: expressive activities when students are creating their own models and exploratory activities when they are working with someone else's model. When learners are using a tool in an expressive mode the final model they produce and its closeness to their own internalized ideas or 'mental model' will depend on a number of things, amongst which the primitives available in the tool, play an important role — sometimes constraining, sometimes facilitating.

Good modelling tools will present learners with structures that helpfully allow their thoughts to find expression. In addition these structures, if they are well chosen, and provided that they are internalized by students, can be of value as tools for thought in other situations. Once the model is there, students can experiment with, and reflect on, their own ideas in this 'concrete' form. The tool provides a way for ideas to be externalized and, more important, to be acted upon.

When the model expresses someone else's ideas, learners can explore how well these ideas fit or conflict with their own. They can try out the model, and perhaps modify it to represent alternative ideas. The model's behaviour may be startling and unexpected, leading to reflection on, and critical appraisal of, the model. Since it is rather reasonable not to want to change one's own conceptions until having tried out other ideas, exploratory learning can provide a relatively safe way of moving forward in learning.

What cognitive abilities are involved in modelling? People of course bring their everyday and other knowledge of the world to bear on most cognitive activities. It is particularly important for students when modelling to sort out how to use this knowledge. This means learning about the special relation of models to reality. We find that young pupils sometimes 'explain' the behaviour of a model by using an aspect of the real world which they know about, but which is not represented in the model. They have to learn that a model is artificial, doing what it does only because of the rules given to it. But also pupils need to ask to what extent and in what way the model is 'like' the real world, and here their mental models of the world are crucial. A mismatch between the two may be fruitful.

Models are always simpler than reality: in building a model a lot has to be left out. By contrast a pupil's knowledge of the world is dense and lived. Thus knowing which entities or variables are relevant to making a model is no simple matter; indeed too much real-world knowledge can get in the way.

Most people's everyday thinking works by imagining real entities and events. Until recently modelling programs have usually required more abstract thinking, particularly the use of variables. Such forms of modelling are not likely to be appropriate for many pupils below the early teens.

People do not readily reason using syntactic operations on formal rules. In many situations, rules of plausibility are used to judge the validity of a set of conclusions rather than any formal consequences. Here again everyday knowledge is used to back up judgments of plausibility.

Testing a model can be cognitively demanding. Systematic manipulation of variables requires changing one variable at a time, keeping others constant, until the effects of all variables have been studied. Research shows that students do not master separation and control of variables until about 15 years of age. Faced with complex models involving many interactions, pupils may have difficulty in seeing how the system works as a whole.

In conclusion, although computer-modelling tools need to be matched carefully to pupils' cognitive abilities, they can if this has been done provide a means for learning, both, new tools for thought and new thoughts about the world, through interacting with external but artificial worlds.

Learning new thoughts about the world may involve clarifying or modifying ideas the pupil already holds, or may require coming to terms with new ones. Any such learning will be refracted through the pupil's current ways of thinking. But it is not necessary to suppose that in every case the pupil has clear-cut prior notions. One may hold, with Norman (1983), that people's mental models are often incomplete, unstable, nebulous, easily confused with one another, and not always able to be 'run' in dealing with a task. If so, interacting with a model in a computer which is clearly structured and runnable provides at least the possibility of clarification and crystallization of ideas.

Learning new tools for thinking is a deeper matter. The very way a model works, and the way it uses a certain set of primitives (whether variables, logical rules or rule-bound objects) to construct a representation of an aspect of reality are themselves potential tools for thought. Tools for thought will not usually be acquired at a first acquaintance, since their value lies in their use in many different contexts. This fact points to the need for repeated use of modelling tools which make their inner 'tools' as visible and transparent as possible.

Finally, a computer model looks to the pupil not like a thought but like a thing. But it is in a way a thought, brought into existence as an artificial world, which can act or respond. 'To make a model on the computer is to create a world, but a world which evolves or changes in front of one's eyes' (Ogborn, 1990). Thus models offer some possibility for active engagement of pupils with ideas, whether these are representations of their own thinking or are part of what our culture has to offer by way of understanding reality.

Chapter 5

Computational Issues in Modelling

Jon Ogborn and Rob Miller

What Is Special about Computers for Modelling?

This chapter discusses computational aspects of modelling. They include the question: 'What is special about computers for modelling?' and an analysis of the nature and characteristics of a variety of kinds of computational model. We conclude with a matter of particular concern for the present book, the design of a modelling system to support everyday practical reasoning about quantities.

The immediate answer to the question above is simply that computers are fast. A computational model can generate rapidly, results which would take a long time to do by hand. The fact is trivial but its consequences are not. One consequence is that the grain size of computational and cognitive elements one uses gets bigger, more interesting and more useful. We know that human beings lump cognitive material into a few meaningful chunks in order to be able to deal with it, and that they cannot handle more than a few chunks at a time. Thus the computer affords the possibility of thinking about larger, more interesting and more important chunks.

This can be illustrated from the history of statistics. When factor analysis had to be done by hand, one analysis took from days to weeks to do. Disputes about the meaning and interpretation of factor analysis were difficult to resolve because of the impracticality of repeating an analysis several times in different ways to see what difference it made. Nowadays one can investigate such questions easily.

This makes the grain size of the primitive elements of a modelling system important. Is a graph to be one complete primitive element, or should the elements be its x and y axes, scales and plotted points, for example? Most computer languages take the second option, whilst many modelling systems take the first.

A less obvious answer to the question is that the computer is a machine. It follows prescribed steps without considering their context or meaning. The computer is a symbol-processing machine. That is, its prescriptions operate only on syntactic, not semantic, information about symbols. That a computer is a symbol-processing machine is of fundamental interest because of the deep connection between formalization and mechanization. A formalized model is one which is built from a strictly defined vocabulary using strictly defined syntactic rules. No room is left for *ad hoc* interpretation or variation. In this way a formal model appears 'objective'. It is this which drives mathematicians towards axiomatic systems and formalization. The question whether *all* of mathematics could be reduced to mechanizable principles occupied mathematicians earlier in this century. The current answer seems to be 'No'.

The idea of a mechanized and explicit basis for a model remains, and is still part of the notion of 'rigour'. In modelling, the distinction between the formal model and the real world it represents is crucial. And the physical computer itself can stand as an image for the much more abstract notion of a mechanizable set of rules; it can be seen as a 'theory machine'.

What Kinds of Computational Modelling Are There?

Some computational models model change and others model fixed relations between parts of a system. We may call the first 'evolutionary' models and the second 'constraint' models. Some examples of tasks such models might perform may make the distinction clearer:

1. Evolutionary
   - prediction of the trajectory of a space craft;
   - visualization of turbulent flow;
   - prediction of the effect of a tax cut on an economy;
   - prediction of cash flow in the future in a business;
   - weather forecasting;
   - study of crystal growth;
   - model of the early stages of the Universe.
2. Constraint
   - a business profit-and-loss spreadsheet;
   - prediction of stress distribution in an engineering structure;
   - modelling of visual appearance of objects in a scene;
   - medical diagnosis by an expert system;
   - modelling of fractal structures;
   - statistical models of data structures.

A model can include both aspects. A model for predicting the course of the failure of a power station will have a constraint model which interrelates the components, and a dynamic model which describes how this pattern of relationships can change.

Many computable models of both classes require numerical calculation, and what they model are patterns of relationship between magnitudes of quantities. But others, such as expert systems, models of languages and some models of cognition, require symbolic or logical computation. The latter are often but not exclusively associated with constraint rather than evolutionary models. Thus we can roughly distinguish quantitative and qualitative models.

Perhaps the stereotypical model is deterministic: given appropriate input it predicts one outcome. But there are non-deterministic models which give alternative outputs for a given input. One such would be a computational grammar which generates many sentences of a given form. And a business executive can use a spreadsheet for 'What if?' calculations, in a non-deterministic mode.

The majority of computational models are built around the serial conception of a computer. A few owe their inspiration to the parallel conception, in which many interconnected processors cooperate or divide work between them.

Many models are variable-oriented. Elements in the model are symbolic variables which take on values, quantitative or qualitative. In such a system to exist as an individual is to be the value of a variable. Some models are more object-oriented. Their primitive elements comprise objects modelled on objects in reality, individual or generic, each of which has associated possible behaviours.

Kinds of Modelling Formalism

One approach to constructing a computational model is simply to program it as best one can, much as a physical modeller might use clay, sticks, glue and string in any *ad hoc* way which seems helpful. The deficiency of *ad hoc* modelling is the difficulty of analysing the model to see what it could possibly do or not do.

For this reason, a number of types of modelling formalism have been developed, which are more or less well-understood. One of the best known formalisms is the discrete approximation to differential equations, in which formal rules specify small increments in the values of some variables. Other rules specify how to sequence the calculation and minimize the effects of the finiteness of steps in the calculation. A related formalism is that of difference equations, for which changes in independent variables are no longer required to be small. Both are by their nature formalisms for evolutionary models. Both are essentially inspired by serial computing.

A somewhat related constraint formalism is the finite-element formalism, developed for calculating patterns of stress in engineering structures. The structure is imagined divided into small elements, each interacting with neighbouring elements. The model seeks stresses and strains at each element such that all elements are in equilibrium. This formalism has proved very adaptable. It can be used to calculate parameters in complex electrical networks, or the intensity of the electric field in a given region.

Algebraic equations are a simpler and well-known constraint formalism, which of course underlie profit-and-loss spreadsheets. Where algebraic relations include inequalities (greater than, less than) we have the formalism of linear programming, well adapted to finding the range of values possible for some variables given the values of others. An obvious example is a model for diet which keeps total energy, fats, carbohydrates and fibre within certain limits.

Statistical modelling again involves constraints, attempting to examine the fit of data of various kinds to predetermined structures. A great number of important and useful structures which data may fit have been developed and exhaustively studied, so that their properties are generally well understood.

Geometry is another possible basis for modelling. What Crick and Watson did with metal shapes, seeing if the geometry of certain molecules was consistent with a proposed structure for DNA, could nowadays be done with a geometric design program. Geometric models are unlike those mentioned so far in being less oriented towards variables and more towards objects.

Another very general formalism is that of graph theory, well adapted to problems which can be modelled as a structure of nodes connected by links. It played an important role in the early development of semantic net models of memory.

Some other formalisms owe their very existence to the computer. Monte Carlo methods, which compute values by averaging over a large number of randomized trials, are only practicable with the computer.

Another offspring of the computer is the cell-automaton formalism, created by one of the parents of computing, John von Neumann, and discussed briefly in Chapter 3. Cell automata are clearly prime targets for parallel computing, and are essentially object-oriented.

A different symbolic or logical formalism is that of production systems. These use 'if-then' rules (productions), which link a condition to an action to be taken when that condition is satisfied. The basic idea has been adapted to model grammars, expert knowledge, and cognitive processes. Some aspects of production systems are well-understood, but many features of actual systems remain *ad hoc*, particularly the way they resolve conflict between competing productions.

No better understood are the various kinds of discrete-event formalisms used for modelling patterns of events involving objects, from traffic flows to airline queues. Typically they provide objects, events which may occur to those objects, resources which events consume or provide, paths along which objects may go and places in which they may stay. Most actual models of this kind have significant *ad hoc* elements, and are often programmed from scratch for a specific purpose. Certain languages (e.g., Simula, SmallTalk) were designed with such modelling in view. Again, such models are often object-oriented.

Better understood, because of its basis in first-order predicate calculus, is the logical formalism offered by, for example, Prolog. Originating in work on formal models of grammars, Prolog has evolved into a general purpose programming language. By being such, the primitive elements it provides for the construction of models are fine-grained and abstract: logical constants, variables, logical connectives. Logic models are essentially variable-oriented, though the variables here are logical ones.

Recently, there has been resurgent interest in connectionist or neural net models. They attempt to model the pattern matching and pattern completion ability of the brain, by representing patterns as stable organizations of activity in an interconnected network of artificial neurons. The essential computational inspiration is parallelism.

Between the Qualitative and the Quantitative

Many of the important results obtained from computational modelling are qualitative rather than quantitative. Economic arguments often fall between the qualitative and the quantitative. 'Higher pay must increase incentives, and so increase productivity and profits', or 'Lower pay must reduce employers' costs and so increase profits', are (contradictory) kinds of arguments it is not hard to find in any daily newspaper. Characteristically such arguments mix actual quantities (e.g., pay) with 'quantities' such as incentives, which cannot actually be quantified, but for which at least 'more' and 'less' can be imagined. Sometimes all the imagined terms in the argument are of this kind: 'Increasing pressures on the President reduce the push to reform.'

It is plain that this kind of partly quantitative, partly qualitative thinking is ubiquitous in natural everyday reasoning. It recognizes ordering of quantity but not magnitude, using terms such as 'big' and 'small', 'increasing' and 'decreasing'. For this reason we focused attention on such reasoning, calling it 'semi-quantitative', and developed the computer tool IQON to support and investigate it.

For the same reasons, such reasoning has been an important focus of work in Artificial Intelligence, in which context it is usually called 'qualitative reasoning'. Various computational strategies have been suggested for dealing with it. One common one is that of de Kleer and Brown, and of Kuipers, in which qualitative versions of a formalism like that of differential equations are constructed. Such equations yield a qualitative change (e.g., 'increasing') when given qualitative values (e.g., 'big' or 'small') for various influences.

Such work has thrown up many interesting difficulties. It is hard to see how much everyday knowledge of the world to build explicitly into any such system, and it is difficult to do it, especially as much relevant knowledge holds true 'normally' rather than always. Thus this line of work has been very productive of difficult logical and computational problems, but has been less successful at producing hoped-for practical qualitative reasoning systems.

Design of Computer Tools for Semi-quantitative Modelling

If we identify semi-quantitative modelling as an important and natural mode of expression, how might we design and implement computer tools to support it?

We may attempt to represent semi-quantitative information several ways. Should such information best be regarded as essentially mathematical (albeit vague), or as essentially distinct from classical mathematics? Proponents of the former view might try to express a statement like 'A positively effect B' through some change in a value of B given a value of A. Opponents of this view might argue that such a style deforms the essential intuitive nature of such information, and is contrary to its relation to other types of 'commonsense knowledge', so that an entirely separate formalism for semi-quantitative information needs to be developed.

Other considerations might however influence the semi-qualitative tool designer away from a complex symbolic formalism. Direct manipulation interfaces provide the possibility for diagrammatic models to be drawn directly onto the screen, and diagrams are often a natural means of expression, particularly for semi-quantitative ideas. The tool *IQON* bases its model representation on the idea of causal loop diagrams, borrowed from system dynamics.

Very little work has however been done in computer science on direct computation with diagrams, so that a diagrammatically based modelling tool will have to translate models into symbolic data of some kind, perform calculations or make inferences using this data, and translate the results back into the diagram.

The discussion mentioned above, about whether or not semi-quantitative information is essentially quantitative information vaguely expressed, transforms into a debate about whether or not the underlying computation should be essentially numerical, or of some other form. As mentioned earlier, work in Artificial Intelligence on qualitative reasoning offers alternatives to traditional numerical iterative computation methods. It aims to provide computational methods to process semi-quantitative information directly to forecast future states of a domain whose present state has been modelled.

At a practical level, we must note that such qualitative reasoning methods at present require very powerful machines. The choice will also depend on the type of output or 'model consequences' desired. For dynamic models, we may require the computer to produce a simulation: a single projected time sequence of events. Qualitative reasoning methods by contrast typically output an 'envisionment', which is a map of all future possible states.

The alternative 'vaguely quantitative' approach to qualitative reasoning requires the modelling tool to internally generate quantitative models which somehow adequately reflect the 'vaguely quantitative' specification of the model. *IQON* adopts this approach. In the discussion above it was observed that 'A has a positive effect on B' could be regarded as a quantitative statement to the effect that changes of B can be obtained knowing the value of A. *IQON* generates functions which give the rate of change of each variable, from the values of the other variables connected to that variable. The functions are chosen so that all possible values of variables fall into one fixed range ('as large as possible' to 'as small as possible'), so that their values can easily be represented graphically. The simulated behaviour of an *IQON* model is thus generated using standard iterative computational methods, but yields only one of the possibly many time sequences which could be generated by an envisionment.

In fact, the interface of *IQON* is such that slight changes in initial values can cause the simulation to progress through a qualitatively different envisionment sequence, by causing one variable value to override the effect of another. *IQON* and tools like it may also be criticized in that the underlying computation, and thus the generated model behaviour, does not fully reflect the type of reasoning in which the modeller is engaging. Nevertheless, they may still be useful pedagogically, and do have the advantage that they can be implemented with reasonable efficiency on machines that might typically be found in the classroom.

Chapter 6

Representations and Representation Systems

Haralambos Sakonidis

Introduction

Representation is important not only in education but in most human activities. The question of representations is an ancient one for philosophers, and psychologists have also turned their attention to it. It has remained a long-standing question because of its difficulty and of the lack of a clear framework for thinking about it. The development of Artificial Intelligence has drawn attention back to representations and representation systems, in part by focusing on the problem of bridging novices' (or pupils') existing representations with those of the expert (or teacher), thus making the issue of representations central in thinking about learning.

Cognitive development is closely related to the ability to represent objects, states of affairs and relations, either internally or externally, and to move successfully between the two. But what exactly do we mean by representations and representation systems? How are internal representations and external representations related to one another? How do children gain access to and master representations? How do we decide what representations to use in a given context and how much does the choice of a particular representation system affect the understanding of a problem? How does the multiplicity of representation systems facilitate understanding or indeed cognitive development, and how do we learn how to move from one representation system to another?

Any attempt to answer all these questions would be too ambitious. Here, I will draw attention to some ways of analysing the idea of representation and representation systems. I will then focus on some issues related to the way in which children understand and cope with representations. Finally, I will try to illustrate some of the ideas discussed by examples from school mathematics.

Representations and Representation Systems

Many of the ideas we need to deal with in thinking about, for example, very large or very small quantities, or processes with many successive stages (e.g., fast movements), are cognitively not easily accessible. We lack direct representations of them which 'confer some behavioural, practical, unifying meaning' (Fischbein, 1989) on them thereby making them possible to handle. Perner (1991) states that, '. . . the notion of representation . . . should cover things as diverse as pictures, models, sentences and mental states . . . (which) share one essential feature. They are not just objects in themselves but in their representational capacity they evoke something else'. These quotations point to the fact that the value of a representation is to be found in its power to energize, to make an idea manageable by the human mind.

For the constructivist von Glasersfeld (1987) the individual's choice of a representation to signify other things can be deliberate or can arise '. . . by ordinary inductive inferences by which a cognitive subject organizes experience', but in such a way that whatever is chosen to stand for a segment of experience should be able to be perceived in isolation from the rest of experience and taken as a discrete, coherent item.

Denis and Dubois (1976) distinguish two meanings of 'representation': (i) some material organization of symbols (schema, graph, diagram) which either correspond to other entities or 'model' mental processes and (ii) the organization of knowledge in long-term memory. Similarly, Dufour-Janvier, Bednarz and Belanger (1987), and also Pratt and Garton (1993) from a developmental perspective, distinguish between internal and external representations, the former being internal models of reality, and the latter being publicly accessible external symbolic organizations which represent certain 'external realities'.

Kaput (1987) and Palmer (1977) argue that there are five elements involved in representation: (i) the represented world, (ii) the representing world, (iii) aspects of the represented world which are represented, (iv) aspects of the representing world which do the representing and (v) the correspondence between the two worlds. One or both worlds can be hypothetical or abstract. Kaput identifies five (interacting) types of representation: cognitive, perceptual, explanatory (involving models), representation within a domain and external symbolic representation.

Johnson-Laird (1983) distinguishes propositions (strings of symbols that correspond to natural language), mental models (structural analogues of the world) and images (perceptual correlates of models from a particular point of view). These three types of representation are functionally and structurally distinguishable from one another, and differ in how they encode information.

In summary, we need representations to feed the mind with manageable mental entities with which to think. A representation has three components: the represented entity, the representing entity and the relationship between the two. The relationship is shaped both by the individual, and by the influence of the environment and social context. The organization and coordination of these three components constitutes what I will from now onwards call a representation system (see also Kaput, 1987).

Representation Systems and Children

From an early age, people, as individuals and as social beings, have to deal with a variety of representation systems. The distinction between internal and external representations presents a number of problems. Campbell and Olson (1990), following Piaget, believe that the capacity for coping with external representation systems is an indication of pre-existent internal representations. Vygotsky (1981) on the other hand, advocates the priority of externally mediated representations, followed by internalization. Mason (1987) and von Glasersfeld (1987) criticize the internal/external distinction, on the grounds that for the child inner representations are not a representation of the real world but of the child's inner world. Von Glasersfeld suggests that it is more appropriate to talk about inner experiences, and their expression in terms of pictures, diagrams, words or symbols as a 'presentation' of an inner world.

The relationship between representation and thing represented can be arbitrary (as de Saussure claimed language to be) or be based on some kind of resemblance (e.g., models, paintings). In the former case, the relationship is founded on long-standing and well established social conventions, a fact which can lead to considerable difficulties for children. Durkin (1986, 1993) illustrates this by looking at development in the representation of number, which he concludes '. . . is a social process (where) the learner has to discover what other people mean. . . . People represent number to children, children form representations of what adults want them to do, and these representations form the basis of protracted discourse in which children shift their representations increasingly in the direction of those of their community' (Durkin, 1993).

It is important to ask what the status of a given representation system is for a person, especially for a child. Algebraic symbolism is only at a late stage of learning appreciated as a representation system in its own right. This may be the reason why children, asked to build models using some representation system provided to them, find it hard to treat the model they build as something existing in its own right. When asked to think about the model as itself an entity with its own proper structure and functioning, they tend to appeal to reality to make sense of the model.

The mastery of some representation systems often depends on mastery of others (for example, written/spoken language, algebra/arithmetic). The dependency can have developmental or historical origins. The general problem is the multiplicity of representation systems used in different contexts, and the relationships between different ways of representing the same idea. Which representation systems should come first so as to assist learning and understanding? What makes a representation system appropriate and how does this depend on the subject matter?

The distinction between internal and external representations, and a focus on the latter, is helpful in thinking about educational implications. Teaching to a great extent consists of submitting children to a variety of externally represented ideas. Dufour-Janvier, Bednarz and Belanger (1987) raise four important questions concerning the use of representations in mathematics, which, I believe, have relevance to other subjects:

(i)   Why do we use external representations?

Representations are so closely associated with certain concepts, particularly in mathematics, that they become part of them. In other cases, representations constitute tools for studying concepts. In presenting multiple representations of a concept, we attempt to concretize it, to reduce its difficulty and to make it more interesting.

(ii)   What are the benefits of using external representations?

The use of representations provides the child with a stock of representations to use in a variety of contexts. It aims at developing the ability to select appropriate representations, to pass from one representation to another, and to recognize the value of approaching a problem from different points of view. Dufour-Janvier, Bednarz and Belanger suggest, however, that in mathematics children do not usually seem to select a representation, but just to use the most familiar one, and that moving between two representations is only possible when the child has grasped them both well.

(iii)   How do children gain access to representations?

External representations which are too distant from the child's internal ones are either rejected or create difficulties because they do not fit what the child perceives as significant in the situation studied. Representations which are too abstract for the child lead to rote manipulation of symbols and rules, and to excessive concern with learning the representation at the expense of the concept represented.

(iv)   How do children's own external representations contribute to their learning?

At first, children's external representation systems are mainly drawings and spoken or written language. These need to be capitalized on in developing further representation systems such as graphic codes and symbols.

Acquiring the ability to use a representation is obviously a gradual process. Two levels can be immediately identified, the first level involving:

- identification of the elements of the representing world;
- establishment of relationships between the elements of the representing world;
- transformation of the above relationships to the ideas for which these elements stand for, that is, to relationships between elements of the represented world.

A more advanced meta-level includes:

- appreciation of the equivalence or complementary nature of various representation systems;
- ability to move between representation systems.

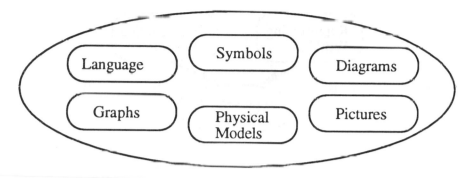

Figure 6.1: Types of representations in mathematics

Representation Systems and Mathematics

In mathematics, representations play a special role in expressing, communicating and manipulating abstractions, and because mathematical abstractions require the use of many kinds of representation, including mathematical symbols, diagrams, pictures, etc. Although a powerful feature of mathematics, these are also sources of confusion if pupils have too little help (i) to identify and appreciate different representation systems and (ii) to establish correspondences between different representation systems. The drawing of a circle (the Euclidean system of representation) and its equation $(x - a)^2 + (y - b)^2$ (the Cartesian or algebraic system of representation) are two different ways of expressing the same idea in two different representation systems, but children need help to see that this is so and that it is a fact of mathematical interest.

Some ideas depend on the representation system used, and others do not: this again is not always made clear to children. An example (Kaput, 1987) is the tendency to ignore the distinction between properties of numbers which are related to the representation system (e.g., binary or decimal) versus those properties of numbers which do not (e.g., primeness).

Multiplicity of Representation Systems

Figure 6.1 shows several of the representation systems used in mathematics.

How, we may ask, do all these representations cooperate in enriching and supporting learning and understanding in mathematics and science?

Representation Systems With the Same Represented World

Sometimes the same idea is represented via two different representation systems, as suggested in Figure 6.2.

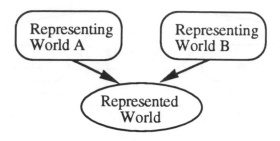

Figure 6.2: Multiplicity of representation systems in mathematics

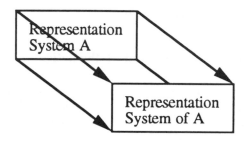

Figure 6.3: Representation systems as interpreters of other representation systems

Examples include fractions represented either as expressing whole-part relationships (e.g., 3/4 means 3 parts out of 4) or as ordered pairs of integers; geometric forms represented graphically or as algebraic equations; and a calculation represented as a system of equations or as a computational algorithm.

Representation Systems Interpreting other Representation Systems

An algebraic expression like $(x + y) - xz$ can easily be thought of — and often is in the school context — as a representation of a statement such as $(3 + 2) - (3)(4)$, which itself is an arithmetic representation of the number (-7) to which it can be reduced. Thus a representation system can be used to interpret or make sense of another representation system (as represented in Figure 6.3). This of course is the basis of many advances in mathematics itself, such as when Group theory was created to represent very general features of systems of algebra.

Overlap of Representation Systems

Representation systems can often overlap (as represented in Figure 6.4). For example, '+' (addition) is an element of the representation system of numbers as well as of that of functions.

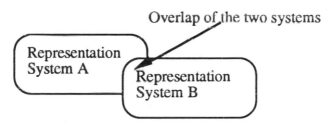

Figure 6.4· Overlap of representation systems in mathematics

Some Concluding Questions

Rather than attempting any general summary, I will conclude with a number of questions which, I believe, need to be on the agenda of those thinking about learning in relation to representation systems in general, and about the role of representation systems in educational software in particular.

In general:

- Can we identify the different types of representation systems used in a given domain?
- Which representation systems best support the initial learning of a domain?
- How compatible are the representation systems used within the domain?
- What are the representation systems pupils are familiar with, and how do they differ from teachers' or experts' representations?

In relation to the use of computers:

- What are the types of representations used by existing software, and how far do they reflect pupils' own modes of representation?
- What are the cognitive demands of switching from one mode of representation to another, and how does this affect children's ability to cope with a problem in a given domain?
- How does the nature of the domain and the context affect the choice of representation system to be used?
- Do multiple representations in a piece of software support or enrich the learner's understanding of and access to ideas?

Part 2

Mathematics and Reality

Chapter 7

Interpreting the World with Numbers: An Introduction to Quantitative Modelling

Richard Boohan

Introduction

Quantitative modelling, or mathematical modelling, has a history which goes back much further than the computer, though the computer has allowed models of greater complexity to be built. The behaviour of many simple systems can be predicted with great accuracy using just a few basic physical principles, given a knowledge of the initial conditions. Thus, Newton's Laws can be used to make predictions about mechanical systems, if initial values of variables such as velocity, distance and force are known. In all quantitative models, the initial conditions are specified by giving values to independent variables; the model uses algebraic relationships to calculate the values of the dependent variables. So, the behaviour of the model depends on both the values of the independent variables and on the nature of the relationships between the variables. In complex systems, it may be difficult to identify and measure relevant variables, or to specify relationships between them. Nevertheless, quantitative modelling has taken on increasing importance in the social sciences. One ambitious and well-publicized attempt was described in *The Limits to Growth* (Meadows *et al.*, 1973), in which a computer model of the social and economic system of the world was constructed and used to make long-term predictions about its possible behaviour.

Different Kinds of Model

We need to distinguish between two fundamentally different kinds of quantitative model — 'static' and 'dynamic' (essentially the same distinction was made in Chapter 5 but the authors of that chapter preferred to use the terms 'evolutionary' and 'constraint' models). In a static model, initial values are given to the variables, and output values are calculated. In a dynamic model, the calculated values are fed back into the relationships so that the behaviour of the system is modelled over time. Some simple examples will illustrate these points.

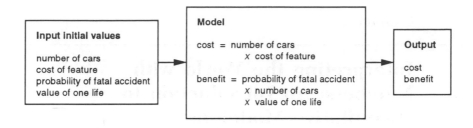

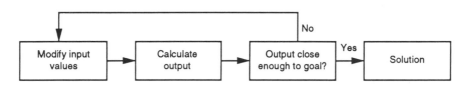

Figure 7.1: A static model

Figure 7.2: Getting a numerical solution

Static Models

Some years ago, there was a public outcry in the US when it was discovered that the Ford Motor Company had decided not to implement a safety feature which would have reduced the risk of the car catching fire in an accident (Henderson, 1987). It was estimated that the feature would have saved 180 lives, while adding only about £8 to the cost of the car. In fact, the company had carried out a cost-benefit analysis, and decided that the cost outweighed the benefit. The essence of the analysis is represented diagrammatically in Figure 7.1. This calculation could be represented on a computer as a quantitative model, albeit a rather trivial one, to calculate costs and benefits from any set of initial values. This is a static model.

Because of the large number of cars requiring modification, Ford calculated that the cost would far exceed the benefit in terms of lives saved — using £138,000 as the value of one life. Whether the choice of model and initial values is seen as rational or outrageous is a matter of human judgment. Having chosen them, though, the conclusion is inevitable. By changing the initial values, 'what if?' questions can be easily answered: 'What if the value of a life is judged as £500,000?', 'or £10 million?'.

Notice that the model allows calculation only in one direction — finding the total cost from the other variables. The model cannot reverse the calculation — for example, finding the cost per car from the other variables. Here, it is easy to find an expression to do this (cost per car = the total cost ÷ the number of cars), but with complex calculations, this may be difficult or even impossible. If so, we cannot get an analytical solution, but we may find a numerical solution by systematically varying the input values until a desired output value is found (Figure 7.2).

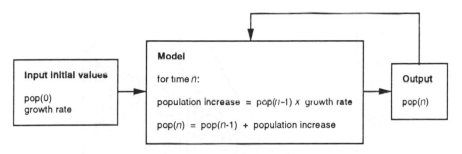

Figure 7.3: A dynamic model

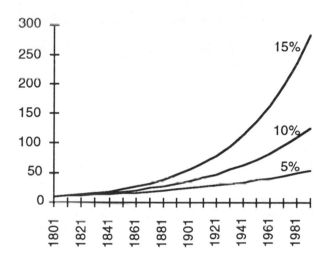

Figure 7.4: Output from dynamic model of population growth

Dynamic Models

In 1801, the first census was carried out in England and Wales. The population was approximately 8.9 million. At around this time, Malthus was arguing the inevitability of poverty since the population would always increase more rapidly than the resources to support it. How might we have predicted the size of the population after two centuries? Figure 7.3 shows how such a calculation might be represented as a computer model. As before, the model uses initial values to calculate another variable, but this time uses the calculated value as input to the model. It is iterative. It assumes a constant growth rate for each time interval, calculating the increase in population during each time interval. This increase is added to the old population size, to get the new population size which is fed back into the calculation, and so it goes on.

This is a dynamic model, since it calculates how the population changes over time. Figure 7.4 shows the behaviour of this model between 1801 and 1991, with

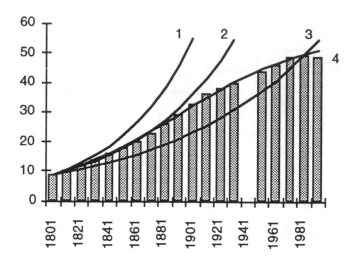

Figure 7.5: Comparing the model with data

growth rates of 5 per cent, 10 per cent and 15 per cent every ten years (from one census to the next).

How do these curves compare to the way the population has actually changed over this period? Figure 7.5 shows a bar chart of the census populations. While the population grows at first, it then levels off. So, line 2 (10 per cent) agrees quite well initially, but then rises too steeply. Line 3 (5 per cent) is closest to the 1991 population size, but does not fit very well earlier. Clearly, no value of the growth rate will give good agreement with the data.

To fit the data we need to change not the initial values, but the model itself. Line 4 shows the line obtained using a different expression, in which the growth rate also depends on a maximum limit:

$$\text{population increase} = \text{pop}(n-1) \times \text{growth rate} \times (1 - \text{pop}(n-1)/\text{limit})$$

with initial values of growth rate = 20 per cent and limit = 57 million. As the population approaches this limit, so the growth slows down. This type of growth is found for many diverse populations — the growth of yeast in a fermentation vessel reaches a limit, since they become poisoned by the alcohol they excrete. Whether similar mechanisms are at work for the UK population is another matter.

Non-deterministic Models

The models discussed above are deterministic. Given the same initial values they will always produce the same behaviour. Monte Carlo modelling is non-deterministic since it involves the use of randomly generated variables. So each time the model is run a different result is achieved. Individual runs are not of interest — the model is run many times, and the results averaged. This kind of modelling was pioneered by Stanislav Ulam and John von Neumann at Los Alamos, and was a key element in development of the hydrogen bomb.

Iterative dynamic models can also be non-deterministic but in a rather different way. The above UK population model is an example of a logistic relationship, which has the general equation $f(x) = ax(b - x)$. Such models can behave chaotically. The effect of increasing the growth rate is illustrated in Figure 7.6, chaotic behaviour appearing when the growth rate is large. This model is still deterministic — the same initial values will always give the same behaviour — but very small changes in the initial values cause the model to behave differently. Figure 7.6d shows the effect of changing the initial population from 8.901 to 8.900 (about 0.01 per cent difference). Initially the behaviour is almost identical, but soon they start to diverge. Over sufficiently long periods, even infinitesimally small initial differences produce entirely different behaviour. This kind of behaviour was first noticed due to rounding errors in meteorological data, and is one reason reliable weather forecasting is so difficult (see Chapter 3).

At a computational level, these two kinds of non-determinism are rather similar since 'random numbers' are in fact generated in a computer by an expression which gives a sequence of pseudo-random numbers starting from an initial seed. Changing the seed changes the sequence; using the same seed reproduces the same sequence, which can be useful when testing a 'random' model.

Different Kinds of Modelling Tools

Some modelling tools can support static models, others are better for dynamic modelling and some support both. What all of these have in common is that variables are linked by algebraic relationships. In some tools these links are made more explicit than in others. For example, dynamic iterative models may be represented by causal diagrams in which causal relationships are shown visually by a directed link from one variable to another. This may help to make the model clearer, but it may be a distraction — we may wish to represent visually some other aspect of the model. Each modelling tool uses a different representation, and this may help or hinder thinking about any particular problem.

Using a Spreadsheet for Quantitative Modelling

Spreadsheets have acquired some popularity as a modelling tool in the school curriculum. One obvious advantage is that they are already commonly available in schools. They are also relatively easy to use and are very versatile, suitable for many kinds of model. They are most often used for static models, and the ease of entering new values makes them ideally suited to 'what if?' problems and to trial-and-error solutions. Some have sophisticated features to assist in obtaining

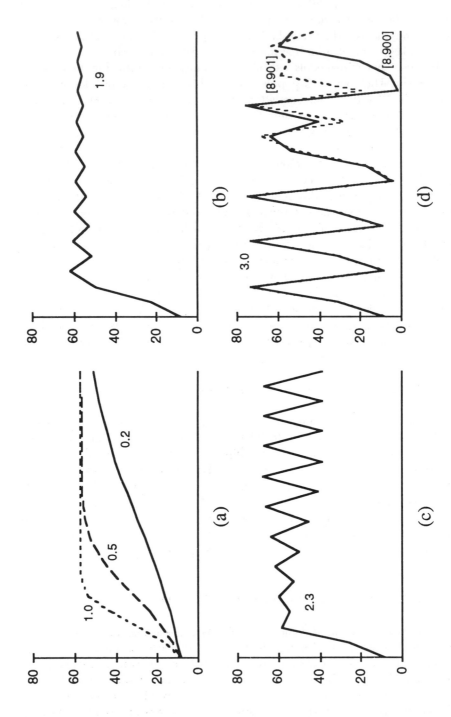

Figure 7.6: Chaotic behaviour of the model

numerical solutions. They can also be used for iterative dynamic models and for probabilistic models.

Spreadsheets have disadvantages. They are limited visually, so links between variables cannot be represented. Also, relationships are usually defined in terms of cell references rather than in terms of meaningful names. In iterative models, changing a formula involves changing a range of cells which can be time consuming. Finally, while many spreadsheets have facilities for good graphical displays, they can be inconvenient to use. Different modelling tools overcome some of these limitations.

Other Quantitative Modelling Tools

When computers were first introduced to schools, any modelling that was done tended to use what was readily available. This was BASIC. Any general purpose programming language can be used to write quantitative models, but for most pupils this is too difficult. The difficulty lies not so much in writing the model itself — typically just a few lines of code — but in the other features necessary to handle the model.

This led to the development of *Dynamic Modelling System (DMS)*, a 'shell' within which models are constructed in BASIC syntax. The shell takes care of running the model and presenting output values and graphs. Older pupils have found it easy to learn sufficient BASIC to construct *DMS* models. To support modelling for younger pupils, *DMS* was developed into the *Cellular Modelling System (CMS)*. This is similar to a spreadsheet, but meaningful names are used for variables, and running the model to obtain graphical output is made easier.

DYNAMO was a programming language specifically developed for dynamic modelling (Roberts *et al.*, 1983), based on representing systems by causal diagrams and diagrams showing flows through the system. More sophisticated computer graphics led to the development of *STELLA* in which variables and links are represented as icons on the screen (Figure 7.7). *STELLA* uses a metaphor of 'tanks' and 'flows', and while this may seem natural for representing money in an economic system or a chemical reaction, it is more difficult to think of quantities like velocity in this way.

Whilst in *DMS*, *CMS* and *STELLA*, the models are represented by difference equations, in *Dinamix* the model is expressed directly using differential equations. Thus, it can be seen as a bridge between using the computer to give numerical solutions to problems and using the calculus to give analytical solutions.

In *Model Builder*, variables are represented as blocks, which can be moved around the screen. Blocks show the name of the variable, its value and where appropriate the algorithm for calculating it. These blocks can be superimposed on a picture, and so this is particularly useful when showing spatial relationships. *Extend* also builds models from blocks, though these represent objects rather than variables. These objects can be represented as pictures, with connections to other objects to represent input and output values. *Extend* provides a way of

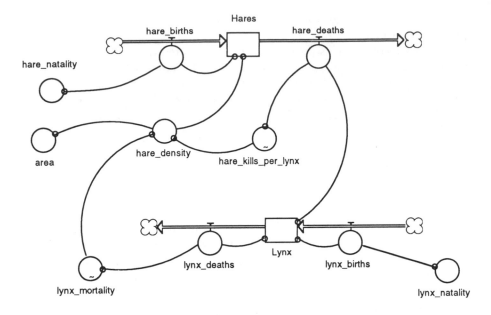

Figure 7.7: A STELLA model of predator–prey populations

building simulations, in which users can easily vary initial values but have no knowledge of the underlying model.

The 'Algebraic Proposer' supports quantitative static models, giving emphasis to the idea that quantitative models are not just about handling numbers but that these numbers refer to quantities in the real world. Thus it processes both values and units of variables — units must be specified when independent variables are defined, and checks are made when expressions for dependent variables are defined. Numerator supports the same kinds of calculations that could be done on a spreadsheet, but represents variables as 'number tanks' which can be 'plumbed together' with pipes, via simple operators. One interesting feature of Numerator is that a number of variables and operators can be displayed as a single 'module' with input and output connectors. Q-MOD was developed as part of the Tools for Exploratory Learning Programme, to support static models. Like Numerator, it uses linked boxes, but does not represent operators separately, relationships being defined in the dependent variable box.

Pupils and Quantitative Modelling

In the chapters in this section, the authors reflect on their experiences of using quantitative modelling tools with small groups of pupils across a range of ages from 10 to 18. A number of different tools are discussed, used by pupils both to create their own models and to explore models made by others. We also see a range of different kinds of model being used. So, Chapter 8 discusses the use by pupils of a modelling tool, *Q-MOD*, specifically designed for building static models. In Chapter 9, we see how pupils can also create static models using a commercial spreadsheet. The versatility of spreadsheets is illustrated in Chapter 10, with a range of static and dynamic, deterministic and probabilistic models. *ProbSim*, discussed in Chapter 11, models a rather more restricted range of problems than the other tools, being designed to simulate simple probability experiments. *Model Builder* was created as a general-purpose quantitative modelling tool for schools, and a case study of its use by pupils is described in Chapter 12. Finally, Chapter 13 is a little different from the others, since it is more concerned with paper-and-pencil ways of making models, and the way that these can complement computer work.

Central to all work with quantitative tools is the concept of variable, though we can see that pupils have very different understandings of its nature. Richard Boohan and Tim Brosnan describe a number of different ways in which pupils used the 'boxes' in *Q-MOD* which were intended to represent variables. In particular, we discuss the use by pupils of what we have called 'situated quantities' — quantities associated with particular objects or events — rather than 'variables', which may be altered to represent different situations. Rosamund Sutherland also discusses 'situation-based' approaches to solving algebraic problems, in which pupils reason within the situation and not algebraically.

Each modelling tool — *Q-MOD*, spreadsheet, *Model Builder*, *ProbSim* — has its own distinctive metaphors, so the extent to which these help or hinder pupils in expressing their ideas is an issue with all of them. For example, Peter Winbourne discusses how *Model Builder*'s metaphor — using a picture as a background to blocks representing variables — helped the pupils to make a start on the model. *ProbSim* has a very specific metaphor — drawing samples of objects from a mixer — and for Peter Wilder this is of central concern, arguing that the metaphor may be unhelpful for representing some real world probability problems.

In these chapters, we see much evidence of pupils using strategies to solve problems — very rarely do pupils work aimlessly with the tools. The importance of having a plan in creating quantitative models with these tools, is that the direction of calculation is fixed, so this needs to be decided at the start. Peter Winbourne is interested in whether pupils can use a plan, made explicit to them, to help them create a model from a broadly-defined problem. Pupils using *Q-MOD* also worked on broadly-defined problems, and we see evidence that some pupils were able to formulate an immediate plan of the model's structure, while others moved step by step from the given variables. Rosamund Sutherland discusses different approaches that pupils use in solving algebraic problems, in which they may work from the given to the unknown or vice versa. She suggests that using computer models can help pupils in moving from situation-based to algebraic models. Tim Brosnan's concern is almost the opposite, using spreadsheets to remove attention from the details of the algebraic relationships, in order to develop in students a better qualitative understanding of the behaviour of the variables.

Richard Boohan

All models are idealizations — within any modelling formalism, only certain aspects of the real situation can be represented. The tools in this section can only represent quantitative aspects of situations, and pupils need to be aware of these limitations. In the work on *Model Builder*, pupils used many qualitative ideas when initially thinking about problems, but were able to move to a more quantitative view in order to build a model. This also arose in the *Q-MOD* work. While many pupils are aware of the idealized nature of a model, they differ in the extent to which they see this as an important limitation. This was a particular issue for the students using *ProbSim*, who found it difficult to represent some features of the real situation within the formalism.

All models are simplifications — even within a formalism, there is always more that could be added to the model, and compromises must be made between simplicity and closeness to the real world. This idea appears throughout the section, but is central to the last chapter, which discusses ways of analysing data — finding simple models, which will not fit perfectly, but which should account for all the pattern we can see in the data.

Chapter 8

Reasoning with a Quantitative Modelling Tool

Richard Boohan and Tim Brosnan

Introduction

Could you get overweight by eating one extra snack each day? How many people can travel down a tube line in the rush hour? Is it possible to get all the energy, protein and fibre you need just by eating bread? What effect do delays have on how fast you can make a journey? All these questions require quantitative reasoning. They are the kind of questions tackled by pupils as part of the Tools for Exploratory Learning Programme (see Chapter 1). This looked at the reasoning used by pupils' working with different kinds of computer model — quantitative, semi-quantitative and qualitative. For each of these kinds of reasoning, computer tools were developed; here we shall look at pupils' use of the tool to support quantitative reasoning.

A Tool to Support Quantitative Reasoning

Q-MOD was developed as a tool for building simple static quantitative models. Models consist of boxes which represent variables, and links which represent simple arithmetic operations. *Q-MOD* was developed after *IQON* (see Chapter 15), and its design was strongly influenced by this (Miller, Ogborn, Briggs and Brough, 1992).

An example of a *Q-MOD* model used in the pupil tasks is shown in Figure 8.1. It can be used to investigate the effect of diet and exercise on body weight. It calculates the time taken to achieve a certain weight change. Each variable has been given a name, a value and units; the signs on the links indicate the relationship used in the calculation. For example, 'time needed' is calculated from 'change per week ÷ change wanted'. Thus, *Q-MOD* supports the kind of simple calculations that could be done on a spreadsheet, but shows a visual representation of the way in which variables are related to each other.

A set of tools are provided for creating, deleting and moving boxes and links, and for changing the values of variables. Changing the value of one variable immediately updates the values of all others — each number changes, and also

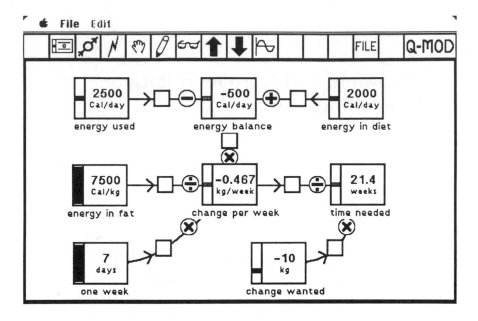

Figure 8.1: A Q-MOD model

the 'level indicator' on the left of the box. This shows its value relative to a chosen maximum and minimum, its appearance differing for independent variables (e.g., energy used), dependent variables (e.g., change per week) and constants (e.g., energy in fat). The tool was so constructed that one direction of calculation had to be chosen. Thus in considering relationships between, for example, speed, time and distance, pupils had to choose which one to make the dependent variable. Which calculation is required depends on the goal of the model, and so the decision requires some strategic plan.

The Tasks

As for the other tools developed by the Tools for Exploratory Learning Programme, there were two kinds of task — exploratory and expressive. In the case of the *Q-MOD* tasks, two domains were chosen: Diet and Traffic. For this study (Ogborn, Boohan and Brosnan, 1992), twenty pupils of middling ability were selected from the second year of a comprehensive school (ages 12 to 13). Five pupils were assigned to each of the four sets of tasks, which are outlined below.

Exploratory Tasks

In these tasks, pupils were provided with computer models which had already been constructed. They were given some problems, and asked to think about

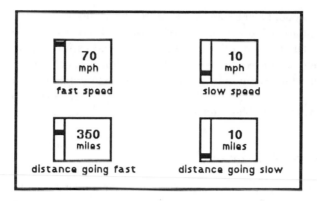

Figure 8.2: Variables provided for an expressive task

them with the help of these models. In the diet tasks, they were asked to investigate problems concerned with the food needed for a healthy diet, or how one's weight depends on food intake. In the traffic tasks, the problems were about numbers of people who travelling down a train line, or walking down a road, or about the number of cars travelling down a road. Pupils were asked to evaluate these models, judging whether they were too simple or too complicated to be useful.

Expressive Tasks

In the expressive tasks, pupils were given some questions, and some relevant data (on paper) and had to construct their own models to help them answer the questions. A number of relevant variables were provided already created, though none were connected, and no task could be completed without creating new variables and links. The diet tasks were about energy and protein requirements from food, and the effect of eating an extra snack each day. The traffic tasks were about the effect of delays when travelling by plane, and of hold-ups on the motorway (Figure 8.2).

Demands of the Tasks

The tasks were designed to be challenging, though not unmanageable, for 12 to 13-year-old pupils, and each task had a similar set of cognitive demands. For example, Figure 8.1 showed a model with three relationships, the result depending on the values of three independent variables; similarly, all the tasks required a structure with more than one relation, involving the simultaneous action of more than one factor. All of the tasks required use of some compound quantities (for example, the model in Figure 8.1 uses calories per day and kilograms per week).

All pupils could make some sense of the tasks, and made an attempt at them, though few constructed complete models or used models to explore a range of possibilities. The tasks and the tool were highly successful in allowing the pupils to use a variety of forms of reasoning. In the following sections we shall focus on those aspects which seem to be most central to quantitative modelling the pupils' understanding of the nature of the quantities used, the relationships they constructed between variables, and their evaluation of models.

Nature of Quantities

It might seem evident that, in using a tool which manipulates quantitative variables, pupils would mainly define and use such variables. In fact, pupils used the 'boxes' in the tool, intended to contain variables, to represent various kinds of entity. Two of these entities which are not variables at all are objects and events. Entities which look more like variables are what we will term numerals, stored reminders, constants, and alterable constants.

Objects and Events

'Variables' which pupils created were sometimes given names suggestive of objects or events, for example 'cheese', 'snack1', 'snack2'. A simple and clear example is the pupil who, in a diet task, created a 'box' called 'boy' with 'value' 13 years:

> I've made a box that says it's a boy and it's 13 years old.

Thinking in objects or events has two big advantages. One is that quantities are associated with particulars which are easy to envisage, which both helps in estimating values and in giving them meaning. The other is that it permits a simple view of the combination of quantities: the calories from one snack just add to the calories from another, or the distance gone in one journey just adds to that gone in another.

Numerals

Most pupils tried to give meaning to quantities, though some tended to regard any quantity merely as a numeral. That is, units were ignored and calculations were described, despite probing, uniquely in terms of operations on numerals. For example,

> It's multiplying 10 times the 12.9 and it's divided the 12.9 into 7

was one pupil's account of a model which gave 12.9 weeks (with 7 days in a week) as the time taken to lose 10 kg at a certain calculated weight loss per day.

Numerals have the great advantage that they can be freely combined: one can add or multiply 2 and 3, but not 2 miles and 3 mph without thought for the meaning of what is being done.

Stored Reminders

It was striking that a few pupils used 'variables' with which no calculations were done. One model contained 8 isolated variables, which included the example mentioned above, of a 'variable' called 'boy' given the value '13 years'. Another example is the pupil who constructed several diet models without ever changing the value of any quantity, and had some quantities which were not linked to any others.

Variables as Constants

Much more frequent, was a view of 'variables' as single correct values associated with relevant quantities, to be found by specifying or calculating them for a single 'one-off' case. Some pupils would create quantities and build links, but never, or rarely, change the value of a quantity once it was decided. In effect 'variables' are seen as constants. In one example, a diet task, the calories per 100 g of each food had been put into two boxes called 'wholemeal bread' and 'cheese':

I've made two more boxes, one is wholemeal bread and the calories in it, and the other is cheese and the calories in it . . . then I'd add them together . . . that gives you 630 calories if you have a cheese sandwich.

Such a view sees a model as appropriate to a single context, and a 'variable' as a singular fact in that context.

Alterable Constants

The most frequent view of variables, in all tasks, was one closely related to the 'constant' view above, but seeing them as 'alterable constants'. This view, of a model as making one of a number of possible specific calculations, using constants altered to fit the situation, is seen in what a pupil said at the end of an exploratory diet task:

. . . if you were trying to work out how many calories you were losing, you'd know how many you would be burning and how many you'd be eating   so you could work it out for yourself — but if you were talking about someone you didn't really know, who wasn't there, you wouldn't know what values to put in.

Richard Boohan and Tim Brosnan

Variables

A few pupils clearly showed a more general understanding of the idea of a variable. For example, where some created separate variables, speed of train and speed of plane, others kept one variable in such cases and entered the different values in it. The pupil who did this with a variable called speed of plane but put speeds of trains in it, and when challenged said, 'It's the speed of whatever you're travelling in' was plainly generalizing away from 'alterable constants' towards variables. There were other such cases, but they were not very frequent.

Situated Quantities

A key to understanding much of the pupils reasoning is the idea of a 'situated quantity'. By this we mean a quantity associated with a particular discrete object or event. Describing the density of people travelling along a road, one pupil said:

> Because if too many people were walking down the road there'd be too much crowding [the name given to the density variable in the task] and that says that the crowding would only be like 5280 people in the crowd walking down the road [5280 was in fact the current value of the 'crowding' in people per mile].

Here, we can regard '5280 people in the crowd' as meaning 5280 people who happen to be walking down a road which happens to be a mile long, and so can be thought of as an amount.

The concept of situated quantity may help to make sense of what otherwise must seem a bizarre way in which some pupils treated speeds. In expressive traffic tasks there were pupils who confidently added speeds and distances. In one task about the average speed on a journey some of which was done at high speed and some at low speed, one pupil immediately formed a plan for the model:

> . . . add the distance going fast and the fast speed, do the same with these two [distance going slow and slow speed] and then join the two [results] together.

And it is not important whether the result is in miles or in miles per hour:

> . . . it finds out the total of how fast it goes and how slow it goes and altogether, and how many miles you can get or go . . . like in an hour or something.

That is, one can add a situated speed (a distance travelled in one particular hour) and a situated distance (a distance travelled at some other particular time). And the strategy for solving the problem — combining distances travelled additively — makes overall sense, though not in the way it is done.

Situated quantities are just what one might expect pupils to imagine and use, if, as is highly likely at the age of 13, they are reasoning with concrete operations. Their use is also consistent with a 'mental models' perspective on the nature of reasoning.

Relationships Between Variables

There appeared to be three main ways in which pupils thought about relations:

- processing mechanics;
- real world connections;
- semi-quantitative relations.

Many pupils would look at relations in more than one way. In the 'processing mechanics' view, which was often found in expressive tasks, relations are looked at as a set or sequence of operations on quantities:

> I've taken the calories and the amount of food . . . and it's 410 calories per portion timesed by 6 portions which the answer was 2460 calories, and I also timesed by the protein needed.

Seeing a set of relations as 'real world connections' meant thinking about how values in a model related to plausible possibilities in reality:

> If you think about it properly it does make sense about gaps between each car. If you're going slow you don't need so much time to slow down, because you're slow already. If you're going faster you need more space to get down your mileage [speed].

The 'semi-quantitative' view of relations treats them as a set of mutual influences:

> Because the faster you go, the bigger the gap has to be between each car, but if you go slower and the gap is smaller, the more cars can get on . . . so in one hour you'd get more cars in the tunnel.

Others do not interpret the relations at all, but just describe the values, most notably in exploratory tasks which they treat simply as a set of connected values, in effect, as a numerical simulation:

> Five minutes between each train . . . that's a five miles gap, the speed is 60 miles for each train, the trains — their frequency is 12 trains per hour, and that's timesed by the five hundred to make the 6000.

In the expressive tasks, there were essentially no cases of pupils constructing 'relations' with no purpose. There was the occasional 'experiment', but in general pupils knew what they were trying to do when they created links, and when the

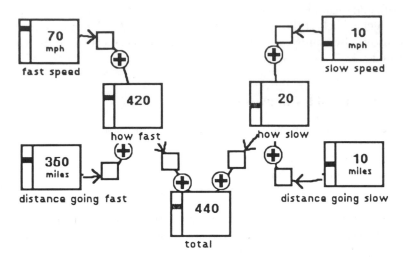

Figure 8.3: One pupil's model for a traffic task

result was not what they had intended. Models were usually built forwards from given quantities, but in some cases a strategic plan was used. In almost all relations, no more than two quantities were linked to the dependent variable. This binary view of relations often led pupils to try to combine two 'boxes' by linking them directly, rather than linking them to a third 'box' as required by the interface.

In all the models built for expressive traffic tasks, there was some basically sound concept, consisting of an integrated set of linked variables. Some pupils constructed useful models with correct relations between speed, distance and time; others showed some understanding of the strategy required, but were unable to construct a useful model.

As an example, Figure 8.3 shows the model built by one pupil following a plan arrived at immediately after starting to think about the problem. Its structure is essentially correct, but both from the model and the pupil's description, speed seems to be regarded as a kind of distance so that they can be added together.

In the models built for expressive diet tasks there were a greater variety of quantities. On the whole they were less structured, though Figure 8.4 shows one pupil's model which performs an acceptable calculation of the calorie and protein yields of a food.

It could be that this difference between domains is due to the greater everyday knowledge pupils have of diet. They could think of more quantities to create, which gave them greater problems in seeing how to organize them.

Pupils' Evaluation of the Models

A model is useful because it is a simplified representation. When asked if the models were too simple or too complicated, several understood this as meaning

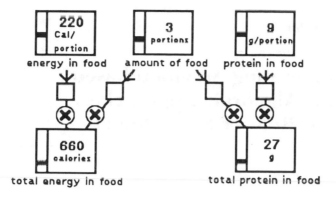

Figure 8.1: One pupil's model for a diet task

'too simple or complicated for me'. Indeed several evaluated models primarily in terms of personal interest and relevance:

> It's not really my stuff to think about all this . . . some people, they're really interested in stuff like this . . . they want to make sure everything's — you know — all right.

No pupil wanted a model made simpler. All suggestions were for adding to the complications, for example, by taking into account the unpredictability of traffic hold-ups, or the variation in the values of variables:

> If they counted the amount of crashes or hold-ups . . . then you'd be a bit more accurate. . . . And trains . . . there's a lot of hold-ups and cancellations.
> They won't walk in equal groups — they will walk differently — like some might walk in twelve's and some in tens.
> It just does the easy side of what happens, but doesn't count the hardest side, so it's not true to life really.

In exploratory tasks, all pupils could give some account of whether the models were useful. Where an expressive model was partially useful, pupils could usually identify what it was able and unable to do; where it was not very useful, some pupils could see that this was so and could say what it would need to do.

Research Tool or Pedagogic Tool?

The quantitative tool proved in many ways very useful as a research tool, particularly in revealing pupils' difficulties with aspects of quantitative reasoning and quantitative models. Had it 'been better' and 'done more', then it might not have been so effective in eliciting these problems. For example, the tool did not enforce consistent units nor compute the units of derived quantities. Had it done so, pupils might have benefited, but we might have learned less.

Chapter 9

Integrating Situation-based and Algebraic Approaches: The Role of Spreadsheets

Rosamund Sutherland

Introduction

Mathematics provides one of the most powerful means of modelling and solving problems across a range of subjects in science and technology. Examples are biology, chemistry, geography and physics, which all make use of mathematical techniques to model situations and solve problems. Many of these mathematical techniques involve using algebraic methods — methods which are considered valuable because of their generalizability. But students find it difficult to use and understand the generalizability of a mathematical model. They do not easily make links between the mathematics they use in different contexts — so, for example, using algebraic methods in a chemistry lesson is different from using algebraic methods in biology. The reasons for this are complex and it is not simply a matter of the student 'forgetting her algebra' or 'never being taught maths properly'. The practice of mathematics differs between subjects, because the situations and objects to be modelled are different.

In order to develop a mathematical model of a situation it is necessary to move from thinking about the more realistic objects and quantities of the situation to thinking about relationships between the more abstract mathematical objects of the model. (I am using the word object to refer both to things in the real world and to manipulable mathematical entities.) Some students find it easy to think within a formal model. Others find it easy to think with the objects of the situation. But to move between thinking about the objects of the situation to thinking within the formal system is clearly very difficult. Within this chapter I shall discuss the ways in which pupils model and solve a number of algebra story problems. The relatively straightforward nature of these problems makes it possible to analyse the diversity of approaches used by students.

Characterizing Approaches to Modelling a Situation

It is now widely recognized that students use a range of situation-based strategies to solve problems. This is the case for street sellers in Brazil (Carraher *et al.*, 1985), supermarket shoppers (Lave, 1988), computer science undergraduates (Hall *et al.*, 1989), and students in school (Lins, 1992). These strategies are often more related to the needs of the situation as opposed to the mathematical knowledge of the student. I cannot recall a time when I have used my formal mathematical knowledge to model a situation in the supermarket or in the kitchen and this is not because I am unable to do so. For me the cultural situation and the problem to be solved do not call for a formal mathematical model. On the other hand practising scientists, engineers and economists, for example, all make use of formal mathematical models. I believe that students should be aware of these practices, not because they themselves will necessarily become scientists, engineers or economists, but because they should experience this aspect of our culture. In the past, school practice has tended to place too much emphasis and status on 'algebraic' and formal thinking at the expense of other types of thinking. This trend is now swinging in the other direction, partly influenced by research on cognition in practice. I suggest that a balance needs to be maintained, which takes into account both the importance of thinking with the more realistic objects of the situation and thinking with abstract algebraic objects.

Situation-based Models

Within this chapter I shall discuss two models which are often used by students when modelling and solving problems:

- a trial and refinement model;
- a whole/parts model.

These are situation-based models, so called because they involve thinking with the objects of the situation (for example width, time). There are many variants of these models described in the literature and it is not my intention here to make a comprehensive study of these approaches, but to use these two models to illustrate a number of important issues related to situation-based thinking. In order to describe these models I shall refer to the following two problems, the first, the 'train problem' used by Hall *et al.* (1989) in a study with computer science undergraduates and the second the 'rectangular field' problem used with a group of 10-year-old pre-algebra students and 15-year-old algebra-resistant students carried out in a study by Teresa Rojano and myself (Rojano and Sutherland, 1992; Sutherland and Rojano, 1993).

The train problem: two trains leave the same station at the same time. They travel in opposite directions. One train travels at 60 km/h and the other at 100 km/h. In how many hours will they be 880 km apart?

The rectangular field problem: the perimeter of a field measures 102 metres. The length of the field is twice as much as the width of the field. How much does the length of the field measure? How much does the width of the field measure?

The Trial and Refinement Model

In this approach the student runs the problem for successive values of appropriate variables. Hall *et al.* (1989) illustrate this by describing the way a student solved the train problem (although they call this a simulation model and not a trial and refinement model). The student carried out and wrote down the following calculations:

first hr 60	100	= 160
2nd hr 120	200	= 320
3rd hr 180	300	= 480
4th hr 240	400	= 640
5th hr 300	500	= 800
6th hr 360	600	= 960

The student then realized that the solution lies between 5 and 6 hours and using proportional reasoning produced a solution of 5.5 hours.

A similar method was used by a 10-year-old pre-algebra student solving the rectangular field problem

> . . . well I tried 40, it was 120 . . . so I knew it must be smaller than that . . . in the 30s . . . and when I tried 36 and it was 108 . . . I knew it couldn't be 35 so it must be 34. . . .

Although this approach may not have been explicitly taught in school it is probably widely used in out of school practices and methods similar to this were used by the ancient Egyptians (Joseph, 1992, p. 79).

The Whole/Parts Model

In this approach the student relates a part quantity to a whole quantity in order to work from the given whole to the unknown part (Lins, 1992). This is illustrated by the following solution to the train problem.

> Let A be the train which travels at 60 km/h
> Let B be the train which travels at 100 km/h
> Every hour train B is 160 km away from train A so the numbers of hours
>   for them to be 880 km apart = 880/160 hrs
>   = 5.5 hrs

This method was used by a 10-year-old pre-algebra student solving the rectangular field problem

> I did 102 divided by 6 . . . I just did two of the lengths to make it sensible. . . . I just thought there must be two of those in one length. . . .

Both the above situation-based models are used extensively by students when solving a range of algebra story problems. They differ in a number of ways from the analytic algebraic model discussed in the following section.

The Analytic Algebraic Model
This is the method predominantly taught in schools as illustrated by the following solutions to the 'train' and the 'rectangular field' problem.

The train problem
Let the number of hours after which the trains will be 880 km apart be x hrs

$$\text{Then} \quad 60x + 100x = 880$$
$$160x = 880$$
$$x = 880/160$$
$$= 5.5 \text{ hrs}$$

The rectangular field problem
Let the width of the field $= x$ metres.
Let the length of the field $= l$ metres.
Then $\quad l \quad = 2x \quad$ (1)
and $\quad 2l + 2x = 102 \quad$ (2)
So by substituting (1) in (2)
$$4x + 2x = 102$$
$$6x = 102$$
$$x = 17 \text{ metres.}$$

The most important characteristic of this approach is that it involves expressing the unknowns in the problem (for example the width and length of the field) in terms of the givens (for example the perimeter). This differs from the whole/part model but has some similarities with the trial and refinement model. The use of algebraic language supports the analytic algebraic method but it is not the algebraic symbols which are the main characteristic of an analytic algebraic method. The method differs from the two situation-based models discussed above in that the focus is on the abstract mathematical objects (e.g., x and l) and not on the more realistic objects (e.g., width).

Possible Tensions Between Situation-based and Algebraic Approaches

I shall now begin to identify the possible tensions between an approach to modelling which is based on thinking with the objects of the situation and the development of an analytic algebraic model. As I have already stressed, the analytic algebraic method, which is emphasized in the mathematics classroom, involves working from the unknowns (called, for example, x) to the givens within a problem. It does not involve manipulating the given quantities within a problem (as is the case in for example the whole/parts model). In this sense algebraic approaches are in opposition to approaches which involve thinking with the givens within a situation. Mathematical modelling involves more than developing a formal algebraic model. It involves moving between the situation and the formal model, and so thinking with the situation is a crucial element in the process of modelling. In other words, while thinking about and with the situation is an important part of the whole modelling process, it is precisely this which must be suspended in order to develop an algebraic model.

There is some evidence that expert problem-solvers in science actually 'work forwards' operating from the givens of a problem, and novices 'work backwards' going from the unknowns to the givens (Heller and Hungate, 1985). This further suggests that the taught analytic algebraic method (which involves working backwards from the unknowns to the givens) could be in opposition to models taught in the science classroom.

Spreadsheets as a Modelling Tool

In a recent study two groups of students were taught to use a spreadsheet to solve a range of algebra story problems (Sutherland and Rojano, 1993; Rojano and Sutherland, 1992). In one group were 10 to 11-year-olds with no previous experience of algebra, and in the other were 14 to 15-year-olds with a previous history of resistance to school mathematics, students in each group being drawn from England and from Mexico. The students constructed their own models to represent a problem and in this sense the tasks are expressive and not exploratory (see Chapter 1 for explanations of these terms). The students were taught a spreadsheet method (called a spreadsheet-algebraic model). This involved working from the unknown to the given as illustrated by the spreadsheet approach to the rectangular field problem presented in Figure 9.1. The unknown is represented by a spreadsheet cell. Other mathematical relationships are then expressed in terms of this unknown (there are some similarities here with the setting up of an algebraic equation). When the problem has been expressed in the spreadsheet symbolic language, pupils can then vary the unknown, either by replicating the rules down the columns of the spreadsheet or by changing the number in the cell representing the unknown (there are some similarities here with the trial and refinement model described earlier).

Although students were introduced to the spreadsheet-algebraic model through working on a number of problems they often integrated this approach into more situation-based approaches. This is illustrated by 10-year-old Mike's solution to the following problem:

Chocolates problem: 100 chocolates were distributed between three groups of children. The second group received 4 times the chocolates given to the first group. The third group received 10 chocolates more than the second group. How many chocolates did the first, the second and the third group receive?

Mike first carried out the calculation 100/3 in a cell and entered the result 33.3333333 in cell A5 (for the number of chocolates in the first group) (Figure 9.2). That is, he started to solve the problem using a whole/parts model which involved dividing the whole number of chocolates by the number of parts. He

Rectangular Field

The perimeter of a rectangular field measures 102 metres.

The length of the field is twice as much as the width of the field.

Use a spreadsheet to work out the width and the length of the field.

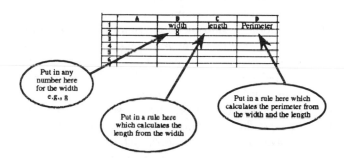

Then change the number for the width until you can answer the question.

Figure 9.1: A spreadsheet approach to solving the rectangular field problem

		A	B	C
No of chocs in 1st group	5	10		
	6			
	7			
No of chocs in 2nd group	8			
	9	=A5*4		
	10			
No of chocs in 3rd group	11	=A9+10		
	12			
	13			
Total No of chocs	14	=A5+A9+A11		

Figure 9.2: Mike's solution to the chocolates problem

then entered the rule 33.3333333*4 (for the number of chocolates in the second group) in cell A9 indicating that he was initially thinking with this specific value. He immediately changed this to the correct rule A5*4 indicating a shift from thinking with a specific object to thinking with a general object (a shift which was possibly provoked by the symbolic nature of the spreadsheet environment). This rule produced a number bigger than 100 which concerned him because 'there are only 100 chocolates altogether' (indicating that he was also thinking with the objects of the situation). However, he continued and entered the correct rule A9 + 10 for the number of chocolates in the third group. He then changed the number in cell A5 (the number of chocolates in the first group) to 22 which reduced the total number of chocolates to less than 100. He finally entered a rule to calculate the total number of chocolates (A5 + A9 + A11) and then varied the number in the first group (cell A5) until he obtained a solution.

The spreadsheet environment supported him in moving from thinking with the objects of the situation to thinking with a more formal spreadsheet-algebraic model. Not all students found this easy. Andrew (aged 10) could not break away from thinking about the situation. He first entered the number 100 in cell B4 and then in cell B5 carried out the calculation B4/3. This was similar to Mike's strategy for calculating a value (although incorrect) for the number of chocolates in the second group. Andrew then entered a correct rule (B5*4) for the number of chocolates in the second group. This produced a number greater than 100 for the number of chocolates in the first group which he knew could not be correct. Instead of changing the number in the first group Andrew then changed the correct rule to B5*4/2 (i.e., he divided by 2) in order to try to reduce this unreasonably large number. This suggests that he was thinking with the objects of the situation at the expense of the mathematical invariants of the problem. It was evident on other occasions that Andrew predominantly thinks with the objects of the situation, ignoring the mathematical relationships within a particular problem, as illustrated by his following comment 'How do we know how many teachers there are, is this a primary school or a secondary school?'. The case of Andrew illustrates the tension between thinking about whether a quantity sensibly fits a situation and thinking with a formal mathematical model which relates to the constraints of the situation.

Finally, I present an example taken from the work with a group of ten 15-year-olds, all of whom had a history of being unsuccessful with school mathematics. Before they started to work with spreadsheets they were asked to solve these problems with either situation-based or algebraic models. All of these 15-year-olds became successful at solving the algebra story problems with the spreadsheet (Rojano and Sutherland, 1992). But, what is more interesting is that when they worked on similar problems in a paper-based test at the end of the study a number of them had developed successful trial and refinement models which were clearly influenced by their spreadsheet work. This is illustrated by Anna's solution to the rectangular field problem (Figure 9.3). This spontaneous use of paper-based 'trial and refinement' models, not used by them before the spreadsheet work, highlights the similarities between these two approaches. Both approaches involve thinking about the objects of the situation and encourage students to move towards developing an analytic algebraic model which is based on working from the unknowns to the givens in a problem. In the paper-based trial and refinement model the unknown is represented by a range of quantities. In the spreadsheet-algebraic model the unknown is represented by a spreadsheet cell within which a range of values can be inserted.

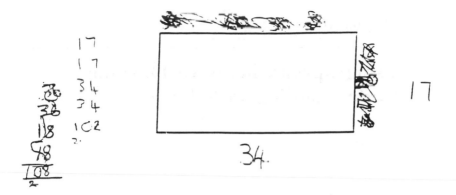

Figure 9.3: Anna's paper-based solution to the rectangular field problem after the spreadsheet experience

Some Concluding Remarks

Within this chapter I have focused on the analysis of relatively straightforward modelling problems. This analysis has highlighted the tension between thinking with the quantities of a situation and thinking with abstract algebraic objects, a tension which is likely to increase within more substantial modelling problems. This tension is further compounded by two different approaches, one which involves working from the givens within a situation to the unknown and the other which involves working from the unknown towards the givens. In a new project ('A Spreadsheet Approach to Mathematical Modelling for Engineering Students' funded by the Nuffield Foundation and directed by Rosamund Sutherland and Alison Wolf) we shall continue to identify the strategies and models which students use within the more 'realistic' modelling problems used by engineering technicians.

Working with a spreadsheet enables students to integrate their situation-based models with a formal spreadsheet model. To communicate this spreadsheet model to others, the algebraic language could then be used, since, for this purpose, the spreadsheet language is not explicit enough. Whether in the future students will need to develop paper-based algebraic models, or whether computer-based ones will be sufficient is still an open question.

Chapter 10

Using Spreadsheets to Develop Understanding in Science

Tim Brosnan

Introduction

At heart, real understanding in science is essentially qualitative yet is often expressed in mathematical relations. Most students of advanced science therefore spend a great deal of time and effort doing calculations. These calculations pose two kinds of demands:

- some of the mathematical models involved are complex and/or
- there is a need for repetitive analysis of large amounts of data.

Both of these can serve to focus students' attention on mechanical mathematics at the expense of their understanding of the underlying scientific principles. Using Ogborn and Miller's phrase (Chapter 5) they reduce the level of cognitive 'chunking'. This a serious hindrance to students' learning and the need is for a tool or tools that can be used to raise the level of chunking so that they can focus on the underlying scientific concepts. Ideally such a system would be capable of being used by both students to model simple systems in which they can express their understanding of the science involved and by their teachers to construct more complex models for the students to explore. This chapter examines a variety of ways in which one tool, a spreadsheet, can be used to promote learning in an important concept area, that of chemical equilibrium.

Why Spreadsheets?

Spreadsheets have a number of attributes which make them suitable for use as a computational tool in the school laboratory:

- They can be used to write both static and dynamic models and can therefore be employed in a wide variety of situations.
- They possess (increasingly) well integrated graphing facilities.

- They can be used in either of two complementary modes. In the first, students use the tool to express their own ideas, usually by testing a variety of models (of their own construction) using fixed data, while in the second, students explore models which express the thinking of others, usually by feeding variable data into a fixed model. The latter category commonly involves exploring the accepted scientific models although it also encompasses students exploring expressions of each others' ideas. The differences between these modes of use are similar to the expressive/exploratory distinction described in Chapter 1. Bliss *et al.* (1992a, 1992b), Kemmis *et al.* (1977) and Schibeci (1989) provide further useful discussions of these ways of using models.
- They are existing well known software packages, capable of being used in many different conceptual areas across the school curriculum.
- They are becoming much more widely used by classroom teachers. Recently a number of articles have appeared in journals including those written for and by classroom teachers. They cover all branches of science and range from the substantial to the brief 'hints and tips' variety (see for example Brosnan, 1990, 1992; Goodfellow, 1990). Attempts have also been made to make the interface of a standard package (Excel) more 'user-friendly' (Beare, 1992).

Spreadsheets thus appear to meet the need for a powerful, flexible and widely available microworld within which students can interact with models both to express their own understanding of a situation and to explore the meanings of others.

The Nature of Students' Difficulties with Equilibrium

Chemical equilibrium is a core chemical concept, an understanding of which is essential for most qualitative and quantitative work in chemistry and thus its study forms a central part of advanced chemistry courses. These courses tend to stress the quantitative aspects of the topic, fulfilling the (necessary) function of teaching students to use the appropriate equations. Studying equilibrium therefore involves both difficult and/or repetitive calculations. In their different ways these provide barriers to conceptual understanding. The topic thus provides a good focus for exploring the different kinds of barriers which both these types of arithmetical demand pose to conceptual understanding.

It is also a conceptual area where previous work has shown that students have well-structured 'alternative conceptions' which are highly resistant to change. Recent research (e.g., Maskill and Cachapuz, 1989) has reinforced the feeling, long held by teachers, that many students find the concept of chemical equilibrium difficult. In particular it has highlighted the way that they base their understandings of chemical equilibria on ideas and meanings associated with other, more everyday, concepts of equilibrium. They have a different qualitative understanding to the scientist of 'the way things are'.

One further difficulty is that chemical equilibrium is commonly portrayed using both static models, which work backward from laws to deduce concentrations, and dynamic models, which stress the process of movement towards equilibrium. Within this latter category there are both probabilistic models, representing the process at the level of individual molecules, and deterministic models based on rate laws. This plethora of conceptual approaches confuses many students who cannot see the links between them. However it provides an ideal forum for examining the ease with which students can move between different representations of the same system.

Addressing the Students' Difficulties

In this section I will list some of the main problems that students have in coming to a full understanding of chemical equilibrium and illustrate some of the ways in which spreadsheets can be used to address these difficulties.

The Ratio of Equilibrium Concentrations

Students often believe that at equilibrium the composition of the reacting species is equal to, or at least in the ratio of, the balanced chemical equation for the reaction. For example, for the reaction:

$$2HI \rightleftharpoons H_2 + I_2$$

they may think that the equilibrium concentrations of hydrogen, iodine and hydrogen iodide are in the ratio 1:1:2. This fits with an everyday notion of balance. As a result many students cannot accept (and therefore have difficulties with) the equilibrium law expression, which in this example is:

$$K_c = [H_2][I_2]/[HI]^2$$

and which relates the equilibrium concentrations to a constant, K_c. One way of addressing these problems is to show that the general form of the equilibrium law 'works' in that it is applicable to a wide variety of reactions with many sets of equilibrium concentrations. Unfortunately the repetitive nature of the necessary calculations soon make them tedious as well as taking a great deal of time. This means that not only is the discussion usually limited to just one or two examples but that the range of alternative equilibrium law formulations which can be tested is also circumscribed. One solution to this problem is for a teacher to enter data sets of equilibrium concentrations on a spreadsheet and allow the students to write their own equilibrium law expressions and see the consequences. Knowing the balanced chemical equations they are free to try any analytic relation they choose on one data set until they find one or ones that give constant values. They

	A	B	C	D	E	F
1	Hydrogen	Iodine	Hydrogen	K1	K2	K3
2			Iodide			
3						
4	4.56	0.74	13.54	0.391	0.25	0.02
5	3.56	1.25	15.59	0.309	0.29	0.02
6	2.25	2.34	16.85	0.272	0.31	0.02
7	0.48	0.48	3.53	0.272	0.07	0.02
8	0.50	0.50	3.66	0.273	0.07	0.02
9	1.14	1.14	8.41	0.271	0.15	0.02

Figure 10.1: Possible equilibrium law expressions for the hydrogen/iodine/hydrogen iodide system

then try and generalize from this and apply their ideas to another data set. In the example shown in Figure 10.1, students are given sets of equilibrium concentrations for the hydrogen/iodine/hydrogen iodide system described above and asked to write different possible equilibrium law expressions. Typically they use expressions such as these:

$$K1 = ([H_2]+[I_2])/[HI]$$
$$K2 = ([H_2]*[I_2])/[HI]$$
$$K3 = ([H_2]*[I_2])/[HI]^\wedge 2$$

It can be seen by inspecting the calculated values that the last of these (K3) produces the most constant value. In this expressive example the students only write an equation once and then use a built-in spreadsheet function to copy the formula into other cells. In this way they are free to concentrate on the models rather than the mathematics. The general nature of the relationship may then be explored further by using another system — such as the ethanol/ethanoic acid/ethyl ethanoate/water system.

$$C_2H_5OH + CH_3COOH \rightleftharpoons CH_3COOC_2H_5 + H_2O$$

where 'common sense' suggests that the equilibrium concentration of all the species should be equal — but they are not.

The Effect of Changing Concentrations on Equilibrium

Another way of examining the non-equivalence of the equilibrium concentrations of reacting species is to use a spreadsheet to perform a 'brute force' calculation

	A	B	C	D	E	F	G
1							
2		React	0.01	Moles			
3							
4		Name	Ethanol	Ethanoic	Ethyl	Water	
5				Acid	Ethanoate		
6		Stoichiometry	1	1	1	1	
7		Initial []	2	1	0	1	
8		Total change	0.7425	0.7425	0.7425	0.7425	
9		Current	1.2575	0.2575	0.7425	1.7425	
10							
11			Book Value		Calculated value		
12			Kc 4.00E+00		K 4.00E+00		
13			lnKc 1.39E+00		lnK 1.39E+00		
14							

Figure 10.2: 'Brute force' calculation of equilibrium concentrations

(Ogborn, 1987). The student is free to choose any initial concentrations of the reacting species and then react or 'unreact' successive amounts of one species until the calculated equilibrium constant matches the book value. The model uses the stoichiometry and amount it is told to react to calculate new concentrations and use these in turn to calculate an 'equilibrium constant'. One particular use of this approach is to allow students to see the effect of adding more of one reagent, the example illustrated in Figure 10.2 shows the effect on the reaction described above of starting with 2 moles of ethanol, one mole of ethanoic acid and of water, and no ethyl ethanoate. The point here is to see how the pattern of equilibrium concentrations relates to the starting concentrations. In particular it can be used to show that the concentrations of species on any one side of the reaction need not be equal — in fact it is unusual for them to be so.

The calculations involved in the examples above are simple but repetitive. However there are other systems, often those involving more than one competing equilibrium, where the barrier to meaningful exploration is that the calculations are too difficult. The technique described above can be adapted for use with these systems also.

A good example is the class of generalized acid/base equilibria. In these there are three competing equilibria — the dissociation of the acid, base and water:

$HA(aq) \rightleftharpoons H^+(aq) + A^-(aq)$
$HB(aq) \rightleftharpoons H^+(aq) + B^-(aq)$
$H_2O \rightleftharpoons H^+(aq) + OH^-(aq)$
(A and B are the acid and base respectively)

The pH curves of these systems are often obtained experimentally and comparing the results of direct experiment with those obtained from theoretical models is

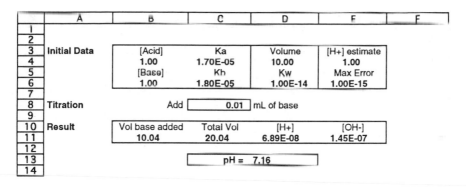

	A	B	C	D	E	F
1						
2						
3	Initial Data	[Acid]	Ka	Volume	[H+] estimate	
4		1.00	1.70E-05	10.00	1.00	
5		[Base]	Kh	Kw	Max Error	
6		1.00	1.80E-05	1.00E-14	1.00E-15	
7						
8	Titration		Add	0.01	mL of base	
9						
10	Result	Vol base added	Total Vol	[H+]	[OH-]	
11		10.04	20.04	6.89E-08	1.45E-07	
12						
13			pH =	7.16		
14						

Figure 10.3: A spreadsheet model to calculate the pH of acid/base reactions

potentially of considerable interest. However while the chemical principles involved are relatively simple, determination of the pH is difficult since it requires solving a quartic equation in $H^+(aq)$. Figure 10.3 shows a spreadsheet model devised to address this problem. In this example the user is free to set the initial concentrations of acids and bases of any strength and the concentration of $H^+(aq)$ is calculated. (It is done by a function macro which uses the Newton-Raphson method iteratively to seek a chemically meaningful root.) Using this model students can 'step through' any acid-base reaction, see the effect of different acid and base concentrations and dissociation constants on the pH values during the titration, and compare the results with those obtained by experiments on the system.

The Dynamic and Probabilistic Nature of Chemical Equilibrium

A complementary approach to the same problem is to use a spreadsheet to model the dynamics of the movement of a chemical system towards equilibrium using a simple Monte Carlo simulation of a system such as that between 'a' and 'b' shown in Figure 10.4 (Brosnan, 1992).

When this model is run, cells are selected at random (by a command macro which performs all the calculations). The chosen probability is used to decide whether to 'react' the contents of the cell — 'beeping' whenever the contents of a cell reacts. A running total is kept of the numbers of each reacting species present, which is used to calculate an equilibrium constant. As well as showing again the non-equivalence of equilibrium concentrations, this example illustrates a number of important points:

- At equilibrium the concentration of each species (and hence the equilibrium constant) fluctuates only slightly but the two reactions are still proceeding — the beeping does not stop. The existence of this fluctuation

	A	B	C	D	E	F	G	H	I	J	K
1											
2											
3		a	b	b	a	b	b	b	b	b	a
4		b	b	b	b	b	b	a	b	b	b
5		b	a	b	a	b	a	b	a	b	b
6		a	a	b	b	b	b	b	b	b	b
7		b	a	a	a	a	b	b	b	b	b
8		b	b	a	b	a	a	b	b	b	a
9		b	a	b	b	b	b	b	b	b	b
10		b	a	b	b	b	b	b	b	a	b
11		b	b	b	b	b	b	b	b	b	b
12		b	b	b	b	a	a	b	b	a	a
13											
14	Probability of Forward Reaction							0.75		[a]	0.24
15										[b]	0.76
16	Probability of Reverse Reaction							0.25		"K"	3.17
17											

Figure 10.4: A simple Monte Carlo model of chemical equilibrium

is itself interesting, being a consequence of the non-deterministic nature of both the model and real chemical reactions. Boxes of different sizes can be used to see that as the size of the system increases the relative importance (although not the absolute size) of the fluctuations decreases. The amounts used in real reactions correspond to boxes about $10^{13} \times 10^{13}$ so the effect of any fluctuation is usually undetectable!

- The students can set the initial concentrations of each reactant and see that the equilibrium concentrations are independent of these.
- The students can also assign the probabilities of the forward and back reactions and see that although the speed of reaction (the frequency of the beeps) depends on their absolute values, the equilibrium concentrations (and hence the equilibrium constant) depend only on the ratio of their values. This can be used to explain the action of a catalyst — multiplying the probability of both reactions by a similar amount speeds up the reaction but as the ratio of the probabilities is still the same the equilibrium constant is unchanged.

The Differing Ways Temperature and Pressure/Concentration Affect Equilibrium Concentrations

All the research evidence stresses that many students have great difficulty in predicting the way an equilibrium mixture will alter when the conditions change. One major reason for this has already been highlighted, i.e., the visualizing of the system as being composed of two independent sides each of which can be

	Reacting Entities	Reactant 1	Reactant 2	Product 1	Product 2
Name		Nitrogen	Hydrogen	Ammonia	0
Stoichiometry		1	3	2	0
Standard molar entropy		191.6	130.7	192.45	0
Standard molar enthalpy		0.00	0.00	-46.11	0.00
Initial Amount (mol)		1	3	0	0
Initial partial pressures		2.5	7.5	0	0
xLN(x)		2.29	15.11	0.00	0.00

Reaction Conditions		Initial Values	
Temperature (K)	400	Extent of reaction	0.87
Step size	0.01	'Enthalpy'	-92.22
Pressure	10.00	'Entropy'	-284.04

x	Pr1	Pr2	Pp1	Pp2	nt	Ssur	Ssys	Stot	"K"
0.87	0.58	1.73	7.70	0.00	2.26	200.58	664.09	864.67	20.05
0.88	0.54	1.61	7.86	0.00	2.24	202.88	661.84	864.73	27.76
0.89	0.50	1.49	8.02	0.00	2.22	205.19	659.56	864.75	39.50
0.90	0.45	1.36	8.18	0.00	2.20	207.50	657.26	864.75	58.08
0.91	0.41	1.24	8.35	0.00	2.18	209.80	654.91	864.71	88.86

Figure 10.5: Spreadsheet model to calculate entropy changes at different extents of reaction

separately varied. It may be important that some of the examples used in school textbooks to explain the differences between chemical and physical equilibrium reinforce the 'two side' view. A common example is to use a person walking up an escalator as an example of dynamic equilibrium. However, the speed of either the person or the escalator may be changed without directly affecting that of the other, whereas in a chemical system a change in any one component necessarily affects all the others.

Rules for deciding what happens when the temperature and/or pressure vary are usually learnt by rote, without any real understanding of why they operate in the way that they do. As a result the rules are often misapplied or confused. For these reasons there is a pressing need to try and develop in students an understanding of the basis of the commonly used rules of thumb — such as Le Chatelier's Principle. Such understanding requires an appreciation of the entropy concept and this can rapidly become very mathematical. Figure 10.5 (derived from Brosnan, 1990) shows one approach to easing this problem. The model allows the calculation of the entropy change and 'equilibrium constant' in any homogenous reaction at any extent of reaction. In this model all the important variables — stoichiometry, standard enthalpy and entropy values, pressure/concentration, initial concentrations and temperature — can be set by the user. Thus, the differing effects of pressure and temperature on both the equilibrium constant and the equilibrium composition can easily be seen. In particular it can be observed that only the temperature has an effect on the equilibrium constant.

This final, exploratory, model seems far removed from the simplicity of the expressive 'calculator replacement' use of a spreadsheet discussed earlier and indeed its purpose is quite different. Rather than replacing boring or repetitive calculations its object is to remove mathematics from an area where its intricacy is often beyond the students (although of course the equations can be as hidden or open as the teacher desires). Instead of becoming trapped in mysterious equations, playing with models like these can lead to fruitful discussions of why the effects obtained should occur, with attention focused on the shape and direction of the change rather than the precise numerical result. It is by providing this qualitative 'feel' that the computational tool is aiding the development of the students' chemical understanding.

Conclusion

The examples briefly described above cover a range of conceptual, arithmetic and programming difficulties. Thus, they are intended to illustrate some of the ways spreadsheets can be used to address the variety of mathematical problems faced by students of science. The key point is that the computational tool is being used to allow students to see the quantitative consequences of differing qualitative conceptions. The apparently paradoxical conclusion of this is that a computational tool's most important attribute may be the help it gives in changing qualitative understandings.

Chapter 11

Models and Metaphors in Reasoning about Probability

Peter Wilder

Introduction

> Probability is a way of thinking. It should be learned for its own sake. In this century probability has become an integral component of virtually every area of thought. (Falk and Konold, 1990)

Probability, and especially conditional probability, can be deceptively difficult. Mathematicians of the past struggled to make sense of probability problems, and sometimes came to wrong conclusions. For example, Leibniz supposed that the probability of scoring a total of eleven from a throw of two dice would be the same as the probability of scoring twelve. One reason for the difficulty is that testing conjectures by experiment is not easy, since repeating an experiment many times takes so much time, and is very tedious. Students face the same problem today and are often quickly bored by lengthy probability experiments. Even then, they may not know whether they have carried out enough trials to be sure of the result.

The computer may offer assistance in two ways: firstly by running a model many times and counting the outcomes, the probability may be estimated from a relative frequency ratio; and secondly by providing a metaphor that enables the student to discern the structure of the problem. Students can now build their own computer models in which they can test their conjectures with large numbers of repetitions very quickly, and can experiment with the effect of varying the number of repetitions.

Probability Models

In many textbooks, three essentially different approaches to measurement of probability are distinguished.

- 'A priori' probability (or theoretical probability) is calculated by consideration of a sample space of events which are assumed to be equally likely;

sophisticated problems. The program simulates the selection of random samples from the mixer of size determined by the user, and the user can count how many times particular combinations of elements occur in a fixed number of samples. It can therefore be used to model situations involving conditional probability.

This metaphor is readily applied to problems that can be formulated with 'a priori' probability. Its use in modelling problems poses three levels of difficulty:

- The problem defines the contents of the mixer.
- The problem statement does not define the contents of the mixer. The elements in the mixer may be abstractions from the problem.
- There is no clear translation from the problem to the mixer.

The problems considered here illustrate these first two levels.

Using *ProbSim* with Students

This work was done with a few students aged 17 years, and with two aged 13 years, on several well-known problems in probability that have been shown to be counter-intuitive, and difficult to reason about (see for example Bar-Hillel and Falk, 1982). During a preliminary discussion about probability, away from the computer, the students were introduced in pairs to the problems. These discussions often produced disagreement between the students about the solutions, and sometimes even about the interpretation of the problem statement itself. Then the students, again in pairs, were introduced to *ProbSim*. They were invited to think about whether the software might help them to resolve difficulties or disagreements over any of the earlier problems.

Problem 1: Red and Green Counters

Falk (1988) identified three sources of difficulty associated with conditional probabilities, and here I shall consider two of these. The first involves an interpretation of conditioning as causality. She presents this as a simple example.

- Imagine: An urn contains two blue counters and two green counters. You put your hand in and draw out a green counter, and place it on the table in front of you. You draw a second counter from the urn. What is the probability that this second counter is also green?
- Now imagine putting the two counters back. This time you put in your hand and place the first counter in your pocket without looking at it. You draw out a second counter and see that it is green. What is the probability that the counter in your pocket is also green?

Falk claims that most novice students will give an answer of 1/3 for the first part, but will claim that the answer to the second part is 1/2, although the correct answer is again 1/3. The explanation she offers is that the students believe the outcome of the second draw is causally dependent on the outcome of the first, but the reverse is not true.

This problem was used to introduce the students to the software for three reasons:

- The students were both already clear about the answer to the problem and could explain it clearly.
- The problem appeared to translate readily into the mixer analogy.
- It raised the issue of replacement versus non-replacement.

When John and Gordon worked on this problem before using the computer they gave different answers. Neither had difficulty with the first part, agreeing on an answer of one in three, and confirming this easily on the computer. The second part gave them more difficulty. John was convinced that the chance was 25 per cent.

There's three counters, one that you took out and the two that's left in there, and them lot come to 75 per cent, and the one in your pocket is like the extra 25 per cent.

Gordon on the other hand gave the correct answer of 1/3, but his reasoning was approximate.

When you look at the green one in your hand, then what you can do is lessen the probability of it [the one in your pocket] being green.

On the computer they set up a mixer containing two elements called G and two called B, and collected one hundred samples of two counters without re-placement (Figure 11.2). They were happy that this represented the drawing of two counters from the bag, but they could not see how to represent the counter that was put into the pocket before you saw it. As John commented: 'The com-puter hasn't got a pocket!'. They were surprised to discover that the proportion of times they got two greens in one hundred samples varied from one experi-ment to another. They tried recording this proportion for several experiments, before they realized that they could increase the number of repetitions. They tried 10,000 repetitions three times and found that the proportions hardly varied at all.

But when they came to consider the conditional probability they had no way to decide what information they needed. They needed help, and, as shown in Figure 11.3, the software only displayed the number of occurrences of each outcome in 10,000 samples.

Both found it impossible to get the conditional probability from this infor-mation unaided. They were given, on a sheet of paper, the table shown in Figure 11.4, showing the same data but as a two-way table which brought out the dif-ferent totals involved in different conditioning events.

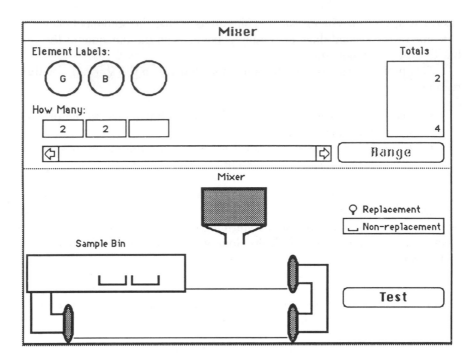

Figure 11.2:   Gordon and John's mixer

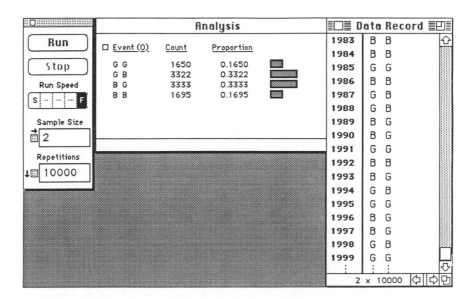

Figure 11.3:   How do you estimate the chance of Green first when you know you've got Green second?

		Second Counter	
		Blue	Green
First	Blue	1695	3333
Counter	Green	3322	1650
	TOTAL		4983

Figure 11.4: Two-way table showing totals of events

After seeing this Gordon was convinced that he had seen something new. He left this session feeling happy that the computer model had confirmed his original reasoning that the probability should be one in three. John was not impressed, but appeared to have understood the argument.

In this case the software seems to be a bigger hurdle than the original problem. When it came to analysing the data, they had no idea what they needed to extract, and when given some help, they still had problems knowing what they needed to do with it. It was interesting that they had some difficulties initially even with calculating estimates of unconditional probabilities from frequency data.

Problem 2: The Three Cards Problem

This second problem of conditional probability caused particular difficulty for the students. You might like to reflect on it yourself, if you have not already seen it. The three cards problem (Bar-Hillel and Falk, 1982) illustrates a second source of difficulty with conditional probability identified by Falk, which lies in the correct identification and definition of the conditioning event. In this case the structure of the problem leads to one condition on an inferred event.

> A hat contains three cards. One card is blue on both sides, the second is green on both sides, and the third is green on one side and blue on the other side. A card is drawn at random from the hat and placed on the table. It shows a blue face. What is the probability that the hidden face of this card is also blue?

The students invariably found this problem difficult in their preliminary discussion. The older students were able to reason about the problem and arrive at a solution, for example, Pedro explained:

> There are two blues. But one of the blues has got a green underneath it and the other has got a blue underneath it ... you pulled out a blue,

so you've already specified that it's one of two blues, and since one of them has got a green and the other has got a blue underneath it the chances of this one having a blue underneath is a half.

The younger pair were both much more confused by the problem. John was convinced that the chance was two in three but could not explain why:

... because you've got one that's totally blue, one that's totally green, and you looked at that one, and it's blue, and it could be green on the bottom or blue, but if it's green on the bottom then ... it's like. . . . I'll just stick with two in three chance.

Gordon found himself switching between answers of '50–50' and 'two in three' as he discussed the problem with John.

Gordon: I'd say it's only 50 if he's just looking at it, the probability of getting a blue card, that'd be 50–50. Just taking one up that has a blue face, all right, no matter which way any of them have landed, that would be 50–50. But with one down, then it's like there's two faces that are blue, and there's three faces that could be green. So I reckon there's two out of three chance.

Interviewers: You're pretty convinced that it's two out of three, Gordon?

Gordon: Yeah, because . . .

John: Because you've already seen one colour, so it has to be two out of three.

Gordon: Because there's another two left.

It appears from Gordon's final explanation of his answer that, by 'two in three', he really means two chances in favour and three against, which is two fifths, rather than two thirds. John's explanations are not clear enough to distinguish whether he agrees with Gordon.

Both pairs went on to try to model the problem on the computer, but found the task extremely difficult initially. This may be because the elements needed in the mixer to model the problem are abstractions from the original problem. Each card needs to appear in the mixer twice, once for each way up. This step is also necessary in order to formulate the problem mathematically in terms of 'a priori' probability.

Each pair needed some practical experience with real cards before they were able to make progress. The older pair built a model which simulated drawing a card from the hat 100 times, and noting each time the colour of the face on top and of the face underneath. They went on to count the total number of times the card showed blue on top, and the total number of times they drew the card with blue on both sides, and used these two counts to estimate the probability.

The younger pair, Gordon and John, wanted to model only the outcome of the hidden face. They reasoned as follows:

Gordon: There's two cards it could be: 'blue blue', and 'blue green'. That's four faces.

John: You know you've got one of the blue faces, so that means it's out of three. Only one of them has green on the back, so its two thirds.

Gordon: Yeah. It's two thirds.

At this stage they were both completely convinced that they were right, and saw no need to use the computer. The model they constructed showed why. It simulated drawing a face from a collection of two blues and one green. The situation was now so simple to them that they did not require a simulation.

These examples illustrate two important points. Firstly, it is not easy to build a computer model of a situation involving conditional probability without some practical experience of the conditioning process. The brief practical experiment that both pairs of students carried out seems to have helped them to understand the conditioning event, and identify it precisely. Secondly, building a computer model focused the students attention on the key aspects of the problem. They needed to identify clearly both the conditioning event and the target event. It seems that reflection on the problem as they built their model, rather than the model itself, which led to the new understanding.

The Possibilities for the Future

The software used in this work poses serious problems for students using it as a general probabilistic modelling tool. Many problems involving probability do not easily translate into the Mixer framework. But for problems closely analogous to the Mixer, the process of modelling may offer some benefits to learners. A spreadsheet with a graphing facility is a much more powerful and flexible tool. As these become more widely available, and easier to use, it will become feasible for students to use them to build these kinds of models.

drawing the picture had helped him to get straight in his mind what sort of model he wanted to build:

> Actually, it helped me to understand that this is the Britain and I have to estimate the way the population will grow. I mean I have to work out for this picture the way its population will grow. But it actually doesn't show the right UK or Great Britain.

Picturing was helpful to Sadaat as a means of focusing on these steps in the process. The fact that neither he nor any of the rest of us were very skilful with the *Paint* program seems not to have mattered too much. The act of drawing was enough in itself. Danny and Neil's model shows that they, too, had been able to identify their problem, define its purpose (Managing Crystal Palace Football Club efficiently) and identify its main elements, though they wanted more in the picture:

> Danny: I would have just liked to have made that more — made the set up better.
> Neil: Make the picture more. . . .
> Danny: Yes, like have a picture in the middle and have all these like icons round it and use these, like, as icons.

Later, we were looking at the way they had defined the actions of their blocks and I asked them if there were any that they thought were interesting:

> Danny and Neil: The players.
> Danny: Actually, I'll go inside and have a look to show what we've done . . .

Danny and Neil had, to use Mason's phrase, 'entered the picture' and I was able to 'follow'. By means of this lovely metaphor, Danny was able to show me how the 'players' block worked. This block linked the power to buy new players to the profitability of the club. Its actions included the command:

> Players
> . . .
> When run
> if profits > 2000 [make me me + 1][]

As they explained these actions, it was clear that they could see that the model was iterative over the number of matches. They had started by 'watching one match' and then decided to simulate a whole season!

Making the Model

Having defined the purpose of the model, students needed to decide on the main factors (step three). They quickly realized that they had to focus on quantitative and not qualitative factors. I asked Jatin and Tony why they had decided to have their particular set of blocks:

Tony:	We had to simulate the amount of cars which were going in and going out for the reason for how many cars there are to start with actually in the car park.
Interviewer:	OK. So you felt that you didn't have much choice about what blocks to put in?
Tony:	In a way, yes.
Interviewer:	I mean, do you think that there were any blocks, any other blocks that you could have put in, that you didn't put in?
Jatin and Tony:	Yes.
Tony:	We were going to go on to a bit about other people travelling different ways.
Jatin:	And the number of tills open affecting the flow rate.
Tony:	Yes, and all that, but we never actually got that far.
Interviewer:	But do you think you could return to that?
Jatin and Tony:	Yes.

Jatin and Tony's answers show that they were aware of the constraints of the software, but they had accommodated well to them.

In defining and explaining the relationships between the factors (step four), *Model Builder* allows the learner to describe these relationships as if they had some material existence. So, while Sadaat was describing the actions he had defined he was at the same time using the 'mouse' to point to the blocks he was talking about:

Interviewer:	Can you show me now the actions you defined for each of your blocks?
Sadaat:	Yes. The action for the birth block is population multiplied by birth rate, so the birth rate increase and the population will increase and the function for the population block is . . . the population add birth and immigration-in and take away emigration-out and death.

Model Builder's iconic representation of the elements of a model allows the use of powerful 'pointing', 'opening out' and 'getting inside' metaphors. Additional help could be given to students were it also able to represent links between blocks showing their interdependence in a similar way.

Awareness of the Modelling Process

I had started by referring explicitly to a modelling process, and although it might seem too crude an approach, I decided to ask Jatin and Tony about this directly:

Interviewer:	. . . do you recall that at one time we spoke about a process of mathematical modelling?
Jatin and Tony:	Yes.
Interviewer:	Can you say what you think the stages were, or might be in that — that you went through — if you did go through them?
Tony:	Yes. Identify the problem and then we went on to thinking about the main factors of it. Then, we wrote a few things down and we sort of tried the Model Builder and improved and looked back at what we were doing.

What can be made of this response? Having watched Jatin and Tony as they worked on their model, I believe that they had done more than understand this modelling process; they had also demonstrated awareness of its imperfections.

Modelling and Mathematics

Mandinach (1990) could find no conclusive evidence to show that modelling may improve mathematical content-knowledge. I do not claim to have provided that kind of evidence here, though I can say that the activities provided ample opportunity for the students to apply such knowledge. I will give a few examples.

In *Model Builder*, relationships and variables are represented symbolically. Consider, for example, Danny and Neil's action for the block called 'Profits':

```
when run
make me me + victory – defeat
if I > 200000 [make me me – 50000][]
```

Though we might say that the variable names 'me', 'victory', 'defeat' and 'I' are pre-symbolic, their use seems to demonstrate a good understanding of the idea of variable. As Danny and Neil worked on their model they would regularly substitute values of their own into these expressions to check up on the reasonableness of their answers.

The students used ideas of probability with the 'pick' random number generator. Neil and Danny used it to model what they called the 'form' of Crystal Palace:

```
Dice
when run
make me pick 10

Form
when run
if dice < 6 [make me 1][if dice < 7 [make me 2][make me 3]]
```

(where 1 meant a win, 2 meant a draw and 3 a loss).

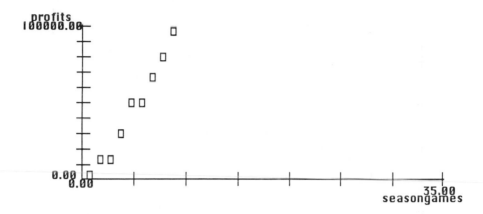

Figure 12.2: One of Neil and Danny's graphs

Tony and Jatin decided to make the number of cars entering their car park a random number between 1 and 100. Jatin's understanding of probability could well be extended through his modelling activity:

Interviewer:	And what made you decide, for example, with the cars-in, to use a random number generator?
Jatin:	That would make it more effective, more lifelike.
Interviewer:	Do you think it is lifelike?
Jatin:	You can't really tell what cars are coming in and coming out in a real store, could you?

Model Builder allows students to create graphs showing how one variable changes with another. Thus, Danny and Neil made a graph to monitor the progress of Crystal Palace's profits against number of games played (Figure 12.2), and used it to assess the validity of their model:

Danny:	. . . I reckon we made a few mistakes on the profits — made the profits too high (Interviewer: Yes) in the end because the graph was just going right up and it would never ever come down again.

Tony and Jatin needed a graph to decide on the most likely peak level of cars wanting to use the car park (Figure 12.3), and found it useful because, as Tony said, 'it peaks where the car park is fullest.'

However, Tony's expectation of what the graph ought to show did not reflect what it was actually doing. The number of cars could rise indefinitely, and did not reach a maximum as Tony had thought. This was because they had defined 'Cars-in' to be a random number between 1 and 100, and 'Cars-out' to be a random number between 1 and 'Cars-in', so more cars were always entering than leaving.

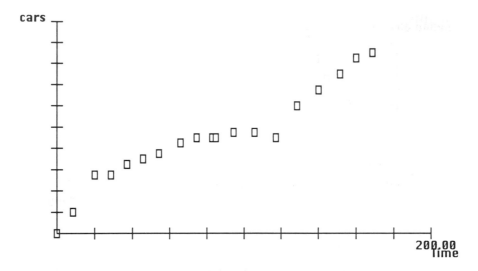

Figure 12.3: One of Jatin and Tony's graphs

An important point here is that the graphs were being generated for a purpose and used as a basis for judgments formulated by the students themselves. The dynamic nature of the graphical representation and its display alongside the other elements of the model were very powerful features.

The Students' Evaluations

None of the students felt that they had built a perfect model, though they felt that they had been successful nevertheless. They accepted implicitly that the context made perfection meaningless, readily acknowledging the need to account for more complex factors. For example, Sadaat commented:

> . . . actually, I've got to have the right numbers, the right values of the population, birth rate and death rate and people coming in and going out.

Later he observed:

> . . . if there is a war (and) the population will not grow, and if there is nothing and the population will grow forever, and the birth rate is greater than death rate, then there will be a point when people will die because of starvation, because there will be not enough food for the population to eat.

Sadaat felt his model could provide some useful ideas about the possible growth of the UK population, even though it was not complete.

The modelling activities seemed also to encourage in the students the sort of 'inner action' which is necessary for involvement (Mason, 1988). It is true that, in terms of motivation, these were not representative students, but their attendance at out-of-school sessions testifies to a special commitment to the activity. I like to think that Neil's short summary of the activity was representative:

Neil: Magic

Conclusion

This study demonstrated to me something of the power of computational modelling. Developing models, and discussing them, encourages in students an awareness of their own learning, and it seems that the potential of modelling in the classroom has only begun to be explored. It has convinced me of the practicability and real value of modelling in the classroom.

Richard Boohan

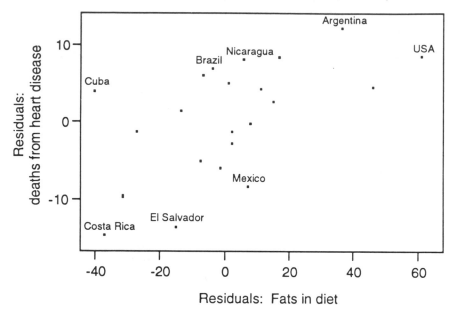

North, South and Central America, 1980–85

Figure 13.3: *Plotting the residuals*
Source: UNEP, 1987

13.1. It is also interesting to note how the positions of countries have changed. In Figure 13.1, Costa Rica seems to be rather typical. In fact, it has quite a high life expectancy, and in Figure 13.3, after this effect is taken out, it occupies a very different position. It now appears with a very low rate of heart disease and fat intake, after taking account of life expectancy.

We could continue, investigating the effects of other factors, but this should be sufficient to give a flavour of the exploratory approach — trying to find a 'model' which accounts for some pattern in the data, then seeing whether there is any other pattern left. Two more examples will show how this idea is used in other analyses with different types of data.

Fats in Diet

For many people, meat is a major source of fat in diet. Meat consumption is low in poor countries, but rich countries with high fish consumption, notably Iceland and Japan, also have lower levels of meat consumption. But does a diet rich in fish, necessarily mean a low-fat diet? We need some data about the fat content of meat and fish to make a comparison. A very simple way of doing this is to make a 'dotplot' as shown in Figure 13.4a. This shows the fat content of a number of

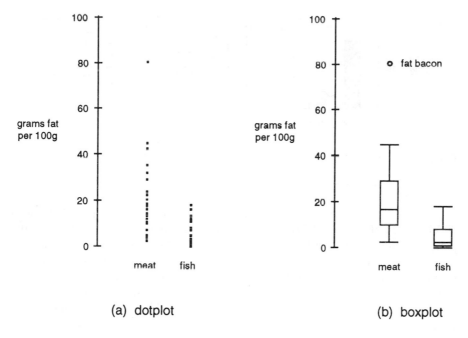

(a) dotplot   (b) boxplot

Figure 13.4:   Fat content of meat and fish
Source: Paul and Southgate, 1978

raw and processed meats and fish. Each value is shown as a dot on a vertical scale.

What can we see from these two batches of values? In general, meat has a higher fat content than fish, though there is quite a lot of overlap. And there is a much bigger spread of values for meat than for fish, with one value for meat being particularly high.

A dotplot is simple, but doing it by hand is quite time-consuming and the eye can be distracted by the detail. An effective display of the same data, making comparisons easier, is a boxplot (Figure 13.4b). The line in the middle of each box shows where the middle value of the batch is (the median), so it tells us in general how big the values are. The box tells us how spread out the values are — it contains one half of the batch (a quarter above and a quarter below the middle line). The lines above and below the boxes show the top and bottom quarters of the batch. The boxplot also displays clearly the distribution of the values; we can see that for the fish there is a skew distribution, with values being more spread out above the middle than below it. The meat values are also skewed slightly, but even allowing for the greater spread at higher values, one value (fat bacon) seems unusually high and has been shown as an individual point, or outlier, separate from the rest of the distribution. Outliers are often of particular interest, with special reasons why they are so different from the other members of a batch.

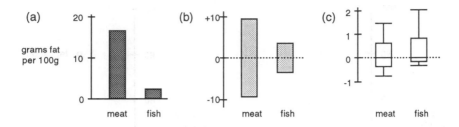

Figure 13.5: Fat content of meat and fish — level, spread and distribution
Source: Paul and Southgate, 1978

Implicitly, what we have been doing here is also an example of the idea 'DATA = MODEL + RESIDUAL'. We have been trying to account for the pattern in the data by first looking at the levels of values, then at their spread and then at their distribution. If we wished, we could make this explicit, by splitting the data, in a way similar to that in Figure 13.2. Thus, Figure 13.5a shows the levels (medians) of each batch, Figure 13.5b shows the spread (the sizes of the boxes), and Figure 13.5c shows the distribution (found by subtracting the median from each value and dividing by the spread).

With only two batches, we cannot really see much more from this than the original boxplots, but it does emphasize the important ideas needed to compare batches. With many more batches, though, displays in which the level and spread are removed can help in noticing things we may otherwise have missed.

Household Spending on Tobacco

By far the biggest factor influencing heart disease is generally believed to be smoking. Figure 13.6a shows the money spent by different income groups on various areas of household expenditure. What can we see? As we would expect, high-income households tend to spend more than low-income households. All groups spend more money on food than on tobacco.

One way of analysing the data to bring out these effects more clearly is shown in Figure 13.6b. The way to carry out this analysis is quite simple, though it will not be discussed here. The column on the right of the table contains multipliers which indicate the typical effect of income group across all types of expenditure. Thus low-income households (0.45) typically spend about a half that of middle-income households (1.00), and high-income households (1.71) typically spend about two-thirds more. Similarly, the multipliers in the row at the bottom of the table indicate the typical expenditure on each category across all income groups. In the bottom right-hand corner is the 'overall effect' which represents a general level for all types of expenditure and income groups (£10.80). These effects are a 'model' from which we can estimate any of the original values, by multiplying the effects together. So, to estimate the money spent on food by low-income households:

(a) Household expenditure by income group (£ per week), 1985

	Food	Housing	Alcohol	Tobacco	Clothing
Low	15.6	11.4	1.9	2.3	3.5
Middle	32.1	25.2	7.1	4.7	10.8
High	51.6	43.0	16.6	4.5	23.7

(b) After 'taking out effects'

	Food	Housing	Alcohol	Tobacco	Clothing	Effects
Low	1.08	1.01	0.59	1.14	0.72	0.45
Middle	1.00	1.00	1.00	1.04	1.00	1.00
High	0.94	1.00	1.37	0.58	1.28	1.71
Effects	2.97	2.33	0.65	0.42	1.00	10.80

Figure 13.6: Analysing a two-way table by 'taking out effects'
Source: Social Trends 18, 1988

Money spent = Overall effect × Type of expenditure effect × Income group effect
$$= £10.80 \quad\quad \times \quad\quad 2.97 \quad\quad \times \quad\quad 0.45$$
$$= £14.43$$

The actual value is £15.60, so our estimate is a little low. That is, low-income households spend rather more on food than we would predict from the model. This is shown in the analysis in Figure 13.6a as the residuals in the main part of the table. For this example the value is 1.08 — that is, low-income households spend 1.08 times as much on food as that predicted by the model. This is perhaps not too surprising — low-income groups are likely to spend proportionately more on essentials than on luxuries.

What else can we see in the residuals from this analysis? If the model was perfect all of these would be '1'. The values for tobacco and alcohol are particularly interesting. Low-income households spend a proportionately high part of their income on tobacco, but a low proportion on alcohol. For high-income households, this is reversed. Perhaps in this example, we could have seen all this simply by examining the original table of data. But with more complex data, such analyses, supported by graphical displays of the results, can reveal patterns that would otherwise be difficult to see.

Data Analysis in the Curriculum

We have only looked at a few kinds of exploratory analysis — for example, there is no mention here of graphs showing trends, or tables showing percentages

— but the selection should be sufficient to suggest possibilities for this approach in the curriculum. The influence of these ideas at the university level has been considerable, particularly in the social sciences (Erickson and Nosanchuk, 1979; Marsh, 1988). More recently, the ideas have been used in developing activities for younger students, for example in the USA (Landwehr and Watkins, 1987; Burrill, 1989), in Germany (Biehler, 1989) and in the UK (Boohan and Ogborn, 1991). Such work has even been extended to pupils in the primary school (Pereira-Mendoza and Dunkels, 1989), where handling data can help develop children's concept of number and its representation.

EDA techniques are simple to learn, but their value lies not in this, but in the way the approach encourages students to ask sensible questions about data. One example is given here. We gave some students, who had studied some EDA, a newspaper article about how much money was spent per pupil on education by different boroughs. The newspaper article, while including the entire set of data, discussed mainly one aspect — which boroughs spent most or least, and how this had changed since the previous year. Such changes may be important, but only if there are substantial differences in spending, and not if the order is altered by very small changes. In their discussion, the students looked at a broader range of important questions — how did the general level of spending compare from one year to another, or in different areas or types of school, and why was there such a large spread of values around the general level. These are the kinds of questions which the EDA approach encouraged the students to ask.

EDA's simple paper-and-pencil techniques allow data to be quickly analysed. But computers are even quicker! What should we use: a pencil or a computer? The advantage of using a pencil is that we are always 'close to the data', and have a better feel for whether what we are doing makes sense. A computer's speed is also a danger — we can use it to make fast, accurate and completely meaningless analyses. Some packages, though, are much influenced by the exploratory approach, and encourage sensible use. *Data Desk* is a sophisticated data analysis and statistical package, with many different kinds of graphical display. The user can interact directly with the data shown on the displays, for example, using a 'knife' to select an area on a scatterplot, then plotting the cases which fall into this area on another kind of display. A simpler package, suitable for school use, is *'ELASTIC'* (see Roseberry and Rubin, 1990), which allows, for example, a fitted line to be moved around directly on a scatterplot. Preliminary work with pencil and paper is valuable alongside this kind of software — the computer manipulates data faster, but in a way which students could imagine doing by hand.

All these developments have a number of concerns in common. One is the importance of modelling real data. Data invented merely to illustrate a technique is of limited value, and does little to provide motivation to students. Also, the emphasis is not on the techniques themselves, but on asking questions and finding meaning in data. There is never a question of a single interpretation or a single appropriate technique, so exploratory work tends to engage students in much active discussion. The relation between EDA and more traditional statistics is not entirely uncontroversial, though it is simplistic to see them as being in opposition to each other. Traditional statistics tends to emphasize levels of significance, while EDA emphasizes the sizes of effects. So, EDA helps in formulating hypotheses while traditional statistics helps in confirming them. By concentrating initially on what seems to be in the data, EDA can help to give a better view of the nature of statistical thinking.

Part 3

Common sense Reasoning about Quantities

Chapter 14

Causality and Common sense Reasoning

Joan Bliss

Introduction

A key innovation of the Tools for Exploratory Learning Programme was to re-cognize the importance, educationally and computationally, of semi-quantitative reasoning and modelling. Semi-quantitative modelling is new and important. It involves thinking about systems in terms of the rough and ready size of things and directions of effects, for example, that opening the throttle of my car increases the flow rate of petrol to the engine, which causes the engine to work faster. It requires an understanding of the direction of a causal relationship (increase or decrease) but numerical values or mathematical relationships are not needed. This section comprises two chapters: the first will describe the different areas in which the notion of semi-quantitative reasoning has been used; the second will describe findings about the reasoning of children between 11 and 14 when working with a semi-quantitative tool, *IQON* in the Tools for Exploratory Learning Programme.

Background

Modelling, until recently, has been an activity limited to older pupils from 16 onwards or to university students since it involved mainly quantitative reasoning. So quantitative modelling is familiar in science and mathematics and also in geo-graphy and economics. Qualitative modelling, on the other hand, uses qualitative rules or structures, as in decision games, expert systems or models of grammars. In the Tools for Exploratory Learning Programme we believed that the creation of a modelling tool (known as *IQON*) which elicited semi-quantitative reasoning would permit children of between 11 to 14 years to model complex situations. Ideas about this type of reasoning come from two very different sources: (i) recent work in AI and cognitive science and (ii) work on descriptions of young children's and students' reasoning.

Causality is fundamental to semi-quantitative reasoning, underlying descriptions of:

- an action performed by an agent in order to bring about an event or a state of affairs, that is, an agent performing an action with the expectation or intent that something will follow;

- a natural event that brings about an event or a state of affairs, for example, a forest fire burning down a village.

In reality individuals do not have too much difficulty in understanding what happens around them, objects acting on one another, one object causing another to do something. However, philosophers have had difficulty in interpreting everyday ideas of causality. For example, Piaget (1963; 1974) has used the idea of cause in a wider sense in which cause is equivalent to explanation. In this sense, he distinguishes between lawfulness and causality. For him, laws are about general relations between objects or events whereas causality contains necessary relations. Also while general laws can remain isolated, causal explanations coordinate several relations into a system where necessity is of the essence. For Piaget, causality could not be reduced to a simple relation of cause and effect.

Work in AI

Semi-quantitative reasoning, under the name of qualitative reasoning, has for a considerable time been a leading concern in AI and cognitive science, with strong connections to work in naive physics (see Hobbs and Moore, 1985). Forbus and Gentner (1990) claim that, 'People have a deep intuition that causality is a central and cohesive aspect of human mental life', but go on to admit that the search for a unified theory to explain human causal reasoning has been unsuccessful thus far. They state that such failures have led a number of researchers in AI (among them Hayes, 1985) to the conclusion that there is no deep theory of causality, arguing, 'Causal reasoning may be simply a family of inferences whose properties will vary according to the content of the argument' (p. 666).

Forbus and Gentner's main interest is in qualitative physics where the central concern lies in describing how continuous physical properties change over time, for example, that pouring more milk into a glass will cause the level to rise. They attempt to characterize three main aspects of causal reasoning: (i) an explicit mechanism, for example, that boiling causes steam, or warming causes melting; (ii) a direction of a causal link determined by the causal mechanism, for example, the level of the milk rising being in response to pouring in more milk; (iii) the way in which a quantity is thought of as changing, notably in a sequence, often ordered in a causal chain.

They claim that this type of reasoning is similar to everyday reasoning and is essentially qualitative in nature. For example, I can understand that if I turn a glass of water upside down, then the water will flow out. Or that when I see steam coming from the radiator of my car then I think something is seriously overheating so I stop the car immediately. Such qualitative reasoning allows us to make inferences quickly and competently in a complex world.

However the main thrust of work in qualitative physics has been the common sense understanding of specialist domains, usually technical, often called 'common sense expert knowledge'. This knowledge refers to the models that we have of objects in a domain, but at an expert level. Gentner and Stevens (1983) argue, 'The reason that mental models research has focused on seemingly technical domains is precisely because those domains that have proved the most tractable to physical scientists are the ones for which there exist the best explicit normative models.' (p. 2). Thus this mental model work strives for a better understanding of the types of mental models or naive theories that experts construct when interacting with physical systems. Such research has undeniably applied utility in technology and industry.

For example de Kleer and Brown (1983) made a case for this kind of reasoning as essential to envisioning the functioning of machines. Thus they attempted to construct systems of human reasoning which reason 'naturally'. An example of such a system would be working out what a device such as a pump might do, given a description of its parts. For them a mental model is built up in four steps:

- the system builds a description of the structure of the device;
- the system works out a number of ways in which the device might function, building a causal model of it, this process is called envisioning;
- the system imagines the model running;
- the system compares these possibilities with what happens in reality, and may revise its model as a result.

Many AI researchers in the past decade have tried to design qualitative reasoning systems for computers, attempts which have however not met with a great deal of success. Nonetheless it is worth mentioning a number of particular examples of qualitative reasoning systems including Forbus' Qualitative Process Theory (1983; 1984), Kuipers' Constraint-based Qualitative Reasoning System QSIM (1984; 1986) and de Kleer and Brown's ENVISION system using Component-based Qualitative Reasoning (1983; 1984; 1985). Although each of these differs from the others importantly in the style of computation and the strategies employed they have in common an insistence on reasoning in a qualitative manner about process and change, recognizing amounts and rates of change judged qualitatively, and so supporting features of variables, entities or processes such as 'big', 'small', 'bigger', 'smaller', 'increasing' and 'decreasing'.

It is important to make the distinction between qualitative physics, which is qualitative reasoning applied to physical situations, and naive physics. In qualitative physics the intention is to derive only correct inferences. By contrast, naive physics attempts to capture the ways humans reason about their physical environments, correct or not. Thus 'soundness' is not a goal since naive physics wishes to describe some of the erroneous conclusions that humans draw about their environment.

Within the Tools for Exploratory Learning Programme we preferred to call this type of reasoning semi-quantitative rather than qualitative because it both indicates the direction of the reasoning and gives approximate sizes of causes and effects. In other words, this type of reasoning involves seeing how in a complex system the rough and ready size of something has an effect on the rough and ready size of something else, which may, in turn, affect other things and might, in the end, feed back to affect the first quantity. Because we needed to maintain a distinction between this kind of reasoning and the categorical or logical reasoning characteristic of, for example, many expert systems, we preferred the terms 'semi-quantitative' for the former and 'qualitative' reasoning for the latter.

Semi-quantitative reasoning is very widely used in social argument such as about whether increasing policing will decrease crime. It is familiar in the political and economic sections of newspapers, for instance: 'Renewed pressure on the pound forced its value down, leading to expectations of a rise in interest rates but also to hopes of increased exports given the recent rise in investment'. Although it can be seen that this type of reasoning is pervasive, its importance has not always been recognized and it is often thought of as 'second best' to quantitative reasoning instead of as the basis and foundation of quantitative thinking.

Semi-quantitative Reasoning: Children and Students

The programme's second source of ideas about semi-quantitative reasoning came from research into children thinking and reasoning. Piaget is often remembered for his early work on causality (1927) but he was to return to this topic in the early 1970s, saying that his earlier work was 'ancient and out-of-date', starting from the point of view of the child and not considering the objects involved. Piaget (1974) argued that, in an understanding of causality, objects are far more important than in the construction of logical schemes, where actions are crucial. He pointed out that when we attempt to understand the real world reality constantly challenges our logical thinking, that objects sometimes 'cooperate' and sometimes 'refuse to do so', so that it is impossible to attribute whatever one likes to objects. In this later work Piaget also showed that an understanding of causality was linked to the general mechanisms of the development of intelligence.

Other researchers have also shown that children are capable of reasoning causally in familiar domains, for example, simple causal sequences, time and temporal ordering. However when asked to reason about unfamiliar domains, such as evaporation or heat flow, they do not have enough knowledge of the domain to know how the causal mechanisms function (Bullock and Gelman, 1979; Bullock, Gelman and Baillargeon, 1982). Miller and Aloise (1989) suggest that,

> Young children (4–6 years olds) may have more knowledge about causal mechanisms relating to human behaviour, that is, intentions or other psychological states, than about mechanical, physical mechanisms relating to physical events. (Miller and Aloise, 1989, p. 265)

Intentionality is often linked not only with human behaviour, where it may or may not be appropriate, but also to the actions of physical objects. For example,

Piaget (1927) had already shown that young children believed that the sun rises 'because he wants to give us light'. Carey (1985) proposed that young pre-schoolers rely on psychological causes to explain aspects of biology because they neither understand or know enough about biology, so that children's theories about biology emerge from their naive theories about psychology. Others believe that this over attribution of intentionality to physical events is because children prefer 'generative transmission' causes, for example, causes that include a clear mechanism generating or producing effects (Shultz, 1982). Aloise and Miller (1989) suggest that a developmental task for young children is to learn that psychological states do not cause either the activities of physical objects nor some of the activities of people.

In developmental psychology, when studying children's ideas about physical causality, one of the main foci has been on causal mechanisms and the direction of causality without special attention being given to the use of semi-quantitative relations. However, in much of the work done on children's common sense reasoning about motion by Jon Ogborn and myself (Bliss, Ogborn and Whitelock, 1989; Bliss and Ogborn, 1993), children often make comments such as 'the heavier it is the harder you have to push it', or 'the more force you give something, e.g., a ball, the faster it will go'.

More recently, research related to semi-quantitative reasoning has also had as its focus older children and students, particularly those destined to study science. Three examples described in this chapter are:

- an attempt to build an intelligent tutoring system which models students' reasoning, in which semi-quantitative reasoning is seen as a step towards quantitative reasoning;
- new approaches to teaching calculus in which the reasoning of students can be described as semi-quantitative;
- students between 16 and 18 engaging with modelling tools that allow them to reason semi-quantitatively.

Learning Qualitative, Semi-quantitative and Quantitative Reasoning

In the first example, Ploetzner, Spada, Stumpf and Opwis (1990) present a framework for a multi-level representation of domain knowledge and reasoning about the physical world. Their framework describes a number of levels for learning about physical domains, starting from qualitative everyday knowledge through to the level of scientific quantitative knowledge. Their major concern is that, 'If the different types of knowledge are not connected with each other within the learning process, directly taught quantitative knowledge dies away and is forgotten' (p. 510).

Ploetzner and his colleagues therefore set out to produce an intelligent tutoring system in which the knowledge to be assimilated is adapted to the learner's cognitive abilities. To this end, they developed a microworld (*DiBi*) to learn about collisions, which becomes an intelligent tutoring system when coordinated with a computerized diagnosis system (*MULEDS*). *MULEDS* permits student modelling through assessment of the student's correct or incorrect domain specific knowledge, categorized as a series of different levels: qualitative, semi-quantitative relational, quantitative relational and quantitative numerical. They argue that, 'An adequate cognitive model describes the acquisition of quantitative physical knowledge as an evolution of a sequence of upwards-compatible mental representations of the problem domain' (p. 507). Effective teaching means that each different level of mental representation has to be addressed by different levels of instructional presentation.

They claim that the type of everyday knowledge possessed by the student is characterized by qualitative and semi-quantitative relational levels and will either support or impede the acquisition of scientific domain specific knowledge. They take their inspiration for these distinctions from work into children's intuitive ideas about science (Carey, 1986; Chi, Glaser and Farr, 1988; Larkin, 1983).

Learning Calculus and Evidence of Semi-quantitative Reasoning

Nemirovsky and Rubin (1992a; 1992b) looked at problems of teaching calculus and more particularly at the relationship between a function and its derivative. They claim that, 'Although mathematically complex, the function/derivative relationship is embedded in many contexts of daily life which allow us to construct intuitions from an early age' (1992a, p. 1). The examples of such intuitions given in their paper are mainly semi-quantitative in nature.

Nemirovsky and Rubin took a small group of American high school students, who had not studied calculus, examining their abilities to articulate the relationship between function and derivative. Students worked in three contexts: motion (translation between position and velocity), fluids (translation between flow rate and volume), and in numerical integration. In each context students were given a set of computer software tools (*Microcomputer-Based Laboratories, MBL*) which enabled them to generate functions and to explore their ideas about the shape of a function. For both motion and flow students could produce curves on a computer screen by manipulating a physical object monitored by a sensor. For motion, there was a small car and a motion detector, while for air flow students controlled a bellows to generate changes in air flow and in the volume of air collected in a bag.

Their study showed that high-school students tended to assume resemblances between the behaviour or appearance of a function and its derivative, that is, that they believed that a function and its derivative changed in a similar way. For example, students would propose in the case of fluids, that if the flow rate went up, then the volume would increase. Nemirovsky and Rubin argued, 'Volume is thought of as varying according to the variation of flow rate. Both vary in the same way; more of one implies more of the other and less implies less' (p. 27). In a teaching sequence they attempted to move students from the resemblance approach to what they called variational approaches. There were several variational approaches but the underlying idea was to focus students on how, for example with fluids, a function changes locally over time and to recognize flow rate as the descriptor for this local change. Expressions suggestive of this would be: 'the amount of increase (of volume) is less and less and it (flow rate) would decrease from what it was before'.

In summary, in the resemblance approach students would force a match of the global features of the two graphs and focus on one of them. The move to variational approaches focused students on the relationship between the function and its derivative rather than the global properties of each graph. Much of the change in reasoning was achieved through the coordination of the physical contexts, the movements of car or the air from the bellows and their immediate representation on the screen. However in both cases it is possible to see the importance of semi-quantitative reasoning in getting insights into complex situations.

Young Students Engaging with Modelling

Kurtz dos Santos (1992) gives an account of 16 to 18-year-old students' ability to manage some different approaches to modelling; namely causal diagrams and two computational modelling tools: *IQON* and *STELLA*. *IQON* is described in the next chapter; a brief description of causal loop diagrams and *STELLA* is given here.

Causal loop diagrams, often used to represent the behaviour of systems, are directed graphs in which nodes represent variables and arcs represent influences of one variable on another. Causal loop diagrams can be a powerful tool to help define a system's boundary, to sort out what should and what should not be included within the study of a social, economic or other system. *STELLA* (Structural Thinking Experimental Learning Laboratory with Animation) is a quantitative modelling tool, developed for the Apple Macintosh computer. *STELLA* uses a metaphor of tanks, pipes, and valves which makes possible the construction of a model through the diagrammatic linking of these basic objects as in a causal diagram. The structure of the model is automatically determined by the structure of the diagram. Links between variables have to be written in algebraic terms but the system itself converts them into program code.

The study posed a number of questions. Can 16 to 18-year-old students achieve success or some valuable work with computational modelling systems? What is required for students to use or make computational models? How good are modelling systems as tools for making models? How is students' thinking with models related to their other knowledge? Figure 14.1 gives a schematic outline of the research design. The survey questionnaire was used as background for the small-scale intensive study. The survey questionnaire was designed in two parts, the first part being about variables and the drawing of causal diagrams for a number of situations; and the second about the relevant mathematical knowledge needed to engage in modelling. It also included questions about students' previous use of software and hardware.

In the intensive study, half the sample worked first with *IQON* and half with causal diagrams, on parallel exploratory and expressive tasks. Both groups then

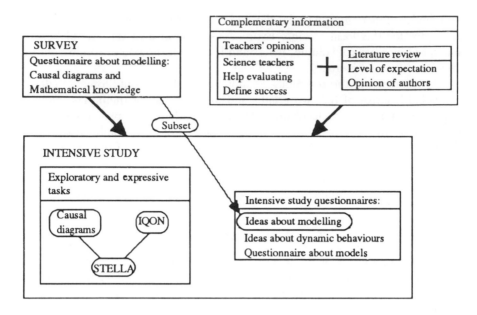

Figure 14.1: Schematic research design

went on to work on exploratory and expressive tasks with *STELLA*. Thus *IQON* could be compared with causal diagrams, both on parallel kinds of task and as a preparation for work with *STELLA*. All students carrying out either the survey or the intensive study were between the ages of 16 and 18. In the survey, questionnaires were completed by sixty-seven students. In the intensive study there were thirty-four students, twelve in physics (eight males and four females) and twenty-two in economics (fourteen male and eight female).

Results of the Survey
In the survey well over three-quarters of the students had some experience of using computers and showed a reasonable initial model-building capability. They could interpret and construct graphs, manage the algebraic relations needed for simple quantitative modelling and cope with iteration in simple cases (e.g., compound growth). They were less good at understanding rates of change expressed using derivatives (mean scores ranging from 30 to 50 per cent). They had difficulty with interpreting models expressed as difference equations in the form of simple BASIC code (mean scores 30 to 40 per cent). They were too strongly inclined to interpret change as likely to be linear and increasing (for example a linear graph or one curving upwards was nearly always the first choice for a graph to express any kind of change).

Results of the Intensive Study
Students who worked only with causal diagrams had some difficulty with them. Those who were given exactly the same model but in *IQON* and ran it,

understood it much better and had less trouble with negative links. With causal diagrams, cause–effect pairs or descriptions of the behaviour of isolated entities were the main focus of over half the students' work (ten out of eighteen) whereas the majority of students working with *IQON* more often gave complex descriptions of model behaviour.

Students using *IQON* to construct their models much more often used variables (rates or amounts) than did students just using causal diagrams. For example, thirty of the fifty-three links constructed using *IQON* were between variables; only two out of seventy links in causal diagrams were between variables. It seems that *IQON* was very helpful to them in this respect. Thus students who worked with *IQON* in general achieved better than those who used causal diagrams, both in exploratory and in expressive tasks. *IQON*, due to its runnability, seemed to help them to think about systems as a whole.

Students who worked with *IQON* did not do significantly better than those who had worked with causal loop diagrams on paper when both later used *STELLA* to construct causal loop models. Students with a physics background did however do better than those without. A number of other features of the students' performance inform us qualitatively about their thinking, each of which is now briefly discussed.

Semi-quantitative Reasoning

Semi-quantitative reasoning was natural even in quantitative tasks. For example, after having seen *STELLA* run, all students reasoned semi-quantitatively when explaining how it worked. It was present when thinking about causally connected entities, and thus in developing or understanding causal diagrams. Semi-quantitative reasoning tends to be complex and seems to depend on subject matter. Students reasoned semi-quantitatively and satisfactorily when working with modelling tasks, in terms of entities, structures and output. About 70 per cent of choices of graphs to represent changes expressed semi-quantitatively were correct; only five out of eighteen semi-quantitative models designed with *STELLA* were rated by teachers as poor. There was some indication that semi-quantitative reasoning might depend on gender and background: female students, and students with a background in physics, were responsible for larger fractions of semi-quantitative descriptions of *IQON* and *STELLA* models, and were more successful in system thinking tasks.

The Idea of Rate of Change

The idea of rate of change is fundamental to quantitative modelling and to understanding models in *STELLA*. The idea that a variable changes seemed not to be a problem. The problem seemed to be the representation of the rate of change of a variable as itself another variable. A further indication of this is that while two thirds of students, after using *STELLA*, could identify rates of change in written problems about cash flow and about diet and getting fat, only about a third could suggest suitable units for these quantities.

System Thinking and Causal Thinking

The ability to manage the relevant facets of a system will reflect students' under-standing of a model. System-level thinking, particularly feedback loops, presented students with some difficulty. It was in expressive tasks that students showed some ability to construct interconnected systems. More than half the pairs work-ing with *IQON* did so, as compared with two out of nine pairs working with causal diagrams, hinting that *IQON* may have some advantage in this respect. System thinking involves causal thinking. A student needs to be able to link entities reasonably in a model and to give mechanisms to explain the links. There was a prevalence of 'linear' causal reasoning (one cause, one effect) over more complex thinking. This does not mean that students did not understand causes. The causal reasoning of students when working with exploratory tasks was often unsatisfactory, though they did better in this respect in expressive tasks.

Students were able to learn *IQON* very quickly so that they were in a posi-tion to explore *IQON* models. Both having been taught *IQON* and working with it in an exploratory mode may have helped students to express themselves with the tool. After being taught, students had few problems in dealing with *IQON*'s basic functions. Similarly, students could quickly learn to deal with the basic operations in *STELLA*, although a few of them asked for help. *STELLA*'s metaphor was powerful in influencing students' ideas about variables. Unlike work with causal diagrams and *IQON*, where the student is free to choose en-tities, *STELLA*'s structure worked as a 'strait jacket', obliging the student to use the idea of rates of change. When not confident of this idea, students could not express themselves with the tool.

In making judgments of models, in exploratory tasks with *IQON* and causal diagrams, students in general considered variables, links and correct structure as the main features in judging a model as accurate. The ability to offer reasonable criticisms of a model may be taken to indicate that students had reached a good level of understanding of the model and of what it represented. About half could reach such a reasonable level of criticism.

Students answered a questionnaire before and after the end of the study about the nature of models. Overall their opinions seem rather reasonable. Over half agreed initially that only a small part of reality can be understood through models, with a few more shifting towards agreement afterwards. Two-thirds agreed that models represent only very simplified aspects of reality, but with some shifts away from this position afterwards. Perhaps students have seen that not every-thing can be modelled, but that which can be modelled may be able to be modelled in some complexity.

Conclusion

Qualitative or semi-quantitative reasoning has been seen in AI as characteristic of experts' common sense reasoning about domain knowledge as well as having parallels with common sense reasoning about the everyday world. To design systems to simulate this type of reasoning has proved difficult. However, such semi-quantitative reasoning is now being used in numerous learning/teaching situations not only because it resembles people's common sense reasoning, but also because it allows the student to focus on the essentials of situations without involving the complexities of exact relationships. Some of the studies here suggest that it is a precursor to quantitative reasoning while others show that complex concepts can be dealt with more appropriately through a refinement of semi-quantitative reasoning than by quantitative reasoning. Overall, it can be seen that semi-quantitative approaches can allow students to approach system thinking in a way that is manageable even from a fairly early age.

Chapter 15

Reasoning with a
Semi-quantitative Tool

Joan Bliss

Introduction

This chapter gives an account of the research that was carried out in the Tools for Exploratory Learning Programme with the novel semi-quantitative modelling tool, *IQON*, looking at how pupils between the ages of 11 and 14, reasoned when working with such a tool. An often cited example of a tool for exploratory learning is that of a microworld. Although there are many different kinds of microworld, common to most descriptions of them is the notion that learners are provided with a collection of 'objects' that have specific behaviours which allow the learners to explore a given set of concepts or phenomena. Initially within the programme a distinction had been made between expressive and exploratory tools, where expressive ones were modelling systems, spreadsheets and shells of various kinds whereas exploratory tools were microworlds, simulations, etc. Such a distinction appeared too limited both in terms of the tools and pupils' activity using them. Thus another major innovation of the programme was to define two modes of learning activity: exploratory and expressive. The exploratory mode permits pupils to investigate the views of another about a domain, views often quite different from their own. The expressive mode allows pupils to represent their own ideas about a domain, reflecting on and exploring their own models. Given software tools can be used in both modes of learning activity.

Our aim in working with *IQON* was to see whether the use of such a tool would facilitate pupils' reasoning about a domain, whether exploring another's ideas or expressing their own. We wondered whether or not pupils could really understand the notion of a 'model', and whether 11 to 14-year-old pupils would actually be able to construct and explore their own models with *IQON*. We wondered about what complexity of model children could profitably explore. We asked ourselves about the extent to which pupils could see a complex model as an interrelated structure.

The Study

The procedures used for data collection and analysis in the study are described in Chapter 1 and the appendix and therefore only a brief outline of these is given

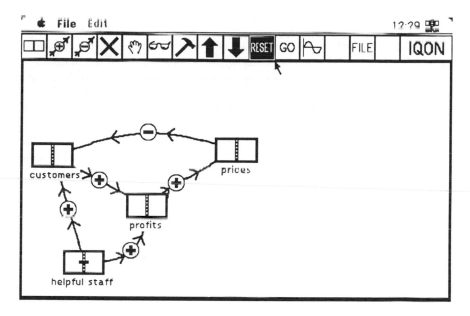

Figure 15.1: The semi-quantitative modelling tool IQON

here as a reminder. Pupils worked individually with a researcher over about two weeks: carrying-out a reasoning task without a computer, learning to use the computer and then the tool, and finally carrying out a modelling task in one of three topic areas in either the exploratory or expressive mode. There were forty-five pupils with a median age of 12; 9 years (range 11 to 14 years).

The Tool — IQON

A tool *IQON* was developed in SmallTalk to support the most elementary aspects of semi-quantitative reasoning and modelling, particularly to represent the idea that the qualitative magnitude of one variable (e.g., 'big', 'small' or 'normal') can change the value of another ('make it bigger', 'make it smaller'). *IQON* allows the user to represent a system in terms of interacting variables. An *IQON* model is built by making and defining 'boxes' to represent relevant variables, and linking them to show their mutual effects by arrowed links carrying a plus or minus sign to represent the direction of the effect. A 'plus' link says that one variable being 'high' causes the one to which it is linked to slowly increase; if 'low' the effect is reversed. A 'minus' link says the opposite. All variables have a level indicator which can be moved up or down with a middle 'normal' level at which they have no effect on others. The strength of the links affecting any one variable may be varied relative to one another. Figure 15.1 gives a picture of *IQON* with the menu of possibilities available for constructing models.

Tasks

All tasks had a broadly common format, and so far as we could manage, made reasonably comparable demands in background knowledge and in complexity of models provided. Parallel tasks for expressive and exploratory work had a very similar content. All the tasks, exploratory and expressive, were formulated as scenarios with a goal to achieve, through three everyday problems: shops and profits, traffic and congestion and fitness and diet. Opinions attributed to a range of people were given to be considered or tested. Thus tasks involved making predictions, considering alternatives, taking decisions and seeing what happened in a model. All tasks were presented in the form of a booklet containing the above material together with open-ended questions relevant to the task. The three topics were chosen on grounds of familiarity, curriculum relevance, and meaningfulness to pupils.

Expressive Tasks

In expressive tasks pupils were asked to build a model for one of the following three goals:

- keeping fit and staying slim;
- keeping a shop in profit;
- dealing with congestion in town.

The variable corresponding to the goal was given: fitness, profits or congestion. Once the model was completed pupils were asked to carry out three tests to see how to get the goal variable (e.g., fitness or congestion) to the best possible level (high or low); to see how to get it to the worst possible level; and to see how to keep it 'normal' (neither high nor low) despite the effect of various other factors on it. Each time pupils were asked to explain their manipulations and what was happening with the model. Three further parts of the task followed:

- modifications to the pupil's original model;
- option to build a new model;
- giving their views about *IQON*.

Exploratory Tasks

Exploratory tasks were parallel to expressive ones, with identical goals. Pupils were invited to test different versions of the basic model in order to see which one best achieved the goal of the task. There were three parts to the task:

- testing of a number of different points of view with the basic model and evaluating the effects;
- possible modifications to basic model and/or possibility of building a new model;
- giving their views about *IQON*.

Structure of Exploratory Models

There were three exploratory models one of which, the traffic model, is shown in Figure 15.2. The model for the shop task was the simplest of the three, with a system containing only one positive de-stabilizing feedback loop. The fitness model was composed of three feedback loops, all going through a central variable. There was a positive de-stabilizing loop and within the positive loop a negative stabilizing loop. In the top half of the system on the screen, there was one stabilizing negative feedback loop. The traffic model is composed of three feedback loops, one positive and two negative.

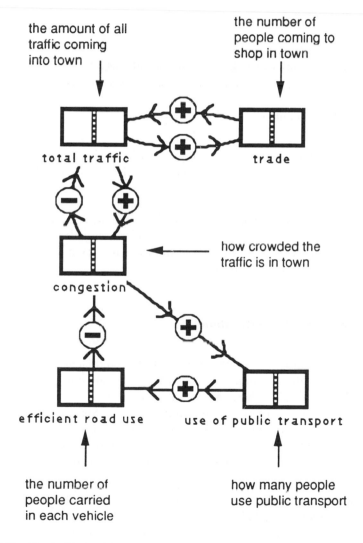

Figure 15.2: The traffic model

Joan Bliss

Table 15.1: Indices of linkage and interdependency of exploratory models

	Number of Variables	Linkage Index	Interdependency Index	Feedback loops
Shop	5	1.40	0.60	1
Traffic	5	1.40	1.00	3
Fitness	5	1.40	1.00	3

We constructed a number of indices to compare the structure and complexity of different models:

- number of variables;
- linkage: number of links/total number of variables;
- interdependency: number of dependent variables/total number of variables;
- feedback: number of feedback loops.

Model structures can also be described qualitatively as 'interdependent' or 'interlinked' 'chain' or 'star'. Interdependent models have complex cross connections, with variables affecting one another in more than one way and often including feedback loops. Chain models have variables each affecting the next in a chain, whilst interlinked models are like them, but with more complex cross-connections. Star models have several independent variables each influencing one dependent variable. The linkage and interdependency indices for the three exploratory models used are given in Table 15.1.

Structure of Pupils' Models

One of our aims was to see whether using *IQON* would facilitate pupils' reasoning so we begin with an example of a model built by one pupil, Nesta, as shown in Figure 15.3, and follow how she reasoned using it.

While carrying out a test 'to keep profits normal', Nesta put her model into an unexpected oscillation by decreasing the independent variable (helpful staff) and the dependent variable (prices). She tried to make sense of this situation, with a causal argument using simple and multiple connections:

> I've put the prices down a tiny bit, and put helpful staff a tiny bit past [down] so there's less helpful staff so they [the customers] would come because of the prices but maybe not because of the staff [it is understood that customers affect profits].

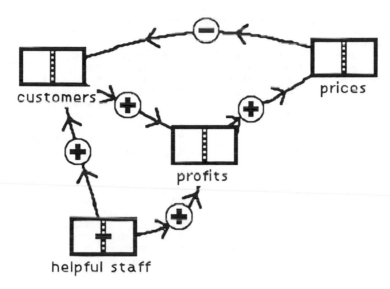

Figure 15.3: Nesta's shop model

She then attempted to explain the oscillation only in terms of the model:

> Profits went down a tiny bit and now its gone up because the prices have gone down but now they're going up again. It keeps going up and down. Now the profits are going down and the prices are up and the prices are going down. It's just going to keep going up and down probably.

However, faced with unexpected results, and not satisfied with her description, she tried to make sense of the situation, calling on her own knowledge of shops and shopping, not represented in the model:

> I suppose sometimes the customers would come and sometimes they wouldn't because it's not anything special, like they could go somewhere else that's cheaper. That's why it keeps going up and down — sometimes they might come and sometimes they might not.

Nesta's reasoning had become more sophisticated during the tests and this progress helped her to make what she considered as necessary modifications to her model. On moral grounds she eliminated the link between profits and prices ('when you get a lot of profits you should not increase your prices') then added a new variable 'attractiveness of the shop', creating a positive feedback loop between it and profits. Nesta's whole performance on the task was one where she appeared to be reflecting on how to use *IQON* to achieve what she wanted rather than achieving results by chance.

Table 15.2: *Indices of linkage and interdependency for pupil models*

SHOP TASK				No. of	
Pupil	Variable	Linkage	Interdep.	Fdbk lps	Type of model
Edna	5	0.80	0.20	0	medium star
Sonia	5	1.20	0.40	0	interlinked
Brian	6	1.00	0.50	0	interlinked
Lester	4	1.00	0.50	2	interlinked + feedback loops
Chloe	4	1.25	0.75	0	strongly interlinked
Nesta	4	1.25	0.75	1	strongly interlinked + feedback loops
Lewis	4	1.50	1.00	2	interdependent + feedback loops
Sam	10	2.00	1.00	3	interdependent + feedback loops
Average		1.25	0.64		

FITNESS TASK					
Pupil	Variable	Linkage	Interdep.	Fdbk	Type of model
Carmen	3	0.67	0.33	0	small star
Margaret	4	1.00	0.50	0	star + one interlink
Basil	6	1.17	0.50	0	interlinked
Mark	4	1.25	0.50	0	interlinked
Nancy	7	1.14	0.57	1	interlinked + feedback loop
Brenda	5	1.00	0.60	1	feedback loop + star
Anthony	6	1.33	0.67	1	interdependent + feedback loop
Judy	4	1.50	1.00	2	interdependent + feedback loops
Average		1.13	0.58		

TRAFFIC TASK					
Pupil	Variable	Linkage	Interdep.	Fdbk	Type of Model
Zillah	5	0.80	0.20	0	medium star
Toby	6	0.83	0.16	0	large star
Linda	4	0.75	0.50	0	star-like
Miles	10	0.90	0.40	0	star-like joined to star
Sally	4	0.75	0.75	0	chain
Marjorie	5	1.20	0.60	0	interlinked
Burgess	4	1.25	0.75	0	interlinked
Average		0.93	0.48		

All pupils who carried out expressive tasks on all three topics, were able to construct a model. Table 15.2 shows indices of linkage and interdependency for each pupil's model, together with a brief description of the model. This table shows that pupils' models were moderate in size, containing between four and six variables. The largest model contained ten variables and the smallest contained three. Pupils could think of at least some ways in which the variables in their model affected one another, since no model contained any variable not linked to some other. More than three quarters of the models have one or more linkages for every variable. Just under one third of the models had a star-like structure and about half show some considerable degree of interdependence or interlinking of variables, with variables affecting one another in multiple ways or with feedback.

The indices of linkage and interdependency are noticeably lower for models on the traffic task than for the models on the shop and fitness tasks. This stems from the fact that over half the traffic models are star-like, this type of model being produced less frequently in the other two tasks. Thus while traffic task models do not contain fewer variables than those on the other tasks, there are fewer links relating variables to one another, and they lack feedback loops. Shop and fitness task models by contrast are mainly interlinked or interdependent.

Do-ability of Exploratory Tasks

In the exploratory tasks it was important that pupils understood the points of view they were asked to test because, if they did not, they would not be able to manipulate the appropriate variables to carry out the tests. Over three-quarters of the pupils gave evidence of understanding the different points of view given in the three tasks. Just under two-thirds of them re-iterated what was written in the text about the situation, sometimes expanding or re-interpreting the content, while the remainder summarized the different view points in their own words.

Problems of misunderstandings of the tasks were few and spread across the tasks. On the shop task a small number of pupils disagreed with a point of view, for example, viewing increasing prices as dishonest. One pupil not only interpreted and expanded but offered a criticism of each viewpoint, based on his everyday understanding of shops. On the fitness task a few younger pupils had difficulty in seeing the difference in meaning between, for example, heaviness of build and body weight. On the traffic task quite a few pupils did not really know the meaning of the terms 'congestion' and 'by-pass'.

When misunderstandings of tasks are set aside, nearly three-quarters of all the pupils were able to cope with all manipulations on the three tasks. The major difficulty that pupils experienced was understanding the resulting indirect effects of the manipulation of a variable. For example, pupils sometimes wished to increase both the input to the independent variable and its effect, not seeing that an effect is passed on. Such difficulties usually occurred at the beginning of a task later these pupils usually manipulated the model appropriately. Children in the expressive tasks also had a similar difficulty, sometimes arising from the stage of building of the model, where the focus is on creating links between pairs of variables and not on the system as a whole.

Reasoning with Models

In carrying out tasks, children were first asked to predict the results of a model running, then to describe the model running and lastly to explain what was happening in the model. The reasoning used varied in each of the parts. Whether in the expressive or exploratory mode, many were fascinated by the model functioning, observing the screen with great attention. At this stage non-causal reasoning dominated their commentaries because they tended to focus on what they saw happening on the screen. Pupils would, for example, notice: 'Congestion is going up, public transport is up, efficient road use is going up'.

Predictions varied, tending to be non-causal at the beginning of the task, but more causal in nature towards the end of the task. When explaining why certain results were obtained with a model, the great majority of pupils used some form of causal reasoning. The few who did not were carrying out exploratory tasks. Overall, just over half used complex causal reasoning not restricted to the effect of just one variable on another, whilst simple causal arguments were used by about one quarter.

There was a greater variety of types of reasoning on exploratory tasks than on expressive ones, the latter splitting roughly equally between those who used complex causal reasoning and those who used simple causal connections in explanations. On exploratory tasks the reasoning pupils used ranged from complex causal reasoning, simple causal reasoning to non-causal reasoning.

Expressive Tasks — Reasoning Carrying Out Tests

Approximately two-thirds of the pupils on all tasks could manipulate their models successfully on the simpler tests and could explain how they functioned using complex causal reasoning. On a more difficult test just over half the pupils across tasks were able to carry out the test or make some sensible attempt at it, and again use complex causal reasoning. What is of interest is that while we might expect pupils with complex models to be able to reason in a sophisticated manner we also found this with pupils whose models were only relatively complex. The somewhat simpler models appeared to help pupils to understand what was happening in the whole system. The most crucial factor with these simpler models is that they need to be interlinked in type, not to be star or star-like models.

Those pupils who had difficulty manipulating their models on the three tests gave only simple causal reasoning limited either because their models were too complex or because the star-like structure of the model required no other type of reasoning. In star-like models reasoning followed the nature of the links, simple causal connections, with a series of independent variables each linked, in turn, to the same central dependent variable. Nothing other than simple connections is required to describe what is happening in the model or to explain how the model functions. In this way, the child's imagination is hindered by the structure itself.

The case of pupils who built more complex models than they could manage is worth noting. Pupils would build their models step by step, sometimes generating fairly complex structures of chains and interconnected variables. These were often models which scored high on the linkage index but low on the interdependency one. However, having built them in this manner, when they observed them running as a system in which effects were not limited to the simple connections constructed but affected the whole system, the results could be unexpected and they could not cope.

Exploring Models with Feedback Loops

A model with a feedback loop shows system behaviour: behaviour to be understood in terms of the structure of the model as a whole. Pupils found both the fitness and traffic exploratory tasks difficult, the fitness one being a little more complex. On the shop task, where there was only one feedback loop, children coped more easily or could more easily ignore the feedback loop. There were two types of argument: in the first pupils paid attention to feedback loops but with the second they ignored them.

When making arguments which deal with feedback, some pupils reasoned about the whole system, attempting to link feedback loops. They often followed one loop like a chain and passed to another, only closing the second loop afterwards. Another kind of argument was more localized, concentrating on only one loop within the system, ignoring the other.

Children who avoided considering feedback had several kinds of argument. In one, pupils saw that changes in one part of the system had effects elsewhere, but just reasoned in terms of chains of effects. In another, pupils did not seem to see the connections between the different parts of the system. They focused on one loop but without closing it, then jumped to the other. Finally there was a localized argument where a loop was treated as an unclosed chain.

On both traffic and fitness tasks just over half the pupils attempted to reason with feedback loops. Well over half of this group used mainly strategies for dealing with feedback loops, while the others sometimes dealt with feedback and sometimes avoided it. For example, on the traffic task (Figure 15.2), one child tried to deal with a positive feedback between a pair of variables, and saw how they each affected one another:

> The total traffic and trade they're both plus . . . well when traffic goes up . . . because when traffic goes up it'll make the trade would go up, wouldn't it? So that's how it's a plus, so when the trade goes up, it'll make the traffic go up.

The remaining pupils used strategies that mainly avoided reasoning about feedback. For example, another child on the traffic task, in avoiding feedback loops, treated them as a chain:

> If people park in car parks, there'd be less traffic [putting together congestion and total traffic] so trade probably go down — but because they'd still be able to go into shops though, wouldn't they — so trade will probably go up.

The conclusion is correct according to the model, but appears to be based on experience rather than on understanding how the model works.

Modifying Models or Building New Ones

In expressive tasks pupils were asked, after having carried out the tests, if they wished to modify their models or to build a new one. About two-thirds of the pupils did so, one pupil doing both. The difference between the pupils who modified models and those who built new ones is worth noting. On the whole, those pupils whose first models were fairly sophisticated chose not to modify them, they did not feel the need for a new model since the one they had created was already quite reasonable. New models were built by pupils who had relatively simple first models or who had experienced some problems with testing their first models. These second models — new or modified — were usually more sophisticated and better structured than the first attempts.

On exploratory tasks pupils behaved quite differently, none suggesting a very different model from that given to them, with one exception. Only two (of the eight) pupils who explored the shop model (in which the task itself, unlike the others, did not involve adding new variables) made modifications. On the traffic and fitness tasks all pupils, except one, made some modifications. All changes increased the size of the model, adding to the model rather than simplifying it. Since in general extra independent variables were being added, the interdependency of models generally decreased, making them more star-like. Linkage did not change much, indicating that about one link was added for each new variable.

Modelling Complex Systems

Initially we asked whether pupils could really understand the notion of a 'model'. Through the tasks we were able to identify a range of pupil activities which seemed to provide evidence that pupils were, in some reasonable sense of the term, modelling. Such activities ranged from testing a model in some way or another, formal manipulation of and reflection on a model, to learning about models by modifying them, or building a new model after having experimented with a first. Examples of these modelling activities are given.

Controlling Variables

A number of pupils adopted the approach of attempting several trials for a given test, and trying to control the variables through the trials. One pupil carried out numerous trials with a fitness model (Figure 15.4). On the most difficult test he ran seven unsuccessful trials, always trying to vary three or more variables at a time. He realized the need to be systematic but never quite managed it enough to help him. Towards the end he argued:

> Nothing is happening — this is a good sign. Fitness is staying — oh it's moving over slightly a bit now but really slowly so that's good. Exercise is still moving. Now that's what happened last time, they sort of like catch up with each other and then it goes wrong. [He notices the effect of a positive feedback loop]. I don't know what happened, it always happens like this. It was doing well and as soon as exercise started really

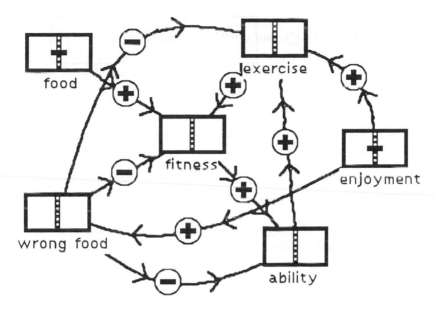

Figure 15.4: A fitness model

decreasing — that was a bit annoying. [He then added] What this would work on is a slightly simpler model.

Other Examples

Do the results the model predicts actually correspond to the reality that is being modelled? In part of a fitness model one pupil had created a positive link from 'exercise' to 'fitness' but also a second positive link from 'exercise' to 'fat'. He then made an appropriate change increasing 'exercise', which increased 'fitness', but this increase also affected 'fat'.

that's what it seems like because exercise goes into fitness and then it goes into fat, and the more exercise you do the more fat you get.
[He pauses] When I exercise I don't get fat!

Understanding compensation between links shows modelling through formal manipulation of the model. For example, when two independent variables link to the same dependent variable, as in Figure 15.5, where one link is positive and the other is negative, such that the two independent variables can balance one another out. In this instance one child focused on the two single links 'bad eating' and 'good eating' to 'fitness'. She increased both links, saying: 'because if good eating went up and bad eating went up they wouldn't affect it [fitness] because

Figure 15.5: Part of a second fitness model

they'd just balance themselves out . . . the good things you ate would just balance out with the bad things'.

Conclusion

The semi-quantitative tool *IQON* was created to provide an environment to support reasoning about complex systems in terms of rough and ready sizes of effects of one thing on another. Other available modelling tools, for example *STELLA*, require too much mathematics for them to be able to be used with younger pupils.

In general, models made by pupils in expressive tasks were simpler than models they could reasonably easily understand in exploratory tasks. However, the complex nature of the exploratory models led to some quite sophisticated and complex reasoning, the majority of pupils taking some account of the complexity of models, and a minority going further and dealing with the model as an inter-connected system. Pupils doing expressive tasks had no hesitation in criticizing their own models and, when asked if they wished to change them, could think of interesting and fundamental changes. Also, they often felt the need or had the desire to create a new model. The structures of the modified or new models were in almost all cases more complex and more interesting than their original models.

In the exploratory mode, pupils started by exploring already sophisticated models created by someone else. They did not generally see the need to build a new model, and usually only suggested additions and extensions to the model, which made the model larger but less structurally complex. By contrast, changes made to models in the expressive tasks were more often likely to involve an effort to clarify or reorganize a model previously made, and some cases made it more elegant and compact. In this sense, pupils doing expressive tasks and making their own models were a little nearer to the adult activity of modelling, even though the models they made were simpler than those provided for them.

The majority of pupils broadly used reference to the real world and to their own knowledge and experience in a reasonable and appropriate manner. An advantage of having tasks based on everyday knowledge was that it permitted and valued the use of pupils' own ordinary knowledge and experience. The more pupils wished to explain and interpret models the more they tended to seek reasons in the real world. This was not without problems. Sometimes pupils would suggest a real world event, not in any way represented in the model, as a reason for an effect of the model.

In all topics and all areas of reasoning, models were similar in size, containing on average between four and six variables. The fitness and diet topic was close to pupils' immediate experience, and had often been the subject of personal reflection so knowledge about it was extensive and well assimilated. *IQON* helped pupils to represent this knowledge. Knowledge of traffic seemed the least well articulated in pupils' thinking. While they knew traffic jams as an immediate experience, they had little appreciation of the overall problem. The tool captured and exposed through the models the simplicity of the pupils' knowledge structures. Shop knowledge was fairly extensive but one-sided, experienced as the customer and not as the seller. Pupils believed they knew a lot, but when they tried to articulate their knowledge from a different perspective, the lack of sureness about the ideas interacted with the difficulties presented by the formalism of the tool being used.

Our study thus suggests that children between the ages of 11 and 14, using a tool such as *IQON* which permits semi-quantitative reasoning, can create their own models. They can understand that a model is fallible and can be modified or that they may need to build a new one. *IQON* provides opportunities for pupils to learn more about some fundamental aspects of modelling, to find out what 'exploring' a model is all about, either through the experience of expressing some themselves or by trying out and criticizing others' models. In both cases they have the opportunity of thinking about the relation of models to reality or about how a model or modelling system looks at the world in its own special way.

Part 4

Thinking with Objects, Links and Logic

Chapter 16

An Introduction to Qualitative Modelling

Chris Tompsett

Introduction

The selection of models in this section represents views of modelling that attempt to a greater extent than those from previous sections to break free from the confines of the mathematical world.

This chapter starts with a brief overview of the development of qualitative modelling in general and a review of earlier applications in education. Some major distinctions between qualitative modelling tools are raised. This is followed by a framework for discussing the relationship between models and the problems that they are intended to represent. After a discussion of the papers that have been included in the remainder of this section, some pointers to the future are raised.

The Origins of Qualitative Modelling

Computer-based qualitative modelling aims to develop reasoning systems that mimic or reflect human understanding, without the use of mathematics. Early examples, such as *MYCIN* and *DENDRAL* (Waterman, 1986), were created to allow more consistent or more accurate decision-taking by a group of professionals. Two characteristics of these systems needed to be taken into account. Firstly, they needed to be considered in terms of the accuracy of decisions taken by the system. Matching human performance was not difficult to achieve. Secondly, the professionals needed to have confidence in the ability of the reasoning process that generated the decisions. This second factor was the most significant in limiting the adoption of such systems by professional groups. *DENDRAL* has been extended and enhanced to a more powerful system, *META-DENDRAL*, which is still used in industry, whilst *MYCIN* was never used by the doctors for whom it was designed, despite outperforming some of them in overall accuracy of decision-taking.

This initial view of qualitative modelling was restricted to well-bounded problems but few problems were sufficiently bounded to allow all the relevant knowledge to be identified and represented. Hayes (1979) commented 'We are never going to get an adequate formalization of common sense by making short forays into small areas, no matter how many of them we make.' A more radical approach was needed to capture the reasoning power of even ordinary people within a computer system.

In a paper entitled *The Naive Physics Manifesto*, Hayes (1979) characterized a possible solution as a search for a representation of the real world at the level of common language — for example, the language of composite objects (glued, nailed, hinged together), substances (sticky, flexible, liquid) as well as support, movement and forces etc. His proposal required that we model the physical world, not at the level of equations of dynamics and Newton's laws, but rather as a common-sense understanding of the external world removed from quantities and equations.

This view provides two motivations for using qualitative models. Firstly, they only need to be partial representations of the world, sufficient to solve problems up to a given level of detail, without claiming that it is a complete solution, and limiting, as far as possible, the complexity of the model that is created. Secondly, they avoid, as far as possible, the use of mathematics and numbers. Bratko (1988) offers further reasons as to when qualitative modelling might be necessary, as opposed to desirable:

- no numerical model is known to exist;
- the mathematics cannot be solved efficiently;
- critical parameters for running a model may not be known;
- experts do not operate at the quantitative level.

Two significant strands of research, one firmly embedded in the world of mechanics and physics, the other less constrained but potentially more powerful, have arisen from this field. The first strand has focused on the development of modelling systems which describe such problems using qualitative descriptions of the numerical quantities (within the Tools for Exploratory Learning Programme, these models were termed semi-quantitative, see Chapters 14 and 15). Instead of numerical values, only critical values such as zero, infinity or limits are used, together with relationships between such values, such as above or below each other and increasing, steady or decreasing over time.

In essence these systems, notably Qualitative Process Theory (Forbus, 1983; 1984), Qualitative Simulation (Kuipers, 1984; 1986) and Envisionment (de Kleer and Brown, 1983; 1984; 1985), emulate differential equations, each with its own characteristics. Relationships between variables are captured within a formalism and the modelling system simulates the interaction of these relationships to show how the variables change over time. For example, Qualitative Simulation has a precise mathematical description which represents a class of problems to a well-defined degree of accuracy. Each of these systems has limitations in the scope of what can be represented and some are often simple to characterize.

Qualitative Simulation, for example, whilst retaining mathematical validity, is non-deterministic and can produce a range of potential behaviours when only a more limited set would be expected from commonsense understanding of the real world. Current research in this strand emphasizes the need to cope with other modelling problems, such as order of magnitude, time, and the kinematics of structures.

The less constrained approach to qualitative modelling is best typified by the work on the Kardio Project (Bratko, Mozetic and Lavrac, 1989). In contrast to the previous approaches, this work is based on the use of logic to describe and integrate components of a model. This particular project modelled the electrical components of a heart and the way in which signals are combined. The model did not provide a specimen electrocardiogram but produced the verbal description that would apply — such as whether significant features were regular, in phase, synchronized, or accentuated. The system included rules that model the composition of electrical signals, such as: 'if two cyclic signals of the same frequency are summed, the resulting signal is cyclic with the same frequency', as well as more conventional ones, e.g., 'adding two positive values results in a positive value'.

In using logical reasoning, rather than an approximation to differential equations, two distinct advantages can be identified. Firstly, although the development of the model might suggest that the system only allows a description of an electrocardiogram to be predicted from a description of the condition of a particular heart, the logic can also be applied 'in reverse'. The range of heart conditions that could give rise to a particular electrocardiogram pattern can also be derived. Secondly, the generic nature of this approach, representing all information as logical statements, provides its inherent power — but the lack of an underlying mechanism other than logic, requires that each system is built from first principles.

Background to Qualitative Modelling in Education

The underlying techniques of qualitative modelling have been pursued in education since the first tools became available on microcomputers in schools. An initial concentration within the United Kingdom, on logic for problem representation (Ennals, 1984) and logic-based microworlds (Nichol, 1988), has since led to a wide range of applications across all phases of education, supported by an international community of developers and practitioners. In addition to work with commercially available reasoning products or expert system shells such as *Xi+* (see, for example Thorne, 1986), other general systems have been developed specifically for education, such, as *Adex*, *Knowledge-Pad*, and *Expert Builder*.

In commercial applications, the intention is to use human decision-taking to enhance the power of computer decision-taking. In education we are interested in the reverse, where reasoning reflected in a computer model is used to develop the understanding of the student or pupil. This shifts the focus from decisions to

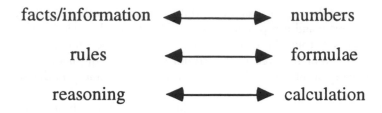

Figure 16.1: Relationship between qualitative and mathematical modelling

reasoning. Partial models which cannot guarantee to produce the correct decision are of little value in commercial terms, but they are still of educational value if the limitations of the model, as well as its potential, can be perceived by the pupils.

At a simple level, qualitative models in education apply 'general rules', which represent subject knowledge, to facts that describe a problem, in order to deduce new information which is interpreted as a solution to a problem in the real world. This shows strong parallels (see Figure 16.1) with mathematical modelling, replacing computation with reasoning in general.

Beyond this simple analogy, however, a wide variety of approaches has been investigated. Apart from the distinction between exploratory and expressive modes of model building (described in Chapter 1), approaches have differed, for example, in the method of representing knowledge, the 'power' of the inherent reasoning mechanism, and the extent to which the reasoning is subject specific. Simple 'rules' and 'facts' remain the most common approach for representing knowledge, partly because of the apparent simplicity with which they can be created, but more complex representations have also been considered, such as semantic networks and frames or objects.

The power of the reasoning mechanism depends on the extent to which statements are decomposed and matched with each other. For example, the statement 'the weather is fine' is related in common sense to the statement 'the weather is rainy', but this is not an association that is made within all reasoning systems (no such link is made within *Expert Builder*, though the link would be made by *Adex*). The two statements above are exclusive, but a similar pair of statements, such as 'the material is soft' and 'the material is shiny', are not. If a reasoning system is to distinguish between these two situations, it must be explicitly instructed to do so. Although this appears at first to be a trivial matter, the facility is not necessarily available in a straightforward manner even in some commercially available reasoning systems. However, the lack of such a distinction can lead to unnatural or convoluted methods for representing what students or pupils might consider as simple knowledge.

The extent to which modelling systems encapsulate subject-based reasoning is less well-developed, though see Nichol's (1988) logic based microworlds in the domain of history and Bateman's work (1988) in chemistry.

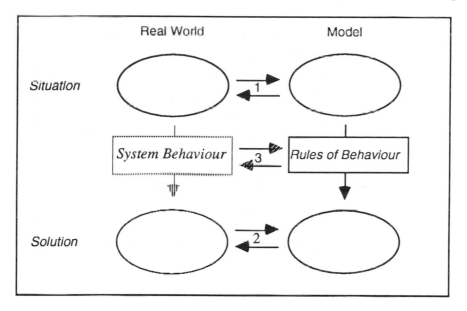

Figure 16.2:   The relationships between a model and the real world

Real Problems and Qualitative Models

Although the term 'model' can be used in many ways, it assumed here that a model cannot exist in its own right but must always function as a model 'of some other system', normally considered to be the real world. At their simplest, models only require a mapping between the elements of the 'real world' and elements in the model.

A stronger notion of a model is implied, however, if the intentionality of modelling is considered. Within education, models are used to explain some particular aspect of a real world problem, whether this is in the exploratory mode, helping the teacher to explain some subject matter, or the expressive mode, creating models as possible explanations of the world. The implication, that the underlying mechanism or theory defines or determines the behaviour of the model, plays a key role in creating such models. It is possible, though not necessary, that there is a close connection between the rules that determine the behaviour of the model and rules that determine the behaviour of the real world.

The essential relationships between problems, reasoning, solutions and models are illustrated in Figure 16.2. These relationships include the ability to correlate descriptions in the real world, both of the problem scenario (1) and the solution (2), with those in the model world and the intermediate process of 'solving' problems by using the rules of behaviour and implicit reasoning within the model. No attention is placed necessarily on the existence of a related real-world system behaviour to match the rules of behaviour within the model (shown by the arrows

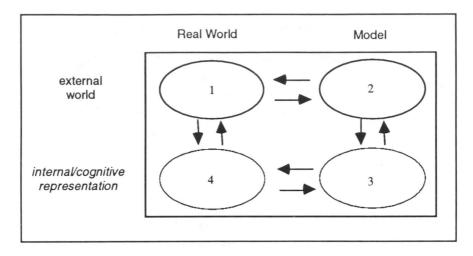

Figure 16.3: Relationship between internal and external models

labelled 3), nor whether such a system could exist (see earlier comments on the nature of qualitative models).

The Papers in this Section

These differences between approaches to modelling become more evident if we recognize, in addition, a separation of the external world from any internal representation that may be developed by the pupil or student (see Figure 16.3). From this point of view, the pupil's personal conception (mental model) of either the real world or any computer-based qualitative model do not necessarily coincide with any objective description of them. For example, the pupil may fail to notice some central aspects of the real world problem, or misunderstand the way in which the model processes information.

In the purely exploratory mode, the emphasis is on the use of the model to develop understanding of the real world. A real-world problem (1) is presented, together with a model (2). The pupils are intended to develop their own understanding of the model (3) in order to improve their understanding of the real world (4). The effectiveness of this approach relies on the transparency with which the model reflects the real world (from (1) to (2)) and the ability of the pupil to follow the behaviour of the model (from (2) to (3)). The rules of behaviour act as the explanation for the real-world system and the processing power of the model demonstrates how this knowledge can be used in any particular situation (see, for example, the 'hydra' model in Chapter 19 on *WorldMaker*). They need to be simple to understand, though not necessarily simple to create.

In the expressive mode, the sequence of transformations is followed in reverse order. The pupils are presented first with a real-world situation (1), for which they must develop their own, suitably complete understanding of the situation (4). In order to create a computer-based model, they must then formulate an appropriate internal 'model' (3) and then represent this as an external model on a computer (2). The last two of these steps illustrate different aspects of understanding the reasoning within the qualitative model. The step from (4) to (3) requires that the pupil understands the type and power of the reasoning that is required. The step from (3) to (2) requires that the pupil is able to represent this effectively on the computer — an interface design issue (see comments in Chapter 18 regarding *Expert Builder*).

The three articles that have been included in this section can only represent an introduction to the field, but all of them address some central issues in modelling in education. Some differences between them result from different modes of modelling, as described above, whilst others reflect different intentions in the use of the models themselves. The motivation for each chapter is different, Chapter 17 describing a research project and is included as much to illustrate the problems which arise in describing work in this field, as to promote the modelling tool. Chapter 18 describes the use of a modelling tool, with well understood properties, for use at an early stage within the curriculum. Chapter 19 describes a modelling system which combines apparent simplicity with potentially significant power to 'explain' phenomena in the real world through the use of exploratory models.

Chapter 17, relating work on qualitative modelling in the Tools for Exploratory Learning Programme, emphasizes the research process, as opposed to significant modelling aspects. Three related features distinguish the system that was created from other work in this field. Firstly, the tool includes no processing power — it is not possible for the information that is 'put in' to the model to be reproduced in any other form. Secondly, since there is no inherent processing, the intended processing of information, either by the originator of the model in exploratory mode, or by a pupil in expressive mode, cannot be made explicit — generating, perhaps, some of the problems in using the model that are reported. The system is closer to simulation of a real-world problem that evolves over time than a qualitative modelling system. Thirdly, the lack of processing removes the constraint imposed by a more formal structure. Understanding the intended scope of the descriptions that can be entered is unsupported by the modelling system itself, leaving this aspect to be managed by the researcher, or teacher, through examples.

Many of these comments relate to the way the modelling system was used within that particular study, which sought to develop different models, quantitative, semi-quantitative and qualitative, that could be compared for analysing the same problem. Other less procedural models, for example replacing the action → result model with a situation → justification view to analyse reasons underlying an historical conflict, might be more suited to the modelling system.

Chapter 18, on *Expert Builder*, reports extensive work with younger pupils creating expressive models. The *Expert Builder* system was designed to allow these pupils to begin modelling, increasing the importance of the pupils' understanding of the AND/OR representation and reasoning power that is used in the system. The focus on visualizing both the representation and the processing of the knowledge in the model restricts the overall power of the processing that can be used. However, as an introduction to modelling, the existence of a professionally developed simple system, with extensive curriculum applications, provides a confident starting point for teachers wishing to begin work in this field.

Chapter 19 presents an object-oriented modelling system that has again been designed to provide a simple interface for pupils. In contrast to *Expert Builder*, the model is time-based, but the accessibility of the representation and the inherent simplicity of the processing of a model highlight the authors' intention to explain, rather than merely emulate the situations that the models represent. When viewing modelling as described in this introduction, it is, perhaps, unsurprising that the pupils found difficulties in interpreting behaviour rules that have no correspondence with commonsense. However, the creative possibilities that such an activity supports should not be overlooked and suggests that further work might lead to interesting developments within the field. The potential of the system, for example to explain 'global' behaviour patterns in terms of the simple 'local' behaviour rules, is well illustrated, even though the work is at an early stage of development in comparison with other qualitative reasoning tools such as *Expert Builder*.

The Future of Qualitative Modelling

Early work in this field has been hampered by the limitations of the available technology. The ever increasing power of technology has begun to allow a closer examination of the relationship between the complexity of the underlying modelling problems and the weaknesses created by limited computer resources, but this direction of work is still in its infancy within the school curriculum. The systems described here allow us to begin this important phase of investigation and it is at this stage that the experience of ordinary teachers working within the constraints of the curriculum and classroom management will become most important.

For the developers, this work outlines the problems in presenting even simple reasoning tools to children. The development of more sophisticated tools is in essence simple — it is making the increased power accessible that requires the major developmental effort. The multi-media lobby beckons with the promise of increasing the ability of pupils to understand what is being conveyed and in enriching the scope of the modelling environment. Where this potential can extend the power of the tools we offer to pupils, this is an exciting concept. Where it only encourages pupils to listen more and detracts from the reasoning power of the tools that we could make available, I, personally, am concerned that the pupils will lose out.

Chapter 17

Reasoning with a Qualitative Modelling Tool

Joan Bliss and Haralambos Sakonidis

Introduction

This chapter describes the work of the Tools for Exploratory Learning Programme that examined the nature of children's reasoning with a qualitative modelling tool. The overall research programme focused on the following questions; firstly, can reasoning with modelling tools containing representations (models) of a domain facilitate reasoning in that domain, and secondly, are learners helped to reason about a domain by using modelling tools to represent and explore their own ideas about that domain?

The study followed the same methods as the other parts of the project (see Chapter 1 and the appendix). Two tasks, either in exploratory or expressive mode, were designed for the two different topics: (i) shops and profits, and (ii) traffic and congestion.

A total of twenty children were interviewed, ten in each learning mode, ranging in age from 11 to 14. Researchers worked with pupils individually over a two-week period. In the first week children carried out a reasoning task without the computer, and were then taught to use a Macintosh computer. In the second week, pupils were taught to use the modelling tool and, shortly afterwards, were asked to carry out one modelling task, either expressive or exploratory. Those carrying out the expressive tasks undertook some informal work on the topic on which their task was based. The data collection and analysis were qualitative.

Choice of Tool

Although there is now a wider choice of tools, including *Expert Builder* (see Chapter 18) and *SemNet*, a program supporting the construction of semantic nets, when the project started there were few systems designed for qualitative modelling with school pupils. Of the few available, *Knowledge Pad* and *Linx88*, both implemented in Prolog on IBM and Nimbus machines, were considered as the basis for the study.

Knowledge Pad is a simple rule-based system which makes inferences from rules supplied by the creator of the model and/or by the user. An important argument in favour of using a simple expert system model, was that the system had significant and interesting behaviour, being able to 'compute' consequences. If it were merely a passive display device, it could be argued that pencil and paper would do just as well. *Linx88* maintains a text data structure and guides the user's exploration of that structure by posing a sequence of choices, applying logic based on these choices to determine the next text to display. In favour of using *Linx88*, or *SuperLinx* (described in Turner, 1990) a version prepared for the Tools for Exploratory Learning Programme, was that it offered a simple and accessible concept — a story composed of episodes with links between episodes based on the previous choices of the user. Unfortunately the versions available, unlike the other tools on the project, had no direct manipulation interface and were available only on IBM or Nimbus machines. Since the project had previously committed its resources to Macintosh machines (partly so as to have access to direct manipulation), this would have meant relying on schools' machines for use in the research.

The decision hinged also on which type of program we could most convincingly fit into the existing framework of exploratory and expressive tasks on the topics of fitness, shops, and traffic. We invested considerable effort into devising tasks for both systems but we found it particularly difficult to develop convincing material for an expert system. We had not anticipated such difficulties, thinking that these domains would yield reasonably accessible and simple rules. There was also a difficulty with *Linx88*, in that, when engaged in expressive activities, pupils tended to produce 'stream of consciousness' stories, changing focus as they went along. The interlinked structures, which would have used the computer more effectively, were hard to achieve.

In the event it was decided to build a specialized version of *Linx88* in HyperCard2. This *Linx88*-like program, called *Explore your options*, permits the construction of a hypertext view of related situations and actions. Any situation can be associated with up to three possible actions in that situation. An action leads to a new situation and several actions can lead to the same situation. Both situations and actions are expressed as text, the tool displaying a graph of the paths between situations and actions. It shows the text of a situation and the action, that has either been selected or has led to the situation selected. A technical report giving further details of the tool and study is available (Bliss, Sakonidis *et al.*, 1992).

The outline graph of the exploratory traffic task is shown in Figure 17.1, below. The reason for introducing the graph of all situations and actions into *Explore your options* was to avoid the well-known effect of 'getting lost in hyperspace'. This may have the effect of making the tool seem less impressive, since one can see, as opposed to having to guess at, just how simple or complex the structure of the model is.

The Tasks

All tasks were formulated as scenarios with a goal to achieve, the scenarios being similar for expressive and exploratory tasks on a given topic. The topics and goals

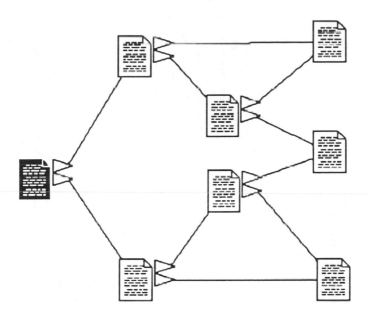

Figure 17.1: Outline structure of exploratory traffic model

were: (i) helping a Town Council with its traffic problems, or (ii) helping a shop-keeper use her profits to expand her business.

In expressive tasks there were three major phases: firstly, introduction to the idea of a model and modelling, by exploring the beginnings of a model; secondly, construction of the model — pupils were asked to build a model which allowed them to set out the options available for one of the above goals; and finally, evaluation of the model produced.

In exploratory tasks there were two major phases, an exploratory and an evaluative phase. In the exploratory phase pupils investigated the model step-by-step, attempting to make sense of the model locally. In the evaluatory phase, they were looking at the model holistically, considering paths through the model and their outcomes as a whole, or comparing different types of paths and their outcomes.

The pupils were asked to evaluate the results of the model in the following terms:

- evaluation of convergent paths;
- evaluation of a path with a bad outcome;
- evaluation of two unsuccessful paths;
- comparison of unsuccessful and successful paths.

Figure 17.2 shows the content of the exploratory traffic model.

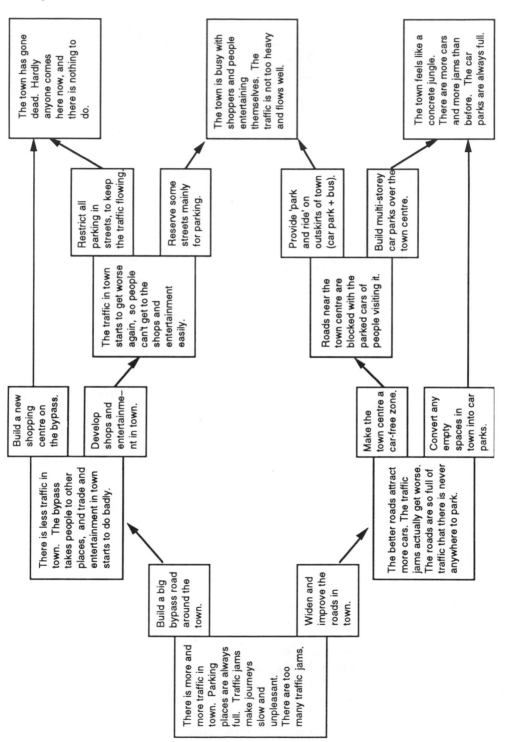

Figure 17.2: Situations and actions in the exploratory traffic model

The Results

This particular part of the overall study highlighted two issues, the first of general interest to the creation of qualitative models and the second of interest to the exploration of models with tools which are essentially display devices. The first issue concerns expressive tasks and the ease or difficulty that pupils experienced in moving from narrative, that is talking about a problem, to modelling it as interconnected choices.

The second issue is to do with exploratory tasks, where, because the tool is a display device, the model is laid out in detail. In these circumstances, what is the role of pupils' experience and their real-world knowledge in the interpretation of a model? When faced with exploring the model sequentially, can pupils see the model as a system of options?

Narrative or Interconnected Choices?

All qualitative tools require the use of some fixed and disciplined framework of qualitative decisions, distinctions or rules. In the case of *Explore your options* this is a set of interlinked, alternative choices of actions in situations with a single-problem focus. This kind of framework can be distinguished from a narrative approach, in which ideas flow in a time sequence, shifting focus and direction as the narrative develops.

In expressive activities, we found that pupils began in a narrative mode and had to try and shift toward the modelling approach required by the tool. Thus, we distinguished two phases: a 'negotiation' phase and an 'execution' phase. During the former, pupils were simply discussing the ideas they wanted to incorporate into their model, whereas in the latter they had to represent them on the screen. As might be expected, the ideas in the 'negotiation' phase were much more detailed and complex, with pupils tending to provide whole paths of ideas. Some pupils were reluctant to simplify these composite constructions in order to make possible the representation of their ideas during the 'execution' phase.

A number of pupils found it easier to talk imaginatively about both actions and situations related to the task rather than to give a specific 'action' or a 'situation'. Because of the use of their own knowledge and experience in the task discussion, both pupils and the researcher often found it difficult to know what the actual situation or action destined for the model was going to be. We give two examples to illustrate this.

In the first example, Jean, on the traffic task, initially believed that the action 'more car parks' would relieve congestion. Later she realized that it would attract cars, and so created the situation 'more traffic' instead. Although Jean knew the task, and what she was supposed to do next, she preferred to talk about it further, as can be seen in the dialogue.

Jean: Yes, traffic — there will be more traffic.
Interviewer: Traffic there will be more — Right, OK, so you are in a new situation now, what actions could you think of taking.

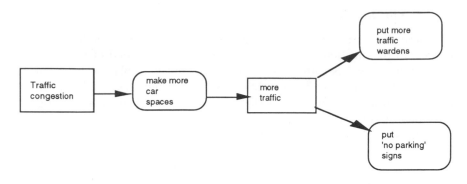

Figure 17.3: Schema of Jean's negotiation of her next actions

Jean: Like you could put yellow lines but they don't really help because sometimes people just park on them anyway. So if you put more traffic wardens on the street then people ain't going to park on them — the yellow lines.

Interviewer: But you need to take some actions, which ones do you think? Can you think of two that you think it would be reasonable to take?

Jean: I'd put more traffic wardens out and I'd put 'no parking' signs.

When she constructed the model, the action of 'placing of yellow lines', and the situation 'people just park on them', were omitted from the model (see Figure 17.3, for a schematized extract from her model). Whether she viewed the action as implicit in the model is unclear.

Isaak, another pupil, also realized, like Jean, that one of his suggested actions, 'make flyovers', would probably attract more cars and so give rise to the situation of 'more traffic jams'

Isaak: And there'll be more traffic jams.

Interviewer: Right, so what are you going to do about that?

Isaak: Where the traffic jam is, go to a road where there's no traffic jams, and if there's a big space there, build a few more roads, going somewhere.

Interviewer: What's a short way of saying that, that you can write in the box?

Isaak: More roads, build roads. Shall I put — look for a clearing to build roads.

Interviewer: Fine.

Isaak: Look for a clearing to build more roads. They [roads] might destroy wildlife.

Interviewer: Yes, Good idea. You need a new situation box now.

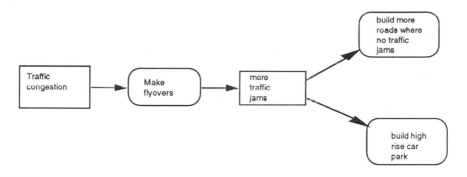

Figure 17.4: Schema of Isaak's reflections on actions to be constructed

Isaak:	To do with the wildlife?
Interviewer:	Preferably to do with wildlife and traffic.
Isaak:	And I'll build a car park, a high rise one.
Interviewer:	Are you suggesting that as a different action?
Isaak:	A different one.

Isaak's reflections on the actions to remedy this situation led him finally to worry about the destruction of wild life. His final model, however, did not reflect this concern (see Figure 17.4).

To say that it is easier to talk about a situation or an action than to represent it, hides the differences between these two levels of thinking. In a narrative phase, pupils could elaborate on the situation, using their everyday knowledge. Pupils must pass from the complexity and richness of the narrative to a simplification of the situation as represented in the model. In order to make this passage, pupils need to be committed to an idea they wish to represent. Also, when modelling, large amounts of detail have to be thrown away, and that which is finally contained in a model must be explicit, representing what really counts. Nonetheless, in spite of some reluctance to move from negotiation to representation, all pupils who were interviewed constructed a model.

A further distinguishing criterion for modelling, as opposed to narrative, is whether or not the paths, which pupils were building in their models, had a sense of consequentiality. That is, whether the actions that emerged from a situation, or the situation that resulted from an action, could, or might, be expected to follow. If this was the case, we could claim that the pupils were attempting to think about the situation and suggest what was essential for a model. In a narrative, the arbitrary and the unexpected are permitted, and often add to the interest of the narrative.

Two factors, those of relevance and continuity, permitted an examination of consequentiality. Just under half of the models made sense according to these two factors. Just over half the pupils' models had some difficulties meeting the factors, though usually only in a single path.

Reasonableness and progression towards a goal were criteria which allowed the examination of necessary or probable consequences in qualitative modelling. The majority of choices of actions or situations were reasonable. Pupils attempted to make sense of all steps, taking 'reasonable' decisions rather than exaggerating or fantasizing. Most models showed progression, and even when pupils' models followed their own goals, rather than task goals, choices and development were reasonable.

Interpreting Models as Systems of Options

Different modelling questions arose in exploratory tasks where the model and its structure are given to the pupil. Firstly, what was the role of pupils' experience and knowledge of the world in exploring and interpreting a model? Secondly, could pupils see the model as a set of options, forming a system?

Role of Pupils' Experience and Knowledge in Interpreting Models

On the exploratory task, just over one-third of the pupils were very circumspect and stayed within the frame of reference of the task, either using their own experience of the topic in a limited manner or refraining from such use. The remaining pupils either used their own experience or their knowledge of the real world to explain the models. For example, on the traffic task, one pupil argued that, with the installation of safety belts, there would be safer cars and so less accidents. But then this pupil argued that, because there were fewer accidents on the roads, the cars might speed up. His own experience of car drivers' behaviour was clearly being used to explain the model. Another pupil, Vera, also used her knowledge of the real world to judge the option in the model of opening a delicatessen in the exploratory shop task:

> Because like, like if it was advertised on TV, advertise new stuff like in Tescos, and all that. And they would go in there and they would see new stuff in there and more customers go by like that, and I thought the same thing would happen if I put a new, like a delicatessen, I thought new customers would come in and buy stuff from there.

However, even though pupils did import their knowledge and experience into the task, to judge the model and paths within the model, they rarely allowed their comments to lead them too far astray. The goal of either 'reducing congestion' or 'making a profit' continued to direct their commentaries.

Evaluating the Model as a System

In the last part of the exploratory task, we wanted to see whether pupils could evaluate and compare paths as totalities, and see the model as a set of options. Answers were given at four levels of sophistication and generality:

(i)   re-descriptions of the contents of the model;
(ii) re-descriptions plus elaborations, that is, adding details not in the model but which have no explanatory power;
(iii) analysis: an attempt to go beyond the model and to give reasons;
(iv) generalized comparisons or general system reasoning.

In both the shop and traffic task, levels (i) and (ii), re-descriptions of the model and re-descriptions and elaborations, were fairly frequent. While there were arguments of the level (iv) type, they tended to be about choices which might or might not work, rather than seeing choices as systematic and interacting. There were fairly frequent arguments of the level (iii) kind, with pupils attempting a more localized analysis. In such instances they did see choices as having alternatives and consequences, set in a complex of background reasons and effects. Alternatively, analysis could use a theme in common between different sets of choices.

Laura, for example, on the traffic task, was one of the few pupils who had some understanding of the idea of interconnected choices. When evaluating and comparing paths, she responded to nearly every question with a commentary about the fact that there were choices, sometimes elaborating them with references to the model. When asked about whether she thought the model useful, she again pointed to the fact that it showed her how to weigh up choices:

> Yes it does because it gives, it advises you what's going to happen next, and you think, so you know what's going to happen — ahead of what you're going to choose, so it's more help to you. At least it tells you like you choose one of them and then like they say that's going to be bad and you know not to choose that one, choose a different solution.

Conclusion

In conclusion, much qualitative thinking initiates in narrative, and it is not trivial for young secondary pupils to move towards simplifying and dissecting a narrative into a structure of alternatives. Nor is it easy for them, in exploring models, to synthesize existing sets of choices and consequences into wholes, so as to compare and evaluate them.

Chapter 18

Learning by Building Expert System Models

Mary Webb

Introduction

Expert Builder was developed by the Modus Project to explore the opportunities for rule-based modelling and was widely trialled by members of the Modus Club (see Chapter 21). Following these trials, the program has been developed further and published. This chapter describes the software, outlines how it has been used, and comments on its strengths and weaknesses as a tool for modelling in schools.

The Need for Rule-based Modelling

A study of teachers' perceptions of modelling activities that could be usefully undertaken by children suggested that many were in the category of qualitative models of reasoning (Webb and Hassell, 1988). Such models are based on 'rules of thumb' rather than mathematical relationships and are concerned with dependence or causality between concepts. They emphasize the declarative (what we know) rather than the procedural (how you do it) aspects of knowledge. Models of this type can be used to guide decision-making, diagnose a problem, make predictions and classify objects.

Similar kinds of computer modelling with pupils had been investigated earlier (for example, Ennals, 1983; Cumming and Abbott, 1988; Galpin, 1989), but these approaches have relied on a textual representation of reasoning and knowledge. Studies in primary schools and secondary schools (for example, Webb, 1987; Hassell, 1987; Wideman and Owston, 1988) suggested that a diagrammatic approach would be desirable. As a result *Expert Builder* was designed and implemented as a rule-based expert system shell, with a graphical interface for developing the knowledge and illustrating reasoning.

The Nature of 'Expert Builder'

In *Expert Builder* a model is constructed by building a diagrammatic structure of the logic on the screen using mouse-controlled tools (see Figure 18.1).

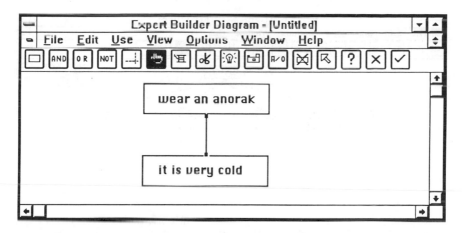

Figure 18.1: The Expert Builder program

Two boxes (clause boxes) linked together, as in Figure 18.1, imply that the statement in the upper box depends on the statement in the lower box. A diagrammatic representation avoids the necessity of adopting a single textual interpretation. Figure 18.1 could be read in several ways, for example, 'wear an anorak *if* it is very cold', '*if* it is very cold *then* wear an anorak' or 'it is very cold *implies* wear an anorak', whichever is appropriate to the problem. *Expert Builder* has a facility for the modeller to provide a page of explanation, which may be an illustration, for each clause. This encourages learners, who are building models, to explain the terms they are using.

This simple representation can be extended with further links and clause boxes and also by using the logical operators AND, OR (one or both) and NOT (see Figure 18.2).

In Figure 18.2 the clause 'it is likely to rain' is linked to two clauses below it by OR. So, 'it is likely to rain' will be true if at least one of:

'the weather forecast predicted rain' or
'it is cloudy' is true.

Similarly 'take an umbrella' will be true if:

'you are intending to walk' is true and either one or both of
'it is raining' or 'it is likely to rain' is true.

Reasoning

In addition to the clause boxes there are special boxes containing the word 'ADVICE'. Advice boxes can be joined to the top of any clause box, designating

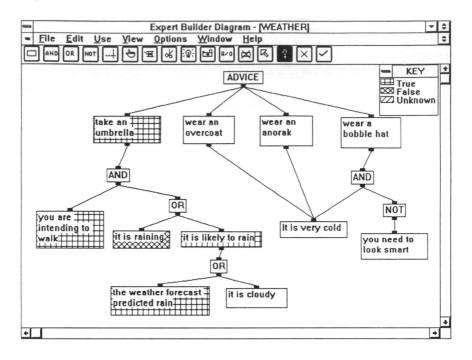

Figure 18.2: Diagram showing the trace of the reasoning used

that clause as advice to be proved by the system. This provides starting points for reasoning in the model. As *Expert Builder* tries to prove a goal the diagram is shaded to show how the reasoning progresses (see Figure 18.3).

When *Expert Builder* is asked for advice, the reasoning mechanism starts with an advice box and attempts to discover whether the conditions on which it depends are true. If this box has other boxes below, it tries to show these are true. This continues till it reaches a box which has no other clause boxes below it. It then asks this clause as a question, storing the answer and then continues, asking any further necessary questions until an advice clause is proved true. As clause boxes are found to be true or false they are shaded to show how reasoning is progressing. Where there is a choice of clause boxes at the same level, the leftmost box is investigated first.

Figure 18.3 shows the sequence followed by the reasoning mechanism in providing the advice 'take an umbrella' where the user answered:

yes, to the question 'you are intending to walk',
no, to the question 'it is raining',
yes, to 'the weather forecast predicted rain'.

The user can also 'volunteer' answers by using 'tick' or 'cross' tool to click on the clause boxes to set them to true or false. The system will then try to prove

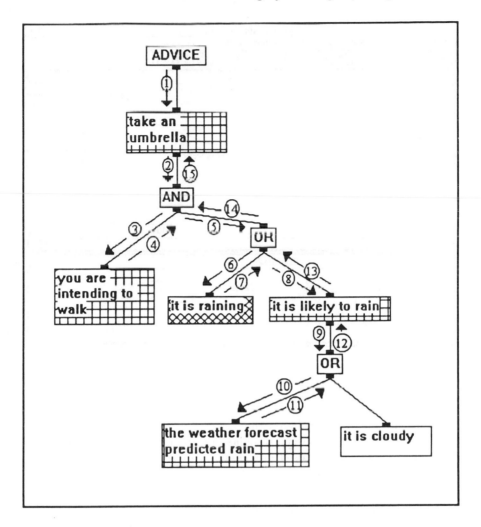

Figure 18.3: The reasoning mechanism

a piece of advice using the facts provided by the user and it is possible for several conclusions to be reached from the same set of conditions.

In order to cope with large models, there are two different views of the model on the computer screen, the normal view and a long distance view (see Figure 18.4). The latter can be used to move around on a large model and, using shading, to view the reasoning sequence.

Expert Builder in Use

Members of the Modus Club in primary and secondary schools have identified a range of ways in which students can develop and consolidate their knowledge

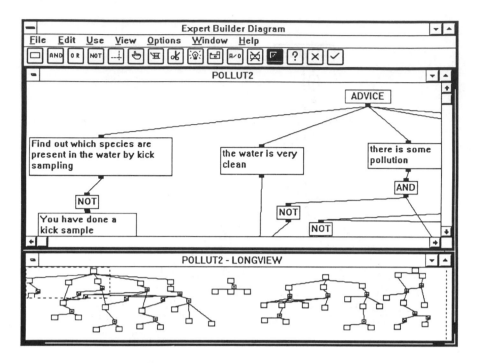

Figure 18.4: The long view

of various curriculum topics by building models in *Expert Builder*. Some older students in secondary schools and students in further and higher education have also studied *Expert Builder* itself in technology or computer-science courses.

Primary Schools

In primary schools *Expert Builder* was typically used for extended project work, complementary to other curriculum activities. Primary-school teachers regarded development of capability in Information Technology through modelling with *Expert Builder*, as of equal importance to the acquisition of knowledge and understanding of other subjects.

Designing and building a model requires a degree of abstract thinking in order to extract important factors and identify rules from one's understanding of a problem or process. It is only likely to be a worthwhile process for those who are at least beginning to engage in abstract thinking, but other students may benefit from interacting with models. Therefore, some detailed evaluations were carried out in primary schools with students aged 8 to 11, at the lower end of the age range of potential users, in order to determine the difficulties students might have and the strengths and limitations of the software. Most students, in this age

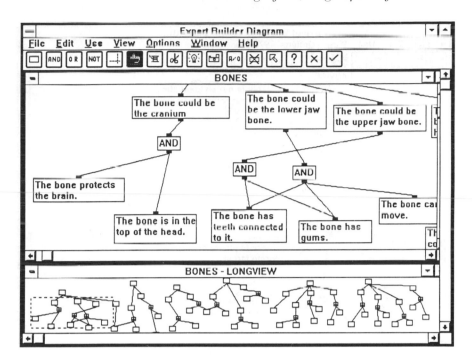

Figure 18.5: Naming bones

range, including those of below average ability, were able to understand how a model with a simple rule structure works, and they were able to make modifications to the rules and/or to provide explanations for clauses, even though *Expert Builder* required them to represent their knowledge in a different way from the resources that they may have been using before.

If students were working on topics in which they were knowledgeable and interested, approximately half of the ability range, in this age group, were able to design, build, test and evaluate their own simple models with *Expert Builder*. Many pupils found such exercises both absorbing and motivating. Their teachers commented that motivation and level of achievement was raised for some pupils. As illustration, in a class that had been studying the skeleton, bones and their functions, two 9-year-old boys built a model that would help to name a bone from its position in the human skeleton (see Figure 18.5). With younger pupils there is a tendency for them to simply transfer information from one medium to another, e.g., copying out of textbooks.

Secondary Schools

The National Curriculum in England and Wales requires students to develop modelling capability including, at Levels 6 to 10, students building and evaluating

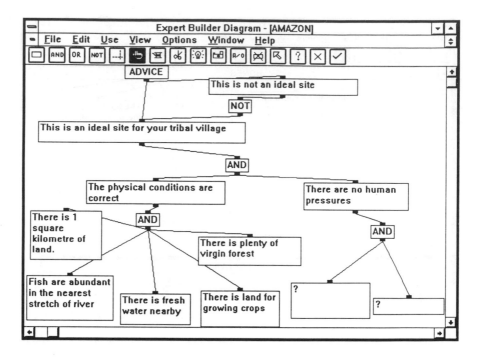

Figure 18.6: Siting an Indian settlement

their own models. *Expert Builder* is designed to support these activities but teachers also found it useful for shorter activities, discussing and organizing ideas about a particular topic. This leads to a range of strategies for its use in the curriculum.

Students can build their own small models as an exercise within one lesson of half an hour to one hour, as long as they have had previous experience with *Expert Builder*. For this to be effective, the teacher needs to specify the purpose of the model and there should be some prior work such as class or group discussion to suggest the important factors to be included.

Students might similarly be involved in extending a model that has already been created. This approach was taken with a class of 13 to 14-year-olds studying the pressures on South American Indians living in a tropical rain forest. Working in small groups, they discussed the conflicts affecting the Indians and devised some rules which might be suitable for Indians to use in order to site new settlements in relation to the pressures of gold mining, ranching, road building, etc. The teacher built the first part of the model (as Figure 18.6) during the following class discussion in which the physical factors were explored.

The students then used their own ideas to extend the model. In a subsequent lesson the students worked on a paper-based exercise to locate a range of pressures in a specific area of tropical virgin rain forest and each group took it in turn to test their model against the site selection they had made.

At a higher level of modelling, students might investigate the important factors which need to be considered when solving a particular problem. They can then explore a model provided by the teacher and compare their own list of factors with those included by the teacher. The students could build or extend the computer model, but do not necessarily have to do so, since the purpose is to provide a critical evaluation of the inherent modelling decisions.

More extended use of the *Expert Builder* has been made by students undertaking a project on a topic which arises from work in science, geography, or technology. If the project is started in subject lessons but is continued either outside of lessons or in time allocated to information technology, the loss of time to conventional subject lessons is reduced.

Review

From these studies it is possible to identify some of the strengths and weaknesses of this style of modelling, and some of the points to consider when undertaking these modelling activities.

It is important that the first modelling exercise can be carried out successfully with a very simple rule structure. Most students develop sufficient understanding of the basic rule structure after a brief demonstration of building a simple model. Starting with a more sophisticated rule structure at this stage led to some groups embarking on an over complex structure which hindered their success in model building. It is likely that pupils would develop modelling skills most effectively by undertaking a series of progressively more complex model building tasks.

Expert Builder is designed for problems which can be expressed as heuristic rules, so task selection is important. Teachers, with some experience of building rule-based models with *Expert Builder*, had no difficulty in identifying appropriate modelling tasks which they felt would be of value to their pupils within the topic on which they were working. Where pupils aged 10 to 11 selected their own tasks, more than half of them were able to identify suitable tasks. Several pupils were able to suggest suitable modelling tasks, within well understood subject areas, after only a brief twenty-minute demonstration of the software.

Expert Builder provides feedback to pupils about how their model is working, but help was sometimes needed in interpreting this, particularly when the model didn't behave as expected. Pupils were sometimes unaware of some relevant feature of *Expert Builder* and made faster progress when advice was available, rather than discovering it for themselves. However, the visibility of the model on which the pupils were focusing enabled the teacher to assess the situation quickly.

Teachers intervened at three levels: manipulating the software, structuring the model and selecting and structuring knowledge. Teachers provided help in manipulating the software but adopted a more exploratory approach at the other two levels, unless the teacher was concerned that the pupils' models should consolidate particular aspects of subject knowledge.

Expert Builder was not designed specifically to facilitate cooperative working although it was expected that pupils would work on a modelling task in groups. Less explanation of individual ideas within groups occurred than anticipated. The need for this may have been reduced by the visible nature of the model, helping them communicate and understand each others' ideas and intentions directly through the representation.

One specific difficulty was observed, especially in older students (and teachers) namely, interpreting the direction of implication between clause boxes to be downwards, rather than upwards, or, sometimes, a combination of the two. It is clearly important for the teacher to monitor the early stages of model building in order to correct this misconception.

These studies were typically conducted with one computer available to a class of up to thirty-two and a modelling task for a pair of pupils could need up to four or five hours at the computer. To develop modelling skills they would need to undertake several such modelling exercises during a school year. The quality of the computers was also important. The computers used in this study were typically Nimbus 186 computers and were only just sufficient for the purpose.

Conclusion

Students, even some 8 to 11-year-olds, are able to build their own simple models with *Expert Builder* provided that they are working with subject matter with which they are familiar and knowledgeable. Activities which involve changing a model rather than just interacting with it, may therefore be a good starting point for developing basic modelling skills leading students through the modelling process to evaluation of their models. Students who have acquired some basic modelling skills and abilities in this way, may then be able to tackle a modelling task based on less familiar subject matter, where an important aim of the task is to develop understanding of the subject matter.

This contrasts with the starting point for computer-based modelling contained in the National Curriculum (DES and Welsh Office, 1990) which states that pupils working towards Level 4 of the Attainment Target for Information Technology Capability should be taught to 'analyse the patterns and relationships in a computer model to establish how its rules operate; change the rules and predict the effect'. It is probable that this starting point was arrived at because it was considered too difficult for students of 8 to 11-year-olds to undertake to build their own model. If so, then experience with *Expert Builder* suggests that an alternative approach is possible. It is easier for students to understand the patterns and relationships in a computer model if it is one which they had been involved in designing and building, rather than trying to guess the basis of the model by examining the output under different circumstances, as suggested in the National Curriculum.

Chapter 19

Creating Worlds from Objects and Events

Richard Boohan

Introduction

It seems a common experience that, after waiting at a bus stop for a long time, three buses will arrive all at once. Is this a real phenomenon, or do we just remember those occasions when this has happened? Is it possible to model the situation in a way which will suggest a reason for the behaviour?

One approach would be to create a quantitative model (see Chapter 7), which might include variables such as the average speed of the buses, the distance between the bus stops, and so on. But the behaviour of this system arises from the nature of the objects in it, like buses, and the things that they do, like travelling along a road. So, it may be better to try to model this situation directly, by representing with the computer the objects, places and events in the real world.

More importantly, children trend to view the world in terms of objects and events, not in terms of variables and algebraic relationships. This chapter describes a software package, *WorldMaker*, designed to make modelling accessible to young children by allowing them to specify the behaviour of objects. While simple in conception, it can also be used to construct models of some sophistication.

Cellular Automata

The concept of *WorldMaker* is derived from that of cellular automata. While the name sounds daunting, the idea of a cellular automaton is essentially simple. It consists of an array of cells where each cell can exist in one of a small number of possible states, e.g., 'on'/'off', 'high'/'medium'/'low'. It evolves over time, with the same rules applied to all cells in every iteration, to determine what the state of the cells will be in the next generation. The rules which determine the subsequent state of a cell are very simple and are based only on the states of the immediately adjoining cells.

The theory of the cellular automaton was developed by John von Neumann, through his interest in the mathematics of self-reproducing structures (Burks,

Richard Boohan

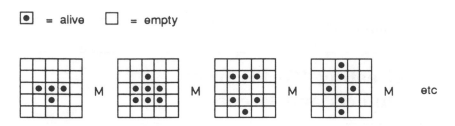

Figure 19.1: A cellular automaton

1970). Perhaps the most well-known example of a cellular automaton is Conway's *Game of Life* (Gardner, 1970), which acquired something of a cult status. In this, cells may either be 'live' or 'empty'. A 'live' cell survives to the next generation if it is surrounded by two or three other 'live' cells, otherwise it 'dies' of over-crowding or loneliness, leaving the cell 'empty'. An 'empty' cell becomes 'alive' in the next generation if it has exactly three neighbouring 'live' cells. Figure 19.1 shows the three generations that follow on from an initial configuration of live cells. Of course, different arrangements of starting cells lead to different patterns.

These simple rules can show an extraordinary range of phenomena as different initial arrangements evolve — some eventually die out, some lead to stable patterns, and others oscillate or cycle through different arrangements with a regular period.

Cellular automata have been used extensively to model phenomena arising from the interaction of many particles (Toffoli and Margolis, 1987). These include models of the behaviour of gases, crystallization, propagation of sound waves, fluid flow and genetic drift.

Extending the Concept

The concept of the cellular automaton seems well suited to enable young children to create their own models. The rules are essentially simple, and the models created can show visually appealing and interesting behaviours. *WorldMaker* extends this concept, by allowing each cell to contain two entities — a 'background' and an 'object'. While the backgrounds behave like a cellular automaton, objects are treated rather differently — for example, they are able to move from one cell to another, which would not be allowed in a cellular automaton. Introducing 'objects' makes the concept of a cellular automaton simpler for children to understand.

Many interesting object-based models have been suggested, for example by Eigen and Winkler (1983). Marx (1981a, 1981b, 1984a, 1984b) has produced further examples for microcomputers, though the rules are inaccessible to the user. Another interesting program, *The Picture Simulator*, does make the rules

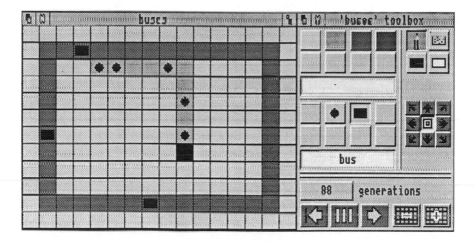

Figure 19.2: The 'buses' world

accessible, but it takes a rather different approach from *WorldMaker*, using a more restricted range of rules and entities. What is distinctive about *WorldMaker* is that it allows children to create rules *graphically*.

WorldMaker

Now let us return to the problem posed at the beginning — 'Do buses really tend to travel in threes?' and see how this situation can be modelled in *WorldMaker* (see Figure 19.2). It has been conceived in terms of two kinds of objects — buses and passengers, and four kinds of background — grass, road, pavement and a shopping centre. Using the plotting tools in *WorldMaker*, these objects and backgrounds have been placed on a grid, with the buses initially spaced equally around the road.

When the model is run, 'passengers' come out of the 'shopping centre', walk along the pavement and form a queue at the end. The 'buses' travel around on the 'road', stopping to pick up passengers if there are any waiting. After a relatively short time the buses will all group together. The initial situation is inherently unstable, and any random fluctuations will cause the buses to group. More passengers to pick up means the bus is delayed, which means even more passengers next time. We have here an example of positive feedback.

In *WorldMaker*, the behaviour of each object or background is determined by a list of rules. The rules for a bus, as shown in Figure 19.3, are accessed simply by 'opening up' an object.

An object can have up to four rules. Each rule has a slider bar which determines the probability that it will 'fire' at each turn. For a bus, each rule has

173

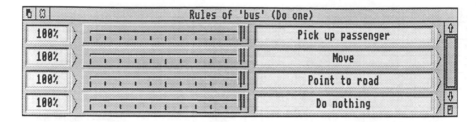

Figure 19.3: The list of rules for 'bus'

been given its maximum setting (probability = 100 per cent). Each rule is defined graphically to show what should happen. 'Opening up' a rule in the list gives a window which displays the picture of the rule. Figure 19.4 shows the three rules for a 'bus'.

The picture of each rule shows a condition, and an action to be taken if the condition is met. Rules are created or modified simply by putting the desired entities or relations into the appropriate slots in the rule. As with a cellular automaton, the condition depends only on what is in the 'target' cell and in the immediately adjoining cells. The first rule shows that if a bus is next to a passenger, then the passenger will 'disappear'.

The next two rules illustrate other ways in which objects and backgrounds can interact. Objects may be given a direction when they are placed on the grid, and the second rule uses the direction of the bus to determine to which cell it should move. In the third rule, the direction of the bus is changed if it would run off the road.

When an object has more than one rule, the user needs to decide on their order and the 'rule logic'. Both will affect the behaviour of the model. In the rules for 'bus', 'do one' logic has been chosen, meaning that in each iteration only one rule is fired (the first whose condition is satisfied). So the bus's priority is to pick up passengers. If it cannot do this it moves along the road in the direction it is pointing. If it cannot do this (it has run out of road!) then it changes direction.

'WorldMaker' in The Classroom

The purpose of *WorldMaker* is to make the creation of rules simple enough to allow young children to construct their own models. The previous example has been used to illustrate a range of rules and possible behaviours, but it is rather more complex than those which would be built by children. Nevertheless, worlds can be constructed in *WorldMaker*, with just a few simple rules, that show both interesting and complex behaviour.

In developing tasks for classroom use, we have found that pupils using *WorldMaker* are able to come up with many ideas that they would like to try. The

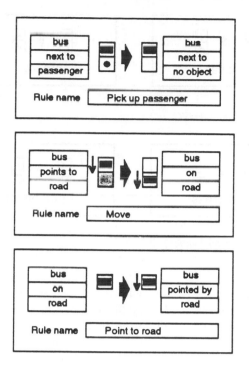

Figure 19.4:   The rule definitions for 'bus'

problem has not been to encourage children to explore, but to ensure that their exploration is productive. In general, we have found that the most successful kinds of task are those in which they are given a limited range of resources and a clear problem to solve with those resources. Learning about *WorldMaker* falls essentially into three stages:

- *Exploring a world* Pupils are given backgrounds and objects which have already been created. They investigate models by choosing how to place backgrounds and objects on the grid;
- *Changing a world* The behaviour of backgrounds and objects can now be altered by changing the 'slider bars' of their rules;
- *Creating a world* Pupils create new types of backgrounds and objects by writing new rules.

Tasks have been developed for each of these stages based on a wide range of models. Many are related to science — bacterial growth and decay, epidemics, predator-prey systems, desertification, forest fires, diffusion, crystallisation, radio-activity, nuclear chain reactions, rates of chemical reaction and chemical equilibrium. But there are plenty of opportunities elsewhere — in mathematics, models

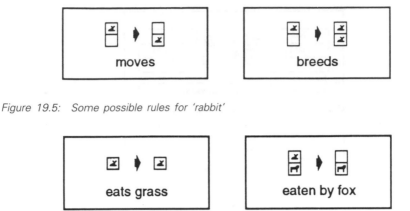

Figure 19.5: Some possible rules for 'rabbit'

Figure 19.6: Further rules for 'rabbit'

can be used to study number patterns and probability, and in geography, models which have been developed include rainfall, coastal erosion and the formation of volcanoes. Two examples will be discussed here.

One world which children have enjoyed exploring is 'rabbits'. Initially, the object 'rabbit' has no rules, so when it is placed on the grid it does nothing. Figure 19.5 shows some possible rules which children can think of and easily construct for themselves. With just the 'moves' rule, the rabbit moves randomly around the grid. With the 'breeds' rule, new rabbits are created — rapidly at first and then more slowly as the limits of space are reached. Rabbits can also be made to interact with other entities, for example, they can 'eat grass' or be 'eaten by a fox' (see Figure 19.6). These other entities can also be given simple rules, such as making the grass grow, or making foxes breed and die.

Children can explore the effects of changing the rules' probabilities, to investigate, for example, what happens if the breeding rate of the rabbits is varied. Some changes may simply cause the equilibrium position of the population to shift. Others can cause the populations to fluctuate or can lead to extinction. There are important lessons to be learned here about the balance of Nature.

One important aspect of these kinds of models is that while the rules are strictly *local*, the system shows *global* behaviour. An example is the 'pondlife' world. In the model shown in figure 19.7, a 'hydra' moves about according to simple rules — if it is dark it moves often and if it is light is moves less often. When the model is run, the 'hydra' concentrate in the light region. Though they all move over the entire gird, they spend most time in light areas. Real hydra behave in a similar way — the darker it is the faster they move. It seems that they are 'attracted' by the light, but in fact, this attraction is only apparent — they have no 'long-range knowledge' about where the light region is, but are blindly responding to a local situation.

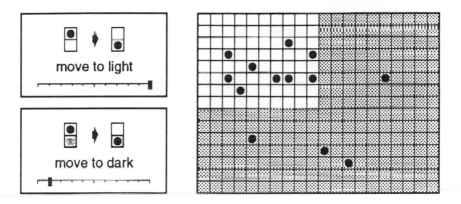

Figure 19.7: Local rules can lead to global behaviour

Children working with WorldMaker

When children start to use *WorldMaker* they do not know about rules. All they see is what happens to objects on the grid. However, they can begin to work out what they do by seeing how they behave in different situations. In one task a group of 11-year-olds were watching a model of crystallisation. One pupil described this:

> 'Sticky' balls stay still all the time and when 'random' balls hit they turn into sticky balls as well.

In these early tasks, pupils are beginning to understand and explain the behaviour of the model in terms of the behaviour of its parts.

The relationship between models and the real world is by no means easy to grasp. A model can help us to explain the real world, but sometimes children use reality to explain the model. A group of 10-year-olds were trying to explain why, in a model of a rabbit population, their numbers were getting smaller.

> Oh, they are less now, because they are moving and they are going away.
> They died.
> Because they were old age.
> And people killed them.
> But there is no one to kill them.

People killing rabbits may be an explanation in the real world, but not, as one pupil realised, in this model.

Even young children are able to make predictions about the behaviour of a model when the setting of one rule is changed. More challenging is to work out

177

the rule settings needed to produce a certain effect. An example of this is a group of 10-year-olds who were experimenting with a 'supermarket' model, and seeing what affected the length of the queue:

> Look how they are going. There is no queue! They stop when it is 100 [shoppers leave].
> Make it 0 [shopper enters]. No-one will come in.
> Go to 10 [shopper enters].
> Put on 10 on both of them.
> Put it [shopper leaves] on 10, and see if the whole thing is crowded. And then put 100 to the entrance.

However, it is not always easy to predict the effects of modifying rules, particularly when pupils are unfamiliar with the structure of the rules. In such cases, they tend to make inferences from the real world rather than from the nature of the model. Such findings suggest that pupils should begin to make their own models as early as possible.

We cannot expect children immediately to identify appropriate problems to model. They can be given support to do this in a number of ways. One approach is to give a context (e.g. rabbits and foxes), asking them to suggest what kinds of behaviours the objects might exhibit.

Another approach is to give pupils some forms of rules, and ask what behaviours these might represent. These may reflect real or imaginary (and perhaps crazy) behaviours. For example, in a world of sharks and fishes, some 10-year-olds are experimenting with a rule which says that when a shark is next to a fish, the shark disappears. We could think of this as a 'fish eats shark' rule, but because this does not make sense in the real world, the pupils are having trouble interpreting it.

> The shark jumps, you see.
> No, the shark ate the fish.
> The shark jumps to an empty cell and then the fish is there.

Eventually a pupil sees what the rule could be, but is not believed.

> The shark jumps away from the fish — maybe the fish ate the shark.
> Oh no, don't be stupid!

Another approach is to construct a new model by using analogous rules from another model. For example, even very young pupils are able to suggest a number of different meanings for a rule which shows a gardener planting a flower, by substituting different objects for the gardener and the flower. Seeing similarities between two real world situations, which on the surface are not at all similar, is an important lesson to be learnt from modelling.

Conclusion

Levels 4 to 7 of the Attainment Target for Information Technology Capability of the National Curriculum (DES and Welsh Office, 1990) include references to pupils using, changing and constructing computer models. *WorldMaker* was created after these statements of attainment were written, and its purpose was to make possible the creation of models by much younger children than these levels, would imply. Even primary-school children are capable of building models by creating entirely new rules. Building their own simple models is important in helping pupils understand models created by someone else.

Sometimes we are clear about what we are trying to model. The 'traditional' approach is to refine our model until it is as close as is necessary to the real thing. Our experience shows that, in an educational setting, there is a lot to be gained from a wider use of exploration. We may start off by looking at one situation, but then find that the model's behaviour suggests something completely different. We can find similarities in models which are about very different things in the real world. *WorldMaker* enables the creation and exploration of children's own models to be part of learning about modelling from an early age, and not the goal of a long learning process.

Conclusion

Part 5

Implementing Modelling in the Curriculum

Chapter 20

Towards a Modelling Curriculum

Harvey Mellar

Introduction

No matter how promising the possible applications of computer modelling to education might be, they will have no effect on schools and colleges if modelling is not used in real classrooms. In this section of the book we turn to look at approaches to curriculum development that suggest ways of integrating modelling into the curriculum. The following chapters describe three projects which explicitly set out to bring about curriculum change. These projects have used very different approaches to trying to bring modelling into the curriculum, and I want to briefly overview and contrast those approaches here.

The Modus Project (Chapter 21) emphasizes software development. The project extends well beyond software development into curriculum support but the central goal remains the creation of an 'Integrated Modelling System'. In this approach, to some extent at least, curriculum change is seen as being brought about through providing certain forms of software — the curriculum being in a sense 'hidden' in the software (this relates to Olson's (1988) description of the Trojan Horse aspects of educational software). This is not to imply that the software is created in some space completely removed from the classroom, indeed, as the authors of this chapter stress, teachers are closely involved in the design and evaluation of the software, but the major products of the project are software packages and guidelines for using them. Such an approach has attractions: the goals of the project are clear, and it responds to the demands of teachers for a product to use. The potential dangers of such an approach are essentially those to do with educational software development more generally: firstly software development (plus maintenance and support) is very expensive in time and money, and secondly an educational approach comes to be confused with the purchase of a product.

The Nuffield Advanced Mathematics Project (Chapter 22) takes a view of modelling as a mathematical technique, which is incorporated into the curriculum as a topic, explicitly taught and assessed. A very different approach is taken to software from that taken by the Modus Project, in the Nuffield Advanced Mathematics Project the emphasis is on software that is already readily available to students rather than on creating new software. Thus the project initially had an emphasis on the use of spreadsheets, but has moved increasingly to base its modelling approach around graphical calculators as these have become more powerful and more readily available. The chief advantage of this approach is that modelling is very firmly and explicitly embedded within the curriculum and its assessment. The major problems are firstly the restricted set of students to which it is addressed, and secondly the restricted definition of modelling that is offered (that is modelling is offered chiefly as a mathematical technique rather than as an approach to learning).

The Computer Based Modelling across the Curriculum Project (Chapter 23) set out to work along with teachers to develop materials to incorporate modelling approaches within the mathematics, science, geography or business studies curriculum that the teachers were presently teaching. The emphasis was on teacher change rather than on software development or curriculum innovation. Materials were developed that could be used with a wide range of existing software so that teachers who had access to specialist software could take advantage of it, and those who had access to more general software, such as spreadsheets, could use them too. The major products were curriculum materials and teacher training materials to help teachers develop their approaches to teaching as well as their understanding of modelling. The advantages of this approach were the significant impact that it had on the teachers taking part, and the development of materials closely tied to teachers' concerns within their own curriculum areas. A restriction of this approach was its limitation to staying within present curriculum boundaries, it offered modelling as a learning strategy for present curriculum objectives. A more serious problem was highlighted by the project itself, the amount of time it took teachers to adapt new approaches to their needs, and the serious cost implications of this.

From a different perspective the three projects could be described as attempting different forms of curriculum penetration. The Modus Project is going for a base general level across all teachers in order to enable teachers to begin to use modelling. The Nuffield Advanced Mathematics Project aims to insert a small but strong wedge of curriculum content within mathematics (and includes assessment as a strong incentive). The Computer Based Modelling Project seeks to integrate modelling closely across a defined range of curriculum areas through helping teachers to bring about changes in the way that they teach.

Modelling Developments Outside the UK

The movement to incorporate modelling into education can also be found in educational systems outside the UK, and the same three themes of software, curriculum and teacher development which we used to identify the defining characteristics of the UK projects are equally applicable to these other developments.

In the area of software (and hardware) developments, the work at TERC in Cambridge, Massachusetts has been particularly interesting (see Nemirovsky and Rubin, 1992a; 1992b). The work at TERC has concentrated on the production of systems of hardware and software that students can interact with by means of physical manipulation. Two widely used systems have been one for motion involving a small car and a motion detector — which enabled students to plot graphs of position and velocity versus time — and one for air flow in which students control a bellows to generate changes in air flow and in the volume of air accumulated in a bag — both of which can be plotted against time. With these systems the students were able to compare their predictions with observations, and more interestingly, were also able to experiment in manipulating the apparatus in order to produce particular graphs, in order that is to bring about a desired behaviour. Aspects of this work and its relation to semi-quantitative modelling are discussed further in Chapter 14. More recently this group have begun to incorporate video with computer measuring tools in their work in order to allow students to capture and examine data on screen.

The kind of curriculum innovation carried out by the Nuffield Advanced Mathematics Project (Chapter 22) has many parallels in other countries. A range of curriculum innovations of this kind from a variety of countries in which mathematical modelling has been incorporated into both secondary and tertiary curricula are described in papers from the biennial International Conference on the Teaching of Mathematical Modelling, see Berry, Burghes, Huntley, James and Moscardini (1984; 1987), Blum, Niss, and Huntley (1989), Niss, Blum, and Huntley (1991), and de Lange, Keitel, Huntley, and Niss (1993).

The System Thinking and Curriculum Innovation (STACI[N]) Project based at the Educational Testing Service (ETS) at Princeton is an important example of a project that has looked closely at teachers (Mandinach, 1989; Mandinach and Cline, 1989; Mandinach and Cline, in press). This work makes explicit reference to Forrester's (1968) work on systems, and is based around use of the program *STELLA*. They have looked at the use of the systems approach within a range of school subjects, and have examined teachers' and pupil's evolving use of the systems approach. With the project's origins in the area of educational testing it is of no surprise that they have also paid particular attention to ideas about assessment, seeing modelling, and the cooperative group work that is often associated with it, as posing particular problems for assessment, but also seeing modelling as offering useful insights into students' ways of working, allowing more valuable forms of formative assessment to be given to students than are possible with traditional testing methods.

Modelling in the UK National Curriculum

The way that modelling is presented in the National Curriculum (DES and Welsh Office, 1990) has been criticized by me elsewhere for its over emphasis on technique and lack of emphasis on modelling as an approach to learning (Mellar, 1990). There is some confusion in schools about how to approach the modelling aspects of the National Curriculum for Information Technology. The level of confusion was clearly illustrated by the pilot Standard Assessment Tasks used in

1992, which at Key Stage 3 reduced the National Curriculum IT Modelling strand to the manipulation of a spreadsheet for small-scale administration. Such a view of modelling is a long way from the kind of opportunities for modelling as an approach to learning that we are presenting in this book.

Modelling as an approach to learning will need to be integrated both throughout the pupil's school career and across the curriculum. The Computer Based Modelling across the Curriculum Project (Chapter 23) has shown how this latter goal can be achieved with students in the age range of 14 to 18. There is now a need to create an approach to modelling from primary through to secondary education that will allow students to develop their understanding of modelling, there is a need, in other words, to create a 'modelling curriculum.' Significant steps have been taken in this direction: *WorldMaker* (Chapter 19) allows older primary-school pupils to build models using 'objects', *IQON* (Chapter 15) allows children in the first years of secondary school to develop models using 'semi-quantitative' reasoning, and there is now a variety of tools including spreadsheets offering possibilities for quantitative modelling to older students.

All of these various attempts to teach modelling to pupils have pointed up the importance of the 'expressive' dimension of the use of modelling, that is that pupils must be encouraged to make their own models if they are to understand the nature, possibilities and limitations of the modelling systems they are using. The National Curriculum Statements of Attainment put pupil exploration of other people's models before pupil creation of their own models, we now know that this is (at the very least) an over simplification of the pupil's developmental path. The Tools for Exploratory Learning Programme has provided more evidence to support the contention that we made some time ago (Mellar, 1990) that expressive activities need to be introduced early in children's experience, and that children's first experience of modelling should not necessarily be via exploratory activities. This same point is made by several other authors in this book from work outside the Tools for Exploratory Learning Programme, see in particular Chapter 18 on the use of *Expert Builder* and Chapter 19 on *WorldMaker*.

The work of the Tools for Exploratory Learning Programme has a number of important implications for the development of an improved modelling curriculum:

- **The ability of children to engage in complex causal reasoning tasks**
  Pupils of 11 to 14 can engage in quite complex reasoning about relationships and cause and effect in systems of practical interest and concern. They think most naturally in terms of objects and events, not variables. Semi-quantitative reasoning is a natural form of expression for these pupils. With it they can manage to reason about quite complex phenomena. Given suitable models to explore with *IQON* some pupils of 11 to 14 can produce quite sophisticated causal reasoning about complex systems. Those who produce sophisticated causal reasoning can also begin thinking about the nature of complex feedback systems.

- **The importance of semi-quantitative reasoning**
  The concept of semi-quantitative modelling, and its incorporation into the program *IQON* has been proved practicable and it appears to tap a way people naturally think. Semi-quantitative thinking ought to be given a greater and better recognized role in teaching In planning semi-quantitative modelling activities, opportunities for both expression and exploration should be provided.

- **The value of the modelling tool *IQON***
  IQON models could be used to teach about formal structures, for example how feedback can lead to stability, oscillation, or runaway. They provide useful opportunities to discuss the nature of the relation between models and reality, and about control of variables. The possibilities for computational tools to be used to teach about models as formal entities, whose behaviour follows from their structure, deserve investigation.

- **The value of expressive tasks**
  With the right tools children of 11 to 14 can make their own models. Our data suggests that if they do so they will understand better that a model is simplified, fallible, can be changed and may need to be remade altogether. In this way they may be helped to see what 'exploring' a model is all about, through the experience of expressing some themselves. Pupils given a model to explore are often reluctant to change it much, though they can criticize it. Having made a model of their own, they are more often willing to change or reconstruct it. When pupils in semi-quantitative expressive tasks improve their models, they make more interesting changes than do pupils in exploratory tasks, beginning to seriously engage in the iterative modelling process.

Chapter 21

Developing Software and Curriculum Materials: The Modus Project

Margaret Cox and Mary Webb

Introduction

The Modus Project is a collaborative venture between King's College London and the Advisory Unit for Microtechnology in Education, Hertfordshire County Council. The collaboration was set up in 1987 to research how computer-based modelling could be used across the curriculum and then to develop appropriate software and supporting materials.

During the preceding ten years, both the Advisory Unit for Microtechnology in Education (Freeman and Levett, 1986) and the Computers in the Curriculum Project at King's College London (then Chelsea College) (Cox, 1983) had been systematically gathering data from schools and teachers about their ability to use educational software, and how this use related to the content, design and flexibility of the software (Watson, 1987). This research has shown that an important element in the production of effective educational software is that it be founded on formative evaluation from teachers, students and curriculum developers.

The Computers in the Curriculum Project already had some experience of the design of modelling software and its use in the classroom through its participation in the work on *DMS*, the *Dynamic Modelling System*. *DMS* enabled students to build their own models of dynamic systems and evaluation of its use indicated that it could provide a powerful tool for students to explore their own perceptions of the behaviour of systems (Wong, 1987). The increasing power of computers which enabled the development of more user-friendly and supportive environments suggested that these opportunities for model building might be extended to a wider range of age and ability and to a greater variety of modelling scenarios.

The philosophy of the Modus Project is to develop educational modelling tools and supporting curriculum materials which integrate different aspects of computer-based modelling with different learning approaches and curriculum needs (Hassell and Webb, 1990).

The project's initial objectives were:

- to carry out a feasibility study into the uses of modelling in schools;
- to develop new educational resources for modelling;

- to research the effect of using this software on learning;
- to develop strategies for encouraging the use of modelling software in education.

The outcomes planned were:

- a feasibility study report;
- interim publications of prototype software and materials;
- the Modus integrated software environment;
- curriculum materials and courseware;
- evaluation reports and research publications.

The project had the aid of two professional bodies: a steering committee which consisted of representatives from supporting funders including the two collaborating institutions, and a panel of experts with experience in different curriculum areas.

Feasibility Study

The feasibility study involved an investigation into current uses of non-computer based modelling activities in schools and of two computer-based modelling systems in science classes. Evidence of teachers' perceptions and practice of modelling (Webb, 1987; Hassell, 1987), involving interviews with about forty teachers selected for their innovative approach, revealed that children do carry out a number of modelling activities although teachers do not always recognize these as such. Some use was made of computer models and simulations but most of the modelling involved word descriptions, diagrams, pictures, graphs or physical constructions. Modelling activities were investigated in mathematics, science, geography, history, religious education, economics, craft, design and technology and home economics. Teachers revealed that they carried out modelling with their students in the form of using dynamic systems, data analysis, probabilistic modelling, spatial modelling and logical reasoning.

The only software then available to support dynamic modelling that was appropriate for schools was *STELLA*, spreadsheets and *DMS*. Modus trials using *STELLA* with students aged 14 to 18, suggested that the diagrammatic interface helped to focus the discussion and consideration of the important factors and their general relationships, but deciding what type of variable was required and specifying the mathematical relationships was too difficult for most students.

DMS had been used by some teachers with their A-level physics students and although these teachers felt that *DMS* was very useful in this context they did not consider it suitable for wider use. A development of *DMS* called the *Cellular Modelling System (CMS)*, which enabled variables to be specified in cells, was tried with 13-year-old students and it showed some promise, particularly by encouraging students to think about the important variables in the model.

Although the teachers were able to propose many areas of the curriculum where modelling would be appropriate, they tended to concentrate on constructed models rather than asking the students to build models themselves, resulting in the under-utilization of modelling techniques. The feasibility study thus showed that there were a range of uses which could be made of both quantitative and qualitative computer based modelling if appropriate software were available.

In order to identify the different aspects of modelling which could form part of an integrated computer-based modelling system a classification of the modelling domains that would be relevant for use in education was developed. Model types were broadly grouped into five domains as follows.

Dynamic Modelling

These are models of systems where quantities change over time. They include many environmental and physiological systems, chemical reactions, and economic models of supply and demand.

Spatial Distribution Modelling

These include: static spatial models used in environmental science and geography; animated sequence models of many physical and biological processes in which objects move in space; dynamic spatial models, where the positions of objects in space change over time, such as gas diffusion models; and structural three-dimensional models such as crystals.

Data Analysis Modelling

Although data analysis was not always regarded by teachers as modelling, such an analysis does involve searching for patterns in data and hypothesizing relationships, and these hypotheses are actually models (see Chapter 13 for a discussion of one approach to data analysis). This part of the modelling system would not only provide a range of statistical techniques but also help users to select appropriate methods and interpret the results.

Probabilistic Modelling

In addition to a number of spatial and data analysis models which make use of probability functions, some models, which consist of a number of discrete events that depend on probabilities, e.g., evolutionary models, belong exclusively in the probabilistic domain.

Qualitative Modelling of Logical Reasoning

Many teachers questioned in the feasibility study felt that it would be desirable to provide tools to aid students in structuring and ordering ideas and relationships and enabling modelling of problem-solving and decision-making processes.

Two types of qualitative models were identified: expert systems that solve problems concerned with planning, diagnosis, or advice; and event-based simulations where the events depend on decisions made by the user, rules, or probabilities.

The categorization of different modelling activities by the project based on the evidence from teachers and students provided the foundation for the initial framework for the integrated modelling system, which is described briefly in the next section.

Integrated Modelling Framework

Using the categories of models identified through the feasibility study, the project designed a framework for an integrated modelling system, which included possible interactions between different components of the system. This framework is shown in Figure 21.1. Each part of the system would function separately as well as being linked to other parts as shown. For example, if students were developing a dynamic model and then running this model as a simulation, they could access a database for more data for their simulation and an expert system to check the validity of the simulation. The letter Λ in Figure 21.1 indicates the access points for the user into the system.

Modelling tools and facilities which were to be included in the system were: dynamic modelling, expert system shell, database system, spreadsheet system, the facility to input maps and diagrams by drawing from coordinates, and from digitized data, and the facility to build three-dimensional shapes on the screen, rotate, section, and transform them. Through the use of a hypertext facility students would be able to provide or obtain explanations and textual information.

Using this integrated modelling environment students would be able to assemble a model from components, pictures, tables of data, facts and rules, text, maps and charts, make the components work together using a simple modelling language and present the model as an interactive simulation. For example, in an investigation of the spread of a disease students might collect data about the spread of the disease and then make up a set of rules to describe how the disease is spread. They could then compare the output of their own model with the real data.

Given such an integrated system, students using one aspect of the system in one curriculum area might develop expertise in modelling that they could build upon in another curriculum area. The intention was that this system would provide for a majority of modelling needs in the curriculum. The system would also provide flexibility for students who were unsure of their modelling needs so that

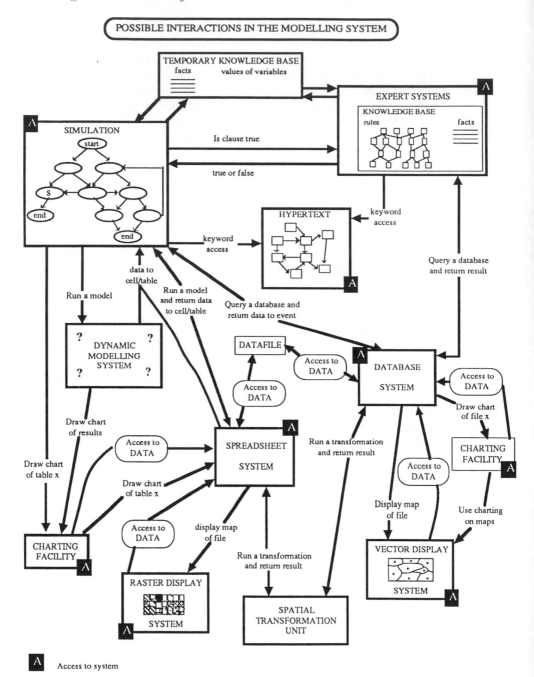

Figure 21.1: Possible interactions in the modelling system

if students started to construct their model using a particular technique and then decided that another would have been more appropriate they would be able to call up a different set of tools and restructure their model.

Before work was started on the development of this integrated modelling system the following criteria for the design were established:

- The modelling environment needed to enable students to start with fairly unclear ideas, by sketching out the problem to be modelled within the modelling environment.
- The metaphors provided should map on to students' own perceptions of a situation.
- Diagrammatic views of the model structure and function should be provided wherever possible to aid model construction and debugging.
- The software should be easy to start using so that students and teachers can undertake worthwhile exercises with only minimal computer expertise.
- The software should be sufficiently powerful to support the variety of modelling activities that might be undertaken in schools.
- The software should be written to run in a *Microsoft Windows* environment for compatibility and ease of use.
- Supporting materials, including a range of ideas for modelling activities in various curriculum areas should be provided with the software.

Developing and Evaluating the Modus System

The integrated modelling system, shown diagrammatically in Figure 21.2 was an ambitious goal and it was recognized that implementation would be expensive in time and resources. It was therefore decided that a realistic method of implementation was to prototype parts of the package and evaluate them at various educational levels. The Modus Project materials are firstly developed by curriculum teams which include subject and industry specialists and sometimes practising teachers and then the materials are trialled extensively in schools and colleges, followed by modifications and upgrades to the materials, and final publication. Evaluation of Modus software is done at both the formative and summative stages. In the formative stage questionnaires are given to both the teacher and the students in order to gather information about their impressions of the materials and descriptions of how they used it in the curriculum, and what models they built.

Prototyping and Evaluating 'Expert Builder'

The first part of the system to be developed was the prototype version of *Expert Builder* (this program is described in detail in Chapter 18). This was produced in the autumn of 1989, together with questionnaires for evaluation in schools. *Expert*

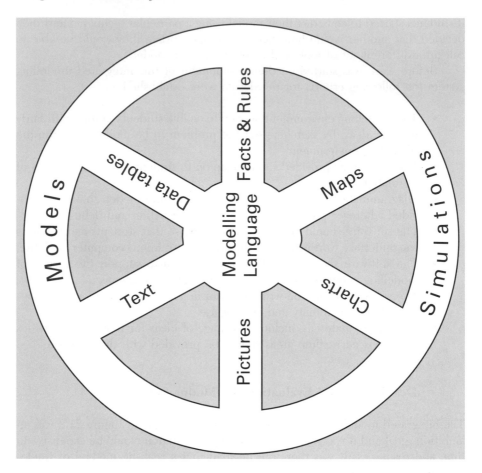

Figure 21.2: The integrated modelling system

Builder is a simple diagrammatic expert system shell that enables rule-based models to be constructed. In the current version, clauses can only be true or false, there are no variables in the rules. The prototype program was supported by a teacher's guide which included instructions on how to create a text or a diagram based system, together with a range of example models.

In order to carry out naturalistic evaluations in classes, the project decided to create a Modus club which would provide a means of supporting teachers in their modelling activities at the same time as obtaining volunteer teachers and schools to evaluate the Modus software and provide feedback to the project. The club was established in the Autumn of 1989 with the launch of the prototype of *Expert Builder* and the first Modus newsletter in 1989. Each Club member was given a copy of *Expert Builder* as well as receiving copies of the newsletter for a small membership fee. By January 1991 membership of this club was 230 institutions The prototype of *Expert Builder* was evaluated in two stages; firstly by Modus club members, and secondly as part of the trials version of the curriculum pack '*Energy Expert*'.

Twenty-three club members returned their questionnaires, of these users, 65 per cent had used modelling software before, and 65 per cent had used other expert systems shells before. A list of other topics in which the respondents would like to use computer-based modelling were given, which included environmental systems, accounting, mathematics, anthropology, population dynamics and equilibrium reactions. Feedback from the students included ideas for building a training schedule for canoeing skills, planning a bike journey, building a conservation management system and constructing and evaluating an expert system on how to grade a jibbock. Feedback from the teachers included suggestions for extending the software, including more tools and other facilities, and positive comments on the value of this type of modelling in education.

Although 66 per cent of the respondents planned to introduce other teachers in their institution to *Expert Builder*, comments from them about opportunities for other teachers to use it included both positive suggestions and reservations about the ability of other teachers to use this software without further training.

'Energy Expert' Pack

Analysis of the data from the feasibility study and the first round of *Expert Builder* trials showed that teachers wanted to have curriculum materials to support their activities in the classroom. In conjunction with British Gas the project developed three themes for the teaching of energy concepts using computer-based modelling:

- **Heating**: Exercises based on the use of the spreadsheet *Excel* to investigate the energy efficiency of a home.
- **Forecast**: Exercises, again based around *Excel*, focusing on the needs and decisions of energy providers trying to maintain an adequate energy supply to the community despite the effects of variations in the weather.
- **Advice**: Exercises in building qualitative models using *Expert Builder* to investigate the relative importance of different factors which lead to energy saving in a home.

A trials pack was produced based on these three modules and was sent for trials in twenty-seven schools during the summer and autumn terms of 1991. Feedback was gathered through questionnaires sent to both teachers and students, sample models and worksheets produced by the students, and classroom observations of four of the schools' classes. One of the most difficult aspects of this trials procedure was that very few schools were using a *Windows*-based environment, and hardly any of the 150 schools first approached had any confidence or experience in using the spreadsheet *Excel*. It was evident from the teachers' and students' feedback that more detailed guidelines were required to enable them to use Excel within the '*Energy Expert*' pack.

As a result of the trials feedback further development work was done during the following year, and an additional module was added to '*Energy Expert*' following suggestions of the trials' teachers and recommendations by the project's curriculum panel. In 1993 the '*Energy Expert*' pack was published after having been extended to include models using *Model Builder* and a fourth module on comfort, and the *Expert Builder* system was also published after revision.

Prototyping and Evaluating 'Model Builder'

The second component of the Modus integrated modelling system to be developed was *Model Builder* (this program is described in detail in Chapter 12). This is a modelling environment with a modelling language based on Logo that enables a wide range of quantitative relationships to be used and provides a range of mathematical functions. The software supports the modelling of dynamic systems using an iterative technique and probabilistic modelling, with the facility to produce graphs of model output that are updated dynamically as the model runs.

Although *Model Builder* does not cover all aspects of the integrated modelling environment, its features include many of the original ones planned and these are exemplified through the provision of a wide range of models, developed by teachers, to show how *Model Builder* can be used in a range of curriculum areas.

Evaluation was done by the project's curriculum panel and subject specialists, and feedback on the modelling ideas gathered through the school trials of '*Energy Expert*', and following modifications *Model Builder* was published in 1991.

There are a number of features that have not yet been implemented in *Model Builder* and it is anticipated that these will be added in future versions. One of the features that has so far proved difficult to design is the provision of diagrammatic views of the model structure and function to aid model construction and debugging. An over-riding consideration in the design was to enable the users to lay out their models as required, possibly on a background picture. This meant that any view showing the interconnections in the model might not superimpose easily on to the model, as laid out by the user, and might therefore need to be in a different layout altogether. It is intended that the next version of *Model Builder* will include some of these features.

Support for the Teachers and Trainers

To support the development of modelling in schools, the curriculum panel and steering committee recommended the development of a video for use by teachers and teacher trainers. This video (*Computer Modelling — Visualising the Solution*) was produced with a booklet showing how modelling is used in industry, linking this to classroom case studies, showing examples of using *Model Builder* to teach about energy, and the hydrological cycle, and *Expert Builder* to teach about energy efficiency, and rock classification.

Model Builder, *Expert Builder* and '*Energy Expert*' all have extensive curriculum materials including sample models to provide ideas and support for the use of modelling at all levels of education.

Integrating the Modelling System

The objectives of the project have been largely met except for the completion of a completely integrated modelling system, and there is always a need for more curriculum materials. In the current version of *Expert Builder*, clauses can only be true or false, there are no variables in the rules. In order to integrate these facilities with *Model Builder* it will be necessary to incorporate variables into the expert system. This is the next step in the Modus implementation and it will require a major programming effort. This will then provide an integrated modelling environment in which it is possible to use both qualitative and quantitative techniques.

Resourcing the Project

One aspect of the modelling project that has not yet been covered is the strategy used to acquire the necessary resources to develop such a system. The original approach was to produce funding proposals which were submitted to the then Microelectronics Education Support Unit (now absorbed within the renamed National Council for Educational Technology), the publishing company Longmans, Research Machines, British Gas and many others. Each of the four organizations named, as well as the two collaborating institutions, have provided funds for the project; British Gas particularly over nearly seven years.

One of the problems associated with obtaining funding has been the conflicting priorities of the funders who prefer to support subject-specific curriculum development and the developers who have the additional need to develop the system software.

Conclusion

The goal of an integrated modelling system was very ambitious particularly given the fairly limited resources available for educational software development. The advent of powerful spreadsheet packages such as *Excel* which enable transportation of data to and from other packages have to a certain extent filled the few missing gaps in the Modus system.

Over a five-year period with three software developers and two curriculum developers on the team, the user interface for the integrated modelling system has been implemented together with quantitative and dynamic modelling techniques. The qualitative modelling facilities have been trialled and the design has allowed for their future integration into the package. In the meantime two modelling packages, *Model Builder* and *Expert Builder* and a widely applicable curriculum pack *'Energy Expert'* as well as a training video are now available for schools to use.

The experience of the Modus Project has shown that the technique of prototyping and trialling the software and developing the system in sections but with future integration designed into the software can enable the gradual development of sophisticated software suited to educational needs.

Chapter 22

Incorporating Modelling into a Mathematics Curriculum

Sue Burns

Introduction

The Nuffield Advanced Mathematics Project was set up in 1990, primarily in response to the opportunity offered by increased access for students to technology. The courses will be available from 1994. The project aims to encourage a larger proportion of each cohort of students to study advanced mathematics, and to engage them in more active ways of learning and in appropriate use of technology. Modelling is an integral part of the material. There is an emphasis on the process of setting up a mathematical model, thinking about the modelling assumptions, and exploring alternatives.

The project is becoming available at a time when the numbers of students electing to study A-level mathematics nationally is dropping dramatically. Information provided by the School Curriculum and Assessment Authority (SCAA) indicates that in 1989 there were 82,987 candidates for A-level and by 1993 only 64,676; there is great concern about this drop. A second change at national level was the production by SCAA in summer 1993 of a new A-level mathematics core which determines 40 per cent of the content of A-level mathematics syllabuses and one of the relevant changes is the explicit inclusion of mathematical modelling.

When the project was started in 1990, it was believed that the time was right to introduce a change in the A-level mathematics curriculum. Many teachers are ready for change, but have felt constrained by their existing syllabuses, their course materials and their lack of confidence in the mathematics at this level.

Issues of Technology

An important idea behind the introduction of curriculum change in the project is that making portable technology available to the students leads to changes in practice. Initially, the evidence available to the project was from two sources: the work of Ruthven at the Cambridge Department of Education working with teachers in nearby authorities (Ruthven, 1990a; 1990b; 1992), and the work of the students and teachers using graphic calculators as part of a 100 per cent coursework A-level centred at the West Sussex Institute.

Recently some research studies in the United States have been reported. For example, Rich at Illinois State University studied two teachers to investigate how the introduction of the graphic calculator affects the teachers' questioning strategies, presentation methods and beliefs about mathematics (Rich, 1993). She observed that the teacher who used graphing calculators:

- used more exploration and encouraged conjecturing;
- asked more higher level questions, used examples differently and stressed the importance of graphs and approximation in problem-solving;
- used more graphs and showed the connection between algebra and geometry in other classes.

Decisions about the level of use of technology to adopt within the Nuffield Advanced Mathematics Project, and which software to assume in the course material, were made after receiving advice and pressure from all sides. On the one hand there was the belief that if a project makes demands, provision will be made; the success in the UK of post-16 projects in other subjects such as business studies may be cited in this respect. On the other hand, publishers and examination boards are under commercial pressure to ensure that their courses are taken up around the country, and they are therefore reluctant to demand a level of technological provision that would make it difficult for teachers and teaching institutions to deliver the course.

Each student taking the Nuffield course will be assumed to have access to a graphing calculator. At the time this decision was shared with teachers, many were very dubious about the feasibility of such a constraint. Over the intervening three years, teachers' perceptions have changed; the calculators are now familiar enough, there are enough such calculators around, and enough support materials, to make such an assumption seem workable on the intended scale of the project.

Initially the project team wanted to assume that all students would have access to a spreadsheet, a statistical package, and possibly a specialized modelling tool such as *Numerator* or *STELLA*, as well as each student having their own graphics calculator. However in practice, decisions about building such assumptions into the course material had to be made in the light of the extra cost in time and money that would be required from an overstretched system and overstretched teachers. Accessibility involves not just providing the technology but also teachers confident enough to use it.

The final product therefore emphasizes the possible role of spreadsheets and statistical packages, and supports these with suggestions and worksheets, but does not require them. The assessment criteria require some work in depth, use of some piece of technology, and some modelling and the integration of these is encouraged.

Why Spreadsheets?

The rationale for focusing on the spreadsheet as the major piece of software was that it would enable us to offer large datasets such as census data on disc. The

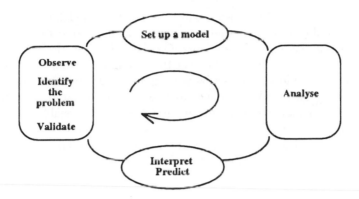

Figure 22.1: The modelling process

spreadsheet had been found to be a very powerful general modelling tool (see for example the work reported in Chapters 9 and 10). The spreadsheet has many other general uses, so once the teachers have invested the initial time, the pay-off extends into record keeping and producing worksheets. In addition, it is a tool widely used in industry and consequently well supported in terms of data, texts and new developments.

Modelling

In all the material, mathematical modelling is presented as the process used when applying mathematics to solve problems. In industry and research the modelling process is often experienced as an iterative one, in which the results from a model are compared with reality and the model consequently modified. The model has a purpose, often to solve a particular problem, and is judged by how well it fits the purpose. The diagram shown in Figure 22.1 is used throughout the course to represent the modelling process.

There is a tradition that many A-level mathematics students study some aspect of applied mathematics, or mathematical modelling. However, in many syllabuses, the applied mathematics ends up as simply an exercise in pure mathematics. Thus topics in mechanics provide practice in trigonometry, geometry and calculus, and statistical work leads to set theory and yet more calculus. There is increasing demand from employers for students who are able to use mathematics interactively with the real world. It is hoped that the emphasis in the Nuffield course on modelling as an interactive process will help to address this need.

We have built two kinds of modelling into the Nuffield course, data modelling and the modelling of dynamic systems. In addition, we have tried to emphasize the final stage of the modelling process: the communication or presentation of results.

There are two further reasons why mathematical modelling and computer modelling should be incorporated into A-level mathematics: the gains for the teacher and the gains for the students. On the one hand, the teacher gains a window into students' thinking wherever there is an opportunity for students to express their own ideas, whether by writing a program or in writing about or presenting their own work. Thus encouraging students to use their mathematics to model real situations, or to solve genuine problems, can enable the teacher to see how students understand the mathematics they choose to use. On the other hand, the students gain motivation, feedback, reflection, and insight from discovering the power to solve problems that they have from mathematics.

How Can Modelling Be Built into the A-Level Curriculum?

There is still a tension between needing to practise and apply new content, and using mathematics to tackle real problems. We have observed that students find it extremely difficult to build their own models using mathematics that they have only recently learned. How can this be taken into account in an A-level mathematics course, in which students are also expected to learn new content? We are attempting to do this in two ways: using the whole modelling process as discussed further below and emphasizing to students which part of the modelling process is being used at any time.

If students are carrying out the whole modelling process investigatively, then they use familiar mathematics. For example students are expected to fit curves by eye to data collected experimentally or from simulations.

Case Studies and Articles

Throughout the course, case studies are used to illustrate how a new mathematical concept may be used by someone solving a problem. The intention has been to put each topic into the context of its use as a mathematical modelling tool, either by citing historical examples or by showing current uses. So for example, the concepts of arithmetic and geometric progression were used by Malthus in the eighteenth century in a population modelling exercise to justify his claim that the population growth at the time would have to be checked, otherwise population would outstrip food supply. This discussion develops into a study of an improved model of limited population growth which uses a logistic model.

Historical Problems

A frequent difficulty with the case-study approach is that modern uses of mathematics assume too high a level of content for A-level students. We have been able to avoid this by focusing on historical problems and by using modern disciplines where mathematical modelling is new.

Data is available for example from the first attempts at traffic modelling when researchers were trying to establish the relationship between the speed of traffic and the flow rate. These early traffic models have been found to be readily accessible to A-level students. Nowadays, the models used are much more sophisticated and incorporate sub-models based on these early results.

Modern Disciplines

Until recently in microbiology, investigations into the growth of organisms such as salmonella were done *in situ*, in the type of food under investigation. In the Institute of Food Research, scientists have been arguing the case for using a descriptive mathematical model. They have built a model using pH, water content and temperature, using data and mathematics which can be made accessible to students. If the model is accepted, it will be used as a basis for future recommendations about food storage.

At an excavation of a Roman site in Baldock, archaeologists found many of the skeletons to be incomplete. They wanted to be able to estimate the height of each skeleton from the available bones, but reliable data about the relationship between the length of a bone and overall height is hard to come by. However, there was a model built by a scientist from data collected after the Vietnam war while bodies were being identified. This model was used to estimate the height of the Roman skeletons, which raises all sorts of issues about modelling assumptions.

Effect on Content

Previous examples illustrate the fact that a mathematics curriculum which emphasizes modelling leads to changed priorities. Traditional A-level mathematics places a strong emphasis on manipulative skills and on analytical calculus as a major tool. In a modelling mathematics curriculum, students can see that there is a choice between approximating when setting up the model, and approximating when solving the model. That is, you can either choose to use functions which approximate to what you need, which you know lead to equations which can be solved analytically, or you can choose to use functions which fit better, but which lead to equations only solvable by approximate methods. This places more emphasis on numerical and graphical methods.

In addition, a modelling curriculum, raises the profile of some areas of mathematics which had traditionally received less emphasis at this level, such as data-handling techniques, probability distributions, matrices and complex numbers. For example, probability distributions are often used in building simulations of situations which involve uncertainty.

An example of the use of simulations came from industry, in the context of risk analysis. If a major exploration project is proposed, planners need to be able to estimate the probable cost and, in case of problems, the maximum cost that they can expect. One approach used to tackle this was to collect from experienced staff three estimates for the cost of each element of the project:

- least possible cost;
- most likely cost;
- maximum possible cost.

A truncated normal distribution was then to be fitted to each element using the following assumptions:

- is the 10th percentile;
- is the mode;
- is the 80th percentile.

By running a Monte Carlo simulation, the resulting distributions could then be used to estimate the probability distribution of the total cost of the project.

Role of Group Work

Students are also encouraged to work collaboratively, and to use additional resources. There is some evidence that there is a parallel between a student's modelling skills and their skills in working collaboratively. The following account draws from the work of Perry (1968), ideas which have been used to devise a prize winning undergraduate course in mathematical modelling at the University of Hertfordshire.

Perry describes the process of growing to full maturity as involving moving from an expectation that someone knows the right answer to a more provisional, relativistic way of looking at knowledge. It can be characterized as having three stages:

- dualistic, in which answers are believed to be either right or wrong, and the student expects the teacher to have the right answer;
- multiplicity, in which everyone's answer must be allowable, since no one knows the right answer for sure, and there are as yet in the student's experience no grounds for making independent judgments;
- contextual relativism, in which students appreciate that answers need evaluation, comparison and judgment, authority does not necessarily have the answer, there exists a justification for a particular opinion, and the student has developed a capacity for making judgments.

Traditional mathematics teaching tends to reinforce dualistic thinking. To some extent those students who choose traditional mathematics courses may tend to be less mature; it is the last repository of dualistic thought at A-level and feels safe to them. Such students did not thrive on the mathematical modelling courses in the research context. Mathematical modelling requires of students that they develop mathematical judgment. It may be that many, at the age of 17, are not ready to move very far towards such a view of mathematical knowledge.

Assessment

The assessment process of traditional A-level mathematics tended to militate against teaching mathematical modelling or mathematics through modelling. Experience in first-year undergraduate courses has shown that coursework or portfolio assessment with appropriate assessment criteria can encourage a mature approach to mathematics. There are, however, two constraints here. One is from government; coursework assessment of A-level is restricted to 20 per cent. The other is from many teachers who, for a variety of reasons, do not wish to take on responsibility for coursework assessment. One approach, used by the Scottish Examination Board in the Revised Higher Certificate in Education, is to offer board-marked assignments, which would be carried out by students under some supervision over several sessions, before being sent to the board to be assessed. This idea was considered by the Nuffield team for a while, but was eventually rejected as presenting too many difficulties. The published syllabus now includes:

- a 20 per cent coursework component, with criteria to show that students understand the modelling process and have been involved in building their own models;
- a comprehension component, to ensure that students are encouraged to read about the use of mathematics in context.

The development of the new course has been influenced by constraints from several sources. The greatest constraint of all has been time. The project was initially conceived as a five-year development project, due to finish in summer 1995. During the lifetime of the project, development of the assessment arrangements for Key Stage 4 of the National Curriculum to be introduced in 1994, and proposals to change the regulations for A-level mathematics, combined to produce a strong commercial pressure to publish materials in 1994.

The role of the SCAA, the regulations for A-level mathematics and the criteria for getting the syllabus agreed by the mathematics committee have provided obvious constraints. What may be less obvious is the effect of these not being publicly available until summer 1993, when the project had already handed material over to the publishers. This meant the project was inevitably working from consultation versions of the core documents, and perhaps has resulted in unnecessary caution.

The examination board (the Nuffield Advanced Mathematics syllabus is published by Oxford University Delegacy of Local Examinations) is another potential source of constraints, but in fact, the examination board has been remarkably supportive and I do not believe they have posed any extra constraints on the project. At the time they were devising a second, more traditional syllabus to fit the new regulations at desperately short notice.

Looking to the Future

The Nuffield Advanced Mathematics Project has made innovations in the way it has built modelling into the course material and into the assessment structure, and there is interest from around the world in seeing the outcomes. There is plenty more scope for development of the ideas, and in conclusion I would like to emphasize two possibilities in particular:

- The role of technology is fast changing and there is already scope for beginning a development at this level that will assume greater access to technology.
- The project has made a start in incorporating case-study material into the course. However, such material is in short supply in the teachers' experience and much more needs to be made easily available.

Chapter 23

Modelling and Teacher Change

Ian Stevenson and David Hassell

Introduction

Enormous changes have taken place in schools as a result of the introduction of a centralized National Curriculum in England, Wales and Northern Ireland. What is taught and how it is presented to students have had to be completely revised in light of the statutory Programmes of Study and Attainment Targets. Teachers no longer have the freedom about *what* is taught, but must exercise their professional judgment and skills about *how* to teach the National Curriculum.

This chapter will discuss the issue of curriculum development and what it might mean within the current context. As a focus, we shall present a case study of the recently completed Computer Based Modelling Across the Curriculum Project (CBMAC, 1989–1992, directed by Professor Celia Hoyles and Dr Bill Tagg). This has produced *The Modelling Pack* — a pack of INSET material for teachers who wish to develop computer-based modelling in the classroom. After describing the background and methodology of the project, we shall discuss the impact that the formal structure and methodology of the project had on the professional development of those teachers involved with it. A contention of our discussion will be that the introduction of the National Curriculum implies that curriculum development means teacher development, but of a specific sort. Further, the experience of the project has important lessons for approaches to professional development and innovations in teaching and learning.

Modelling and Curriculum Development

Using and building computer models of systems has been advocated as a strategy for learning over the past ten years. Mellar (1990) provides an account of the research that has been done over the past ten years concentrating on modelling as a way of allowing students to express and explore their ideas about a particular knowledge domain. However, as he points out, the modelling research had little impact on the curriculum in schools until the Government introduced modelling into the National Curriculum. The majority of modelling software was rather inaccessible, often requiring powerful computers not available to schools.

Introducing modelling into the curriculum through the National Curriculum had a number of consequences. The first was that of surprise. By and large, modelling was new to most teachers. Although they may have used models within their subject area, referring to specific topics, many teachers were unused to the idea of modelling as a process. Further, placing modelling within the Information Technology Attainment Targets added another novelty to the process: computers. Second, because of the cross-curricular nature of IT in the National Curriculum, teachers were asked to look for opportunities for modelling both within their own subject areas and across the curriculum. Taking both of these aspects and the statutory nature of the Attainment Targets, the third consequence at a personal level was anxiety and the demand for INSET. Modelling can be seen to illustrate a central concern of the paper: curriculum development means teacher development.

Interest in modelling was developing in a number of institutions and a range of modelling approaches were starting to be investigated. In 1985 there was a conference of interested parties which discussed the possibilities of developing software for schools and as a result a feasibility study was set up. As a result of this research, King's College, London and the Advisory Unit, Hatfield established the Modus Project (see Chapter 21) to develop software for modelling in schools. The Institute of Education and the Advisory Unit for Microtechnology in Education were approached in the planning stage of the TVEI IT Programme to put together a proposal for the CBMAC Project which then started in April 1989.

The CBMAC Project

On the surface the CBMAC Project appears to be an ideal curriculum development response to the introduction of a strand of the National Curriculum which expects computer-based modelling to be incorporated across a variety of subjects. This project was actually founded on work which was carried out over a number of years in the Advisory Unit, the Institute of Education and other institutions.

What Was It?

The CBMAC Project was one project in an IT Programme sponsored by the TVEI Unit of the Employment Department. The programme supported two groups of projects to develop resources to help teachers and schools come to terms with a range of management and classroom issues related to the use of IT.

The project aimed to promote the use of generic modelling techniques to support individual subject curricula and cross-curricular opportunities in the 14 to 18 age range. The project encouraged teachers to use computers to investigate physical, human and industrial systems, with specific reference to mathematics, geography, science and business education. The main aim of the project was to produce teacher-support materials aimed at individuals and departments which could enable teachers to incorporate computer-based modelling in their teaching. A range of software was used, including spreadsheets, Logo and other modelling packages. The materials included:

- Resources to introduce and develop ideas on modelling.
- Case studies and examples to support classroom/school practice and INSET activities.
- Information on hardware, software and other aspects of applying computer-based modelling.
- Materials to support training in some generic software packages.

Project Organization

The project realized that time was the major factor which influenced the successful adoption of any innovation, especially those relating to the use of information technology. As a result a large proportion of project resources were spent on releasing teachers from their timetable and providing the opportunity for them to become familiar with software and develop their own approaches and materials. This was an expensive but effective approach to curriculum development. The project had the following time scale:

Phase 1 — Preparation
Schools and work practices were negotiated and there was an introductory INSET for the first-year teachers.

Phase 2 — Development
In the first academic year the project concentrated on one or two teachers from two of the departments used in each of five schools. On average each department was provided with one day's release time where the teacher was ensured access to computers and received regular visits from one of the project officers. The teachers had four days of INSET which provided the opportunity to work with people from other schools. The aim of the first year was to develop experience and confidence with software and the time to practise and prepare modelling activities for pupils which could then be tried out with their normal classes.

Phase 3 — Development and Replication
In the second year the ideas and approaches developed before would be used to support staff from the departments which had not had any support in the first year. After some time these teachers would then be encouraged to develop their own ideas and materials. Meanwhile the teachers from the first year would try to disseminate their work to others in their department. Also the project officers started to write up the first drafts of the final resources from the teachers' materials and experiences.

Phase 4 — Production, Trialling and Publication
In the final academic year the materials were written up and trialled with a wide range of schools and student teachers around the country. The trials provided feedback, and together with that from reviewers the final resources were edited and the publication produced.

Issues

Helen Simon (1988) points out that there are at least three elements which need to be considered for implementation of curriculum development: involvement of teachers, formal and informal support structures and institutional values. We shall now discuss these in relation to the project.

Formal Relationships and Structure of Project

A major influence for any project is the formal structure that is set up under the guidance of the project funders. This project was no different as it was a collaboration between two institutions and five local authorities. This resulted in a top–down approach for selecting schools and teachers where the project team had little, if any influence. All the schools worked very hard to enable the project to achieve its goals, but there were situations where the hierarchical approach resulted in some unfortunate pressures or imbalance in the teachers chosen. In some cases the structure of selection and the relationships within the authority or school influenced the perceptions of the results which might be expected, both for the project and the authority, school, department or teacher. This led to a number of inconsistencies or problems, for example:

- The balance of staff was often not what was hoped for, i.e., in terms of experience, IT literacy, confidence with IT, perception of modelling, etc.
- In some cases it was difficult to influence a department or area, because of the person chosen to take part.
- The project sometimes had a low priority, because a teacher was 'forced' to take part or because the perceived school or department outcomes were the reasons for accepting the project.
- Some teachers were placed in difficult positions because particular members of the school organization had not been fully consulted to ensure teacher release in the correct circumstances.

It is accepted that any curriculum-development project is a partnership between the school and the project but it would seem that there might be better ways of approaching schools for this type of collaboration.

Ideology, Practice and Change

Change can provide both challenges and threats. At a personal and professional level, it can call into question values, beliefs and practices that were previously assumed and accepted by teachers. Ball (1987) characterizes this conflict between what a teacher does and believes and new circumstances as ideological. Citing Sharp and Green, he defines a teacher ideology as: 'A connected set of systematically related beliefs and ideas about what are felt to be the essential features of teaching' (p. 14). It includes epistemological and philosophical beliefs about people and how they learn together with a view of the place of schools in society. Coupled to this is a view of the nature of teaching, how it should be performed and assessed and a judgment of the person's own worth as a teacher. A complex process of socialization involving experiences of their own schooling, teacher training, teaching itself coupled to broader socio-political factors help produce a teacher's 'ideological' stance. Teachers see themselves as being inducted into the profession over a period of time (House, 1979). Ideology is formed, therefore, within a professional culture that changes in an evolutionary way over a long period.

Control of the Learning Process

A central strand in any teaching ideology is the issue of who controls the learning process. Teachers are expected to be 'in charge' in the classroom both as managers and as 'the one who has all the answers'. Whether this control is achieved by teacher-centred or child-centred activities will depend on the teacher/school ethos, but the teacher still has the responsibility for ensuring that children meet educational objectives. Moreover, confidence both in oneself and one's professional capacity to control the classroom is related to one's ability to cope with the unforeseen either by being flexible or by minimizing what does not go according to plan. Technology in the classroom represents an area of anxiety. It can 'go wrong' and this will render the lesson useless with possible attendant negative responses of the pupils. The teacher is expected to 'know the answers' by the pupils and by the teacher him/herself. Technical competence is seen, therefore, as a necessity to maintain control and the pupil's confidence.

Many of the teachers involved in the project were relative novices as regards computers. Initially, their primary concern was gaining technical competence of both software and hardware. At the same time, they were being asked by project personnel to identify areas of their current practice which could be presented through computer-based modelling. Clearly these strands are related. As one becomes more proficient with the software, so one sees possibilities for changing one's pedagogy. Changing one's approach to teaching suggests new possibilities which can be exploited using IT. In theory, that is. In practice, a far more complex relationship between personal and professional IT competence became apparent, centred around the ideology of the individual teacher.

Practice and Change

Broadly speaking, the acceptance and integration into routine classroom practice of the approach adopted by the project depended on the extent to which a teacher agreed with the ideology of the project. The CBMAC Project aimed to promote group work and independent learning using a variety of modelling software. Teachers working as part of the project were encouraged to work with students on open-ended tasks that enable them to build their own representations of some system. This entailed that the teacher becomes a facilitator who gives guidance rather than direction to students who were engaged in discovering for themselves about specific domains of experience. A clear 'ideological' stance was taken about the nature of teaching and learning by the project.

The response of the teachers involved in the project varied. If the match between what the teacher believed and what the project advocated was acceptable, there was a good chance that the teacher would translate his/her own experience of modelling into classroom practice. One teacher who was accustomed to an investigative approach found no difficulties in adopting computer-based modelling. Most of the teachers had never considered modelling as a teaching and learning strategy and several were sceptical of the benefits of computer-based modelling. However, they took a pragmatic approach, participating because they had time, hardware and personal support. Some used the time to enhance their personal IT skills, placing a lower priority on changing classroom practice. A handful of the teachers seriously questioned their own assumptions about teaching and learning, changing their practice in light of their experiences. As a result of their experience two science teachers concluded that a modelling approach had made them more aware on a daily basis of the potential difficulties for students. A crucial question for most participants was whether the project enabled them to provide 'effective delivery' of the National Curriculum. More detailed accounts of the teachers' views is presented in the *Modelling Pack* (Computer Based Modelling across the Curriculum Project, 1992).

Materials-led Innovation

A more general question raised by the experience of the project concerns the nature of innovation in the current context. If curriculum development means teacher development, and there is not available generally the resourcing for teachers which something like this project provides, how does teacher development occur? Fullan (1991) argues that change is multi-dimensional centring on methodology, materials and beliefs (what we have called ideology). Using any one of these dimensions as the primary focus and vehicle for innovation must take account of the other two for it to be effective.

In developing the final materials, teachers were directly involved in the selection and implementation of the activities described. As we have outlined, they were resourced and supported in terms of time, equipment and personal guidance. The materials themselves assume that none of these things would be available to a teacher who wanted to start computer-based modelling. In this sense, the CBMAC Project is a materials-led innovation which happens to have occurred at the time when modelling is a compulsory part of the secondary curriculum. Using the perspectives on innovation outlined by House (1979), the CBMAC Project can be described as 'technological': a process of implementation which assumes there is a value consensus amongst implementors. However, the consensus in this case is problematic because the innovation takes place in a situation in which teachers must deliver modelling by law. The statutory nature of the National Curriculum renders unnecessary the need to consider what House calls the 'political' (innovation in context) and 'cultural' (school context) perspectives of the innovation process. In practice, lack of attention to the political and cultural dimensions of the innovation may contribute to its not being fully adopted. Project personnel were aware of these factors and attempted to develop a 'culture of modelling' within the departments of the partner schools. Participants were encouraged to share their work with colleagues both formally through INSET and informally through personal contact. The dominance of the National Curriculum and conditions in schools, however, placed constraints on how easily teachers could translate their experience of computer-based modelling into classroom practice.

Conclusion

Computer-based modelling can be an agent for change. Whether change happens depends on how the innovation relates to the ideological stance of teachers (Fullan, 1991). Some may adopt the innovation whole-heartedly because it reflects their own educational philosophy, others may reject it. A more common response from committed teachers is to try and reconcile a wide variety of constraints on their practice including time, the National Curriculum and resources with their desire to provide pupils with opportunities for learning that computer-based modelling presents. Rather than revolution, our experience suggests that teachers will engage in an adaptation of the innovation to suit their own circumstances. The outcome is naturally complex and, to a degree, uncertain. What can be said is that if teachers are to 'deliver the National Curriculum effectively' they require resources and a clear sense of the need for ongoing professional development at both the institutional and personal level.

Appendix 1: Tools for Exploratory Learning Programme

The Tools for Exploratory Learning Programme formed part of the ESRC's Research Initiative on Information Technology in Education. The programme was co-directed by Joan Bliss at King's College and Jon Ogborn at the Institute of Education who were part of a management team also including Derek Brough at Imperial College, Jonathan Briggs, Kingston University, and Harvey Mellar at the Institute of Education. Other members of the team were Dick Boohan, Tim Brosnan, Rob Miller, Caroline Nash, Cathy Rodgers, John Turner and Babis Sakonidis.

This appendix gives details on the design of the research study, in particular the sampling, the data-collection procedures, and the analytic schemes used. It should be read in conjunction with the last part of Chapter 1 which gives an overview of the programme and a description of the major concepts behind the research and the design of the tasks carried out by the children. Chapter 5 also contains a description of the design of the semi-quantitative tool, *IQON*.

Research Design

For each of the forms of learning (exploratory and expressive) tasks were designed to elicit all three kinds of reasoning (semi-quantitative, qualitative and quantitative) in either two or three of the topics (traffic, shops and fitness). This design is illustrated in Figure 1.1.

Sampling

We worked with pupils in the 11 to 14 age range, the median age being 12.9. It was planned to have eight pupils per cell of the design shown in Figure 1.1, but limitations of time reduced this to five in each cell for the quantitative and qualitative tools (making 88 students altogether). Pupils came from the London area, one Middle and three Comprehensive schools. Pupils were selected by their teachers, as being of near-average ability, excluding the extremes. Pupils with much previous computer experience or with behavioural problems were excluded.

Procedure

Each pupil worked one-to-one with a researcher for about three to four hours over a period of two weeks. The procedure was the same for all studies and had four steps:

(i)   reasoning without the computer (about forty-five minutes);
(ii)   learning to use an Apple Macintosh (about forty-five minutes);
(iii)   learning to use the tool (about one hour);
(iv)   carrying out the task on a given topic (about one hour).

Expressive tasks also included an informal introduction to the topic, carried out between steps (ii) and (iii). This was done in order to raise pupils' awareness of the subject.

Analysis of Data

Tape recordings of the initial interviews without the computer and the task interviews were transcribed and checked against schedules. The data for analysis consisted of these transcripts together with:

- work done by pupils on task sheets;
- screen dumps taken by the interviewers as work progressed;
- observation /interview schedules used for the initial interview and main task.

The process of analysis was essentially the same for all data. The analysis of task-interview transcripts proceeded in stages:

- the transcript was segmented into units, where a unit corresponded to an argument provided by a pupil, including any relevant actions;
- each unit was then coded with terms from an analytic scheme. This initial coding ensured that every part of the transcript had been examined and described in a uniform way. Nearly all codings were checked by a second analyst.
- the coded transcript was used to construct an analytic description of what had happened with each pupil on each task.

These descriptions reported stages of the work done by the child in detail, quoting as necessary, and also summarizing common features of the pupil's behaviour (e.g., frequent interface problems, or frequent use of initiative). With each description was also a summary of the main overall features of the work analysed. Once each pupil's profile was completed, a further synthesis was made of all pupils' work for a given task.

The data collected in this study is inherently qualitative. The essential problem in describing and analysing such data is to arrive at a set of descriptive terms or categories for each aspect of the data, which:

- can reliably and consistently be used by more than one researcher;
- adequately reflect important features of the data, expected or unexpected;
- respect complexity in the data whilst remaining well-defined;
- are relevant to the research questions at issue.

Where appropriate we used the systemic network notation (Bliss, Monk and Ogborn, 1983) to organize such interdependent structures of categories. In this way, it is possible to use larger and more complex category structures than is possible if categories are just defined in an unordered list. A systemic network can be viewed as a context-free grammar which defines a 'language' constructed for describing given data.

It was important to have a systematic method of this kind to inspect the data and to impose a reasonable degree of uniformity between the analyses of work done with different tools (whilst still allowing differences to emerge) for we wished to compare carefully exploratory and expressive work on each topic, and also to look for domain and tool dependencies.

Semi-quantitative Scheme of Analysis

In developing schemes of analysis we were interested in the structure of the arguments given by pupils. This was particularly the case in the analysis of semi-quantitative reasoning with a dynamic modelling tool where we identified two major types of reasoning: (i) causal reasoning about links in the model, and relation to reality; (ii) non-causal reasoning looking only at the behaviour of the model.

With causal reasoning three main categories of complexity of causal reasoning were identified, for both exploratory and expressive tasks: simple, multiple and coordinated connections. 'Simple connections' were where an argument pays attention just to the effect A has on B: $A \rightarrow B$. 'Multiple connections' were arguments containing more than one link. There were three kinds of multiple connections: chain, one-to-many connection, many-to-one connection. A 'chain' argument contains a series of connections: A seen to have an effect on B, and B on C, then C on D: $A \rightarrow B, B \rightarrow C, C \rightarrow D$. 'One-to-many connection' arguments contain one cause which creates more than one effect. 'Many-to-one connection' arguments contain more than one cause to create one effect.

There were three kinds of coordinated connection arguments: feedback, articulated connections, system reasoning. A simple 'feedback' argument articulates the effect that A has on B and that B has on A. However, the feedback loop can be more complex. An 'articulated connections' argument proposes that one connection functions because of a second. In 'system reasoning' the pupil attempts to take into account the interaction between all or a number of the variables in the model. Some system type reasoning only attempts to understand interactions in a part of a model, often a feedback loop.

The language of children's arguments was extremely variable. For example, some of the typical forms of expression for causative links were: 'A makes B go up', 'A pushes B up', 'if A goes up then B', 'A so B', 'A and so B', 'A results in B going up', 'A goes up as a consequence B goes up', 'because A goes up B goes up'. Causative arguments are often linked with the term 'because' but as can be seen from this list there are many other ways of expressing a causal link.

When pupils reasoned non-causally they paid attention only to relations and patterns within the model itself. There were five categories of such arguments: time sequences, collections, lists, isolated variables and scans. In 'time sequence' arguments variables are named but links are only articulated through temporal conjunctions such as 'when', 'then', 'now', 'before', 'after', 'at the same time', etc. In 'collection' arguments variables are named but links are only articulated through additive conjunctions such as 'and', 'also', 'but', 'in addition', 'as well as', etc. 'Lists' are made up of variables but without any form of conjunction between them. Some arguments concerned 'isolated variables', sometimes only a single variable, with no part of the argument concerning a link. 'Scanning' arguments do not look at the model in a sequence defined by the links in the model, but look at variables in any order in which they attract attention.

Qualitative Scheme of Analysis

In qualitative expressive tasks we identified two major modes of reasoning that pupils used when describing actions linked to situations: the subjunctive argument and the forward planning argument. Pupils also used a mix of both of these arguments in their reasoning. In 'subjunctive' arguments pupils first envisaged an action and then their reasoning focused on all the actions and situations that might be preconditions for this initial action. In other words, in their reasoning pupils specify the prerequisites necessary to achieve an action. In 'forward planning' arguments the pupil did not simply sketch out the next action, but anticipated a series of other actions that followed from the first action to permit the achievement of the goal.

In 'subjunctive' arguments the link between an action or situation and a set of pre-requisite actions and situations can be modulated along a scale indicating degrees of obligation. The language exploited by the pupil gave rise to a range of expressions, for example, words such as 'would', 'should', 'may', 'might' express degrees of obligation and inclination. Pupils also used the verb 'need' to express a condition that had to be fulfilled or adverbs such as 'until', 'unless', 'instead' were used to express that one event was conditional on another. The reasoning of 'forward planning' arguments enabled pupils to see links between actions and situations as steps in carrying out a plan. Pupils could use temporal conjunctions to indicate their plan. Examples of these temporal links are: 'then', 'next', 'soon', 'afterwards', 'when', 'before', 'at the end', 'here', 'now', 'at the moment', etc. They sometimes expressed the planning in terms of the verb 'want'.

In the evaluation of qualitative exploratory models we were interested in whether the pupil could see the cause and effect within the development of a path and whether or not they could compare different sets of causes and effects in different paths. The different categories of argument were:

- re-descriptions of the contents of the model;
- re-descriptions plus elaborations, that is, adding details not in the model but which have no explanatory power;
- localized analysis: an argument based on some localized aspect of the model, but attempting to go beyond the model and to give reasoned arguments;
- generalized comparisons or general system reasoning, e.g., systems of choices.

Our subjects generally expressed their arguments as straightforward choices which may or may not work, and tended not to see these choices as systematic and interacting.

Quantitative Scheme of Analysis

Each argument was analysed according to a three-component description: whether the pupil was initiating or responding, what type of action was concerned, and what type of reasoning accompanied that action. The reasoning was characterized both by its kind, using knowledge, comprehension, planning or deciding, analysis and evaluation, and by whether it was (from the pupil's point of view) positive, querying, expressing confusion, or failing to achieve what it had tried to do. The five networks shown in Figure Appendix 1 show the more delicate levels of the five aspects of reasoning which were looked for and coded.

Results

The results of the work on quantitative reasoning are reported in Chapter 8, the work on semi-quantitative reasoning in Chapter 15, and the work on qualitative reasoning in Chapter 17. The implications for the curriculum are discussed in Chapter 20.

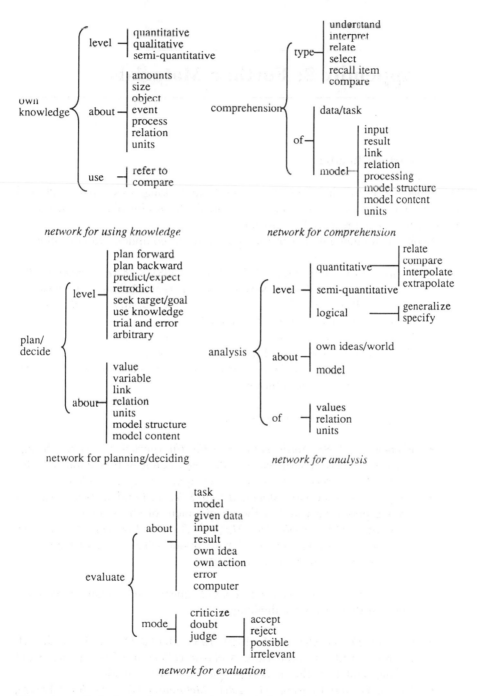

network for using knowledge

network for comprehension

network for planning/deciding

network for analysis

network for evaluation

Figure Appendix 1: Systemic networks for quantitative analysis

Appendix 2: Further Materials

Further Reading

The bibliography for this book is necessarily quite long, so we have collected together here a selection of readings that might be useful places to follow up some of the ideas presented in this book.

Books in the general area of the application of computers to education:

- Forman G.F. and Pufall, P.B. (Eds) (1988) *Constructivism in the Computer Age*, Hillsdale, New Jersey, Lawrence Erlbaum Associates.
- Olson, J. (1988) *School worlds/Microworlds: Computers and the Culture of the Classroom*, Oxford, Pergamon Press.
- Rutkowska, J. and Cook, C. (Eds) (1987) *Computers, Cognition and Development*, Chichester, John Wiley and Sons.
- Turkle, S. (1984) *The Second Self: Computers and the human spirit*, New York, Simon and Shuster.

For general background on modelling:

- Ekeland, I. (1988) *Mathematics and the Unexpected*, Chicago, Chicago University Press. A short but stimulating account of how familiar mathematics has in recent years thrown up quite unexpected ideas.
- Gleick, J. (1988) *Chaos: Making a New Science*, London, Heinemann. A riveting popular account of the development of chaos theory.
- Hofstadter, D.R. (1985) *MetaMagical Themas*, London, Penguin. An idiosyncratic but fascinating debate about what can and cannot be modelled by mathematics or computer.

For a wider view of the psychological and linguistic issues related to people's use of models in their everyday thinking:

- Gentner, D. and Stevens, A. (Eds) (1983) *Mental Models*, Hillsdale, NJ, Lawrence Erlbaum Associates. A classic collection of researches about making models of the models people have of the world.
- Lakoff, G. and Johnson, M. (1981) *Metaphors We Live By*, Chicago, Chicago University Press. An approach from linguistics to questions about how we imagine the nature of the world.

For accounts of specific types of modelling:

- Roberts, N., Anderson, D., Deal, R., Garet, M. and Shaffer, W. (1983) *Introduction to Computer Simulation*, New York, Addison Wesley. An extended and detailed introduction to computer modelling in the framework of general systems theory.
- Richmond, B. (1987) *An Academic User's Guide to STELLA*, New Hampshire, High Performance Systems, Inc. This contains a useful introduction to computer modelling in general.
- Toffoli, T. and Margolis, N. (1987) *Cellular Automata Machines*, Cambridge, Massachusetts, MIT Press. An interesting but rather technical account of what can be done with cellular automata.
- James, D.J.G. and McDonald, J.J. (1981) *Case Studies in Mathematical Modelling*, Cheltenham, Stanley Thornes. A collection of interesting case studies.
- Williams, B.C. and de Kleer, J. (1991) 'Qualitative reasoning about physical systems: a return to basics', *Artificial Intelligence*, 51, pp. 1–9. This paper provides a brief introduction to the special edition of *Artificial Intelligence* on qualitative modelling, and this special issue contains a number of other important papers in the area of qualitative reasoning.

For material relevant to the use of modelling within the curriculum:

- de Lange, J., Keitel, C., Huntley, I. and Niss, M. (1993) *Innovation in Maths Education by Modelling and Applications*, Chichester, Ellis Horwood.
- Computer Based Modelling across the Curriculum Project (1992) *The Modelling Pack: Teacher Resources for Computer Based Modelling in Science, Maths, Geography and Business Education*, Newcastle, NORICC and Hatfield, AU Enterprises Ltd.
- Mandinach, E.B. (1989) 'Model-building and the use of computer simulation of dynamic systems', *Journal of Educational Computing Research*, 5, pp. 221–43.
- Mandinach, E.B. and Cline, H.F. (in press) *Implementing Technology-based Learning Environments: Systems Thinking and Curriculum Innovation*, Hillsdale, NJ, Lawrence Erlbaum Associates.
- Niss, M., Blum, W. and Huntley, I. (1991) *Teaching of Mathematical Modelling and Applications*, Chichester, Ellis Horwood.

Software and Curriculum Materials

Adex
Briggs, J. (1988), in the pack 'Learning With Expert Systems', London, FEU.

Appendix 2: Further Materials

The Algebraic Proposer
Schwartz, J.L. (1987), Hanover, New Hampshire, True Basic.
The Cellular Modelling System (CMS)
Ogborn, J. and Holland, D. (1988), Harlow, Longman Micro-Software.
Computer Modelling — Visualising the Solution, (Video)
Webb, M. and Cox, M.J. (1991), Hatfield, The Advisory Unit For Microtechnology in Education.
Data Desk Professional (1989)
Odesta Corporation, Commercial Avenue, 4084, Northbrook, IL 60062.
Dinamix
Lobo, M.S. and Clérigo, F.C. (1991), Project MINERVA, Technological University, Lisbon.
The Dynamic Modelling System (DMS)
Ogborn, J. (1985), Harlow, Longman Micro-Software. (Republished 1991, Gwent, AVP)
Energy Expert
Cox, M.J., Webb, M., Booth, B. and Robbins, P. (1993), Hatfield, The Advisory Unit For Microtechnology in Education.
Expert Builder
Webb, M., Booth, B., Cox, M.J. and Robbins, P. (1993), Hatfield, The Advisory Unit For Microtechnology in Education.
Explore your options
a program developed as part of the Tools for Exploratory Learning Programme.
Extend
Diamond, B. (1987), San Jose, California, Imagine That.
IQON
a program developed as part of the Tools for Exploratory Learning Programme. Commercial production of this program is presently under negotiation.
Knowledge Pad
Briggs, J. (1989), London, PEG.
Linx88
Briggs, J., Brough, D., Nichol, J.D. (1988), London, PEG.
Microcomputer Based Laboratories
TERC (1990),
2067 Massachusetts Avenue, Cambridge, Massachusetts, 02140 USA.
Model Builder
Webb, M., Booth, B., Cox, M.J. and Robbins, P. (1991), Hatfield, The Advisory Unit For Microtechnology in Education.
The Modelling Pack: Teacher Resources for Computer Based Modelling in Science, Maths, Geography and Business Education
Computer Based Modelling across the Curriculum Project (1992), Newcastle, NORICC and Hatfield, AU Enterprises Ltd.
Numerator
Hunter, P. (1989), Cambridge, Longman Logotron.

The Picture Simulator
Camara, A.S., Ferreira, F.C., Nobre, E. and Fialho, J.E. (1991), Uninova, Portugal, Newsoft Group.
ProbSim (Probability Simulator)
Konold, C. (1992), Scientific Reasoning Research Institute, University of Massachusetts, Amherst.
Q-MOD
a program developed as part of the Tools for Exploratory Learning Programme.
SemNet (1991)
Semnet Research Group, San Diego, California.
STELLA
Pytte, A. and Doyle, J. (1988), High Performance Systems Inc. 13, Dartmouth College Highway, Lyme, New Hampshire, 03768 USA.
Superlinx
a program developed as part of the Tools for Exploratory Learning Programme (for an account of Superlinx see Turner, J. 1990).
WorldMaker: Software and Teachers' Guide
Boohan, R., Ogborn, J. and Wright, S. to be published.

For further details on the availability of software mentioned in the text contact Dr Harvey Mellar, Institute of Education, 20 Bedford Way, London WC1H 0AL.

References

BALL, S. (1987) *The Micro-Politics of School*, London, Methuen.

BAR-HILLEL, M. and FALK, R. (1982) 'Some teasers concerning conditional probabilities', *Cognition*, 11, pp. 109–22.

BATEMAN, D. (1988) A Knowledge Based System as an Aid to Chemical Problem Solving, Unpublished PhD thesis, King's College, University of London.

BATTY, M. (1989) 'Urban modelling and planning: Reflections, retrodictions and prescriptions', in MACMILLAN, B. (Ed) *Remodelling Geography*, Oxford, Basil Blackwell.

BEARE, R. (1992) 'Software tools in the science classroom', *Journal of Computer Assisted Learning*, 8, pp. 221–30.

BENIGER, J.R. (1989) 'The evolution of control', in FORESTER, T. (Ed) *Computers in the Human Context: Information Technology, Productivity and People*, Oxford, Basil Blackwell.

BERRY, J.S., BURGHES, D.N., HUNTLEY, I.D., JAMES, D.J.G. and MOSCARDINI, A.O. (1984) (Eds) *Teaching and Applying Mathematical Modelling*, Chichester, Ellis Horwood.

BERRY, J.S., BURGHES, D.N., HUNTLEY, I.D., JAMES, D.J.G. and MOSCARDINI, A.O. (1987) (Eds) *Mathematical Modelling Courses*, Chichester, Ellis Horwood.

BIEHLER, R. (1989) 'Educational perspectives on exploratory data analysis', in MORRIS, R. (Ed) *The Teaching of Statistics*, Paris, UNESCO.

BLISS, J., MELLAR, H., OGBORN, J. and NASH, C. (1992a) *Tools for Exploratory Learning Programme End of Award Report: Technical Report 2, Semi-Quantitative Reasoning — Expressive*, London, University of London.

BLISS, J., MELLAR, H., OGBORN, J. and NASH, C. (1992b) *Tools for Exploratory Learning Programme End of Award Report: Technical Report 3, Semi-Quantitative Reasoning — Exploratory*, London, University of London.

BLISS, J., MONK, M. and OGBORN, J. (1983) *Qualitative Analysis for Educational Research: A Guide to Uses of Systemic Networks*, Beckenham, Kent, Croom Helm.

BLISS, J. and OGBORN, J. (1993) 'A commonsense theory of motion: issues of theory and methodology examined through a pilot study', in BLACK, P. and LUCAS, A. (Eds) *Childrens' Informal Ideas About Science*, London, Croom Helm Routledge, pp. 158–72.

BLISS, J. and OGBORN, J. (1993) 'Steps towards a formalisation of a psycho-logic of motion', *Journal of Intelligent Systems*, 3, pp. 1–48.

BLISS, J., OGBORN, J. and WHITELOCK, D. (1989) 'Secondary school pupils' commonsense theories of motion', *International Journal of Science Education*, 11, pp. 261–72.

BLISS, J., OGBORN, J., BOOHAN, R., BRIGGS, J., BROSNAN, T., BROUGH, D., MELLAR, H., MILLER, R., NASH, C., ROGERS, C. and SAKONDIS, B. (1992a) 'Reasoning supported by computational tools', *Computers in Education*, 18, pp. 1–9.

BLISS, J., OGBORN, J., BOOHAN, R., BRIGGS, J., BROSNAN, T., BROUGH, D., MELLAR, H., MILLER, R., NASH, C., ROGERS, C. and SAKONDIS, B. (1992b) *Tools for Exploratory Learning Programme End of Award Report: Executive Report, Summary Report and five Technical Reports*, London, University of London.

BLISS, J., SAKONIDIS, B., OGBORN, J. and NASH, C. (1992) *Tools for Exploratory Learning Programme End of Award Report: Technical Report 5, Qualitative Reasoning — Expressive and Exploratory*, London, University of London.

BLUM, W., NISS, M. and HUNTLEY, I. (Eds) (1989) *Modelling, Applications and Applied Problem Solving: Teaching Mathematics in a Real Context*, Chichester, Ellis Horwood.

BOOHAN, R. and OGBORN, J. (1991) *Making Sense of Data: Nuffield Exploratory Data Analysis Project*, Longman for University of London, Institute of Education.

BOOS-BAVNBEK, B. (1991) 'Against Ill-founded, Irresponsible Modelling', in NISS, M., BLUM, W. and HUNTLEY, I. (Eds) *Teaching of Mathematical Modelling and Applications*, Chichester, Ellis Horwood, pp. 70–82.

BOOS-BAVNBEK, B. and PATE, G. (1989) 'Information Technology and mathematical modelling, the software crisis, risk and educational consequences', *Computers and Society*, 19, pp. 4–22.

BRATKO, I. (1988) *Lecture Notes on Qualitative Modelling*, Glasgow, Turing Institute.

BRATKO, I., MOZETIC, I. and LAVRAC, N. (1989) *KARDIO, a Study in Deep and Qualitative Knowledge for Expert Systems*, Cambridge, Massachusetts, MIT Press.

BRIGGS, J. (1988) *Learning With Expert Systems*, London, FEU.

BROSNAN, T. (1990) 'Using spreadsheets in the teaching of chemistry 2: More ideas and some limitations', *School Science Review*, 71, pp. 53–9.

BROSNAN, T. (1992) 'Spreadsheets — of swans and swimming', *Education in Chemistry*, 29, 2, pp. 50–3.

BULLOCK, M. and GELMAN, R. (1979) 'Children's assumptions about cause and effect: Temporal ordering', *Child Development*, 50, pp. 89–96.

BULLOCK, M., GELMAN, R. and BAILLARGEON, R. (1982) 'The development of causal reasoning', in FRIEDMAN, W.J. *The Developmental Psychology of Time*, New York, Academic Press.

BURKS, A.W. (Ed) (1970) *Essays on Cellular Automata*, Chicago, University of Illinois Press.

BURRILL, G. (1989) 'Quantitative literacy in the United States', in MORRIS, R. (Ed) *The Teaching of Statistics*, Paris, UNESCO.

CAMPBELL, R. and OLSON, D.R. (1990) 'Children's thinking', in GRIEVE, R. and HUGHES, M. (Eds) *Understanding Children*, Oxford, Basil Blackwell.

References

CAREY, S. (1985) *Conceptual Change in Childhood*, Cambridge, Massachusetts, MIT Press.

CAREY, S. (1986) 'Cognitive science and science education', *American Psychologist*, 41, pp. 1123–30.

CARRAHER, D., CARRAHER, T. and SCHLIEMAN, A. (1985) 'Mathematics in the streets and in the schools', *British Journal of Developmental Psychology*, 3, pp. 21–9.

CENTRAL STATISTICAL OFFICE (1988) *Social Trends 18*, London, Her Majesty's Stationery Office.

CHAMBERS, J.M., CLEVELAND, W.S., KLEINER, B. and TUKEY, P.A. (1983) *Graphical Methods for Data Analysis*, Wadsworth, California.

CHI, M.T.H., GLASER, R. and FARR, M.J. (Eds) (1988) *The Nature of Expertise*, Hillsdale, NJ, Lawrence Erlbaum Associates.

CLEVELAND, W.S. (1985) *The Elements of Graphing Data*, Wadsworth, California.

COMPUTER BASED MODELLING ACROSS THE CURRICULUM PROJECT (1992) *The Modelling Pack: Teacher Resources for Computer Based Modelling in Science, Maths, Geography and Business Education*, Newcastle, NORICC and Hatfield, AU Enterprises Ltd.

COSGROVE, D. (1989) 'Models, description and imagination in geography', in MACMILLAN, B. (Ed) *Remodelling Geography*, Oxford, Basil Blackwell.

COX, M.J. (1983) 'Case study of the application of computer based learning', in RUSHBY, N.J. (Ed) *Computer Based Learning: State of the Art Report*, Maidenhead, Pergamon Infotech.

CRAIK, K.J.W. (1943) *The Nature of Explanation*, Cambridge, Cambridge University Press.

CUMMING, G. and ABBOTT, E. (1988) 'Prolog and expert systems for children's learning', in ERCOLI, P. and LEWIS, R. (Eds) *Artificial Intelligence Tools in Education*, Amsterdam, North Holland, pp. 163–75.

DE KLEER, J. and BROWN, J.S. (1983) 'Assumptions and ambiguities in mechanistic mental models', in GENTNER, D. and STEVENS, A.L. (Eds) *Mental Models*, Hillsdale, NJ, Lawrence Erlbaum Associates.

DE KLEER, J. and BROWN, J.S. (1984) 'A qualitative physics based on confluences', *Artificial Intelligence*, 24, pp. 7–83.

DE KLEER, J. and BROWN, J.S. (1985) 'A qualitative physics based on confluence', in HOBBS, J.R. and MOORE, R.C. (Eds) *Formal theories of the commonsense world*, New Jersey, NJ, Ablex.

DE LANGE, J., KEITEL, C., HUNTLEY, I. and NISS, M. (1993) *Innovation in Maths Education by Modelling and Applications*, Chichester, Ellis Horwood.

DENIS, M. and DUBOIS, D. (1976) 'La présentation cognitive: Quelques modèles récents', *Année Psychologique*, 76, pp. 541–62.

DES AND WELSH OFFICE (1990) *Technology in the National Curriculum*, London, HMSO.

DUFOUR-JANVIER, B., BEDNARZ, N. and BELANGER, M. (1987) 'Pedagogical considerations concerning the problem of representation', in JANVIER, C. (Ed) *Problems of Representation in the Teaching and Learning of Mathematics*, Hillsdale, NJ, Lawrence Erlbaum Associates.

DURKIN, K. (1993) 'The representation of number', in PRATT, C. and GARTON, A.F. (Eds) *Systems of Representation in Children: Development and Use*, Chichester, John Wiley and Sons.

DURKIN, K., SHIRE, B., RIEM, R., CROWTHER, R. and RUTTER, D. (1986) 'The social and linguistic context of early number world use', *British Journal of Developmental Psychology*, 4, pp. 269–88.

DUTTON, W.H. (1987) 'Decision-making in the Information Age: Computer models and public policy', in FINNEGAN, R., SALAMAN, G. and THOMPSON, K. (Eds) *Information Technology: Social Issues*, Sevenoaks, Hodder and Stoughton.

EKELAND, I. (1988) *Mathematics and the Unexpected*, Chicago, Chicago University Press.

EIGEN, M. and WINKLER, R. (1983) *Laws of the Game: How the Principles of Nature Govern Chance* (translation by R. Kimber and R. Kimber), Harmondsworth, Penguin Books.

ENNALS, J.R. (1983) *Beginning micro-Prolog*, Chichester, Ellis Horwood.

ENNALS, J.R. (1984) 'Teaching logic as a computer language in schools', in YAZDANI, M. (Ed) *New Horizons in Educational Computing*, Chichester, Ellis Horwood, pp. 164–77.

ERICKSON, B.H. and NOSANCHUK, T.A. (1979) *Understanding Data*, Milton Keynes, Open University Press.

FALK, R. (1988) 'Conditional probabilities, insights and difficulties', in DAVIDSON, R. and SWIFT, J. (Eds) *Proceedings, Second International Conference on Teaching Statistics*, British Columbia, Canada, University of Victoria, pp. 292–7.

FALK, R. and KONOLD, C. (1990) 'The psychology of learning probability', in GORDON, F.S. and GORDON, S.P. (Eds) *Statistics for the Twenty-First Century*, Washington, Mathematical Association of America.

FISCHBEIN, E. (1989) 'Tacit models and mathematical reasoning', *For the Learning of Mathematics*, 9, pp. 9–14.

FORBUS, K.D. (1983) 'Qualitative reasoning about space and motion', in GENTNER, D. and STEVENS, A.L. (Eds) *Mental Models*, Hillsdale, NJ, Lawrence Erlbaum Associates.

FORBUS, K. (1984) 'Qualitative process theory', *Artificial Intelligence*, 24, pp. 85–168.

FORBUS, K.D. and GENTNER, D. (1990) 'Causal reasoning about quantities', in WELD, D.S. and DE KLEER, J. (Eds) *Readings in Qualitative Reasoning about Physical Systems*, Palo Alto, Morgan Kaufmann, pp. 666–77.

FORMAN, G.F. and PUFALL, P.B. (Eds) (1988) *Constructivism in the Computer Age*, Hillsdale, NJ, Lawrence Erlbaum Associates.

FORRESTER, J.W. (1968) *Principles of Systems*, Cambridge, Massachusetts, MIT Press.

FREEMAN, D. and LEVETT, J. (1986) 'QUEST — two curriculum projects: Perspectives, practice and evidence', *Computers and Education*, 10, pp. 55–60.

FULLAN, M. (1991) *The New Meaning of Educational Change*, London, Cassell.

GALPIN, B. (1989) *Expert Systems in Primary Schools (British Library Research paper 73)*, Boston Spa, British Libraries Board.

References

GARDNER, M. (1970) 'The fantastic combinations of John Conway's new solitaire game "Life"', *Scientific American*, 223, pp. 120–3.

GENTNER, D. and STEVENS, A.L. (Eds) (1983) *Mental Models*, Hillsdale, NJ, Lawrence Erlbaum Associates.

GLEICK, J. (1988) *Chaos: Making a New Science*, London, Heinemann.

GOODFELLOW, T. (1990) 'Spreadsheets: Powerful tools in science education', *School Science Review*, 71, pp. 47–57.

HALL, R., KIBLER, D., WENGER, E. and TRUXAW, C. (1989) 'Exploring the episodic structure of algebra story problem solving', *Cognition and Instruction*, 6, pp. 223–83.

HASSELL, D. (1987) The Role of Modelling Activities in the Humanities Curriculum, with Special Reference to Geography: An Investigative Study, Unpublished Dissertation for Associateship in Education, King's College, London.

HASSELL, D. and WEBB, M. (1990) 'MODUS: The integrated modelling system', *Computers and Education*, 15, pp. 265–70.

HAYES, P.J. (1979) 'The naive physics manifesto', in MICHIE, D. (Ed) *Expert Systems in the Micro-electronic Age*, Edinburgh, Edinburgh University Press, pp. 242–70.

HAYES, P.J. (1985) 'The second naive physics manifesto', in HOBBS, J.R. and MOORE, R.C. *Formal Theories of the Commonsense World*, New Jersey, NJ, Ablex.

HEALY, L. and SUTHERLAND, R. (1991) *Exploring Mathematics with Spreadsheets*, Oxford, Blackwell.

HELLER, J. and HUNGATE, H. (1985) 'Implications for mathematics instruction on scientific problem solving', in SILVER, E. (Ed) *Teaching and Learning Mathematical Problem Solving: Multiple Research Perspectives*, Hillsdale, NJ, LEA.

HENDERSON, M. (1987) *Living with Risk: The British Medical Association Guide*, Chichester, Wiley.

HOBBS, J.R. and MOORE, R.C. (Eds) (1985) *Formal Theories of the Commonsense World*, New Jersey, NJ, Ablex.

HOFSTADTER, D.R. (1985) *MetaMagical Themas*, London, Penguin.

HOUSE, E. (1979) 'Technology versus craft: A ten year perspective on change', in TAYLOR, P.H. *New Directions in Curriculum Studies*, Lewes, Falmer Press.

JAMES, P.D. (1989) *Devices and Desires*, London, Faber and Faber.

JAMES, D.J.G. and MCDONALD, J.J. (1981) *Case Studies in Mathematical Modelling*, Cheltenham, Stanley Thornes.

JOHNSON LAIRD, P.N. (1983) *Mental Models*, Cambridge, Cambridge University Press.

JOSEPH, G.J. (1992) *The Crest of the Peacock: Non-European Roots of Mathematics*, London, Penguin.

KAPUT, J. (1987) 'Towards a theory of symbol use in mathematics', in JANVIER, C. (Ed) *Problems of Representation in the Teaching and Learning of Mathematics*, Hillsdale, NJ, Lawrence Erlbaum Associates.

KEMMIS, S., ATKIN, R. and WRIGHT, E. (1977) *How do Students Learn? Working*

Papers on Computer-Assisted Learning (Occasional Publications No. 5), Norwich, University of East Anglia.

KONOLD, C. (1989) 'Informal conceptions of probability', *Cognition and Instruction*, 6, pp. 59–98.

KONOLD, C. (1991) *ChancePlus: A Computer-based Curriculum for Probability and Statistics. Annual Review Year 2, NSF Grant MDR-8954626. Technical Report SRRI*, Amherst, University of Massachusetts.

KUIPERS, B. (1984) 'Qualitative simulation', *Artificial Intelligence*, 24, pp. 289–338.

KUIPERS, B. (1986) 'Qualitative simulation', *Artificial Intelligence*, 29, pp. 289–338.

KURTZ DOS SANTOS, A.C. (1992) Computational Modelling in Science Education: A Study of Students' Ability to Manage some Different Approaches to Modelling, Unpublished PhD thesis, Institute of Education, University of London.

LAKOFF, G. and JOHNSON, M. (1981) *Metaphors We Live By*, Chicago, Chicago University Press.

LANDWEHR, J.M. and WATKINS, A. (1987) *Exploring Data*, Palo Alto, California, Dale Seymour Publications.

LARKIN, J. (1983) 'The role of problem representation in physics', in GENTNER, D. and STEVENS, A.L. (Eds) *Mental Models*, Hillsdale, NJ, Lawrence Erlbaum Associates.

LAVE, J. (1988) *Cognition in Practice: Mind, Mathematics and Culture in Everyday Life*, Cambridge, Cambridge University Press.

LEONT'EV, A.N. (1981) 'The problem of activity in psychology', in WERTSCH, J.V. (Ed) *The Concept of Activity in Soviet Psychology*, Armond, NY, Sharpe.

LEVY, S. (1989) 'A spreadsheet way of knowledge', in FORESTER, T. (Ed) *Computers in the Human Context: Information Technology, Productivity and People*, Oxford, Basil Blackwell.

LINS, R. (1992) A Framework for Understanding what Algebra Thinking is, Unpublished PhD thesis, Shell Centre for Mathematics Education, Nottingham University.

LYON, D. (1991) 'The information society: Ideology or utopia?', in MACKAY, H., YOUNG, M. and BENYON, J. (Eds) *Understanding Technology in Education*, London, Falmer Press.

MACMILLAN, B. (Ed) (1989) *Remodelling Geography*, Oxford, Basil Blackwell.

MANDINACH, E.B. (1989) 'Model-building and the use of computer simulation of dynamic systems', *Journal of Educational Computing Research*, 5, pp. 221–43.

MANDINACH, E.B. and CLINE, H.F. (1989) 'Applications of simulation and modelling in precollege instruction', *Machine-Mediated Learning*, 3, pp. 189–205.

MANDINACH, E.B. and CLINE, H.F. (in press) *Implementing Technology-based Learning Environments: Systems Thinking and Curriculum Innovation*, Hillsdale, NJ, Lawrence Erlbaum Associates.

MARSH, C. (1988) *Exploring Data*, Cambridge, Polity Press.

MARX, G. (1981a) 'Some simulations of science I', *Physics Education*, 16, pp. 152–8.

MARX, G. (1981b) 'Some simulations of science II', *Physics Education*, 16, pp. 212–17.

MARX, G. (1984a) 'Simulation games in science education', *European Journal of Science Education*, 6, pp. 31–45.

MARX, G. (1984b) *Games Nature Plays*, Budapest, Roland Eotvos University.

MASKILL, R. and CACHAPUZ, A. (1989) 'Learning about the chemistry topic of equilibrium', *International Journal of Science Education*, 11, pp. 57–69.

MASON, J. (1987) 'Representing representing', in JANVIER, C. (Ed) *Problems of Representation in the Teaching and Learning of Mathematics*, Hillsdale, NJ, Lawrence Erlbaum Associates.

MASON, J. (1988) 'Modelling: what do we really want pupils to learn?', in PIMM, D. (Ed) *Mathematics, Teachers and Children*, London, Hodder and Stoughton, pp. 201–5.

MEADOWS, D.H., MEADOWS, D.L., RANDERS, J. and BEHRENS, W.W. (1973) *The Limits to Growth*, New York, Universe Books.

MELLAR, H. (1990) 'Creating alternative realities: Computers, modelling and curriculum change', in NOSS, R. and DOWLING, P. (Eds) *Mathematics versus the National Curriculum*, London, Falmer Press.

MILLER, P.H. and ALOISE, P.A. (1989) 'Young children's understanding of psychological causes of behaviour: A review', *Child Development*, 60, pp. 257–85.

MILLER, R., OGBORN, J., BRIGGS, J. and BROUGH, D. (1992) *Tools for Exploratory Learning Programme End of Award Report: Technical Report 1, Tools — Expressive and Exploratory*, London, University of London.

NEMIROVSKY, R. and RUBIN, A. (1992a) *Students' tendency to assume resemblances between a function and its derivative*, Working Paper 2–92. TERC, Massachusetts Ave, Cambridge, Massachusetts.

NEMIROVSKY, R. and RUBIN, A. (1992b) 'It makes sense if you think about how the graphs work, but in reality . . .', Internal Working Paper, TERC, Massachusetts Ave, Cambridge, Massachusetts.

NICHOL, J. (1988) 'Models, micro-worlds and minds', in NICHOL, J., BRIGGS, J. and DEAN, J. (Eds) *Prolog, Children and Students*, London, Kogan Page.

NISS, M., BLUM, W. and HUNTLEY, I. (1991) *Teaching of Mathematical Modelling and Applications*, Chichester, Ellis Horwood.

NORMAN, D.A. (1983) 'Some observations on mental models', in GENTNER, D. and STEVENS, A.L. (Eds) *Mental Models*, Hillsdale, NJ, Lawrence Erlbaum Associates.

OGBORN, J. (1987) 'Computational modelling in science', in LEWIS, R. and TAGG, E.D. (Eds) *Trends in Computer Assisted Education*, Oxford, Blackwell Scientific.

OGBORN, J. (1990) 'A future for modelling in science education', *Journal of Computer Assisted Learning*, 6, pp. 103–12.

OGBORN, J. and BLISS, J. (1990) 'A Psycho-logic of motion', *European Journal of Psychology of Education*, 5, pp. 379–90.

OGBORN, J., BOOHAN, R. and BROSNAN, T. (1992) *Tools for Exploratory Learning Programme End of Award Report: Technical Report 4, Quantitative Reasoning — Expressive and Exploratory*, London, University of London.

OLSON, J. (1988) *Schoolworlds/Microworlds: Computers and the Culture of the Classroom*, Oxford, Pergamon Press.

PALMER, S.E. (1977) 'Fundamental aspects of cognitive representation', in ROSCH, E. and LLOYD, B.B. (Eds) *Cognition and categorization*, Hillsdale, NJ, Lawrence Erlbaum Associates.

PAUL, A.A. and SOUTHGATE, D.A.T. (1978) *McCance and Widdowson's The Composition of Foods*, London, HMSO.

PEREIRA-MENDOZA, L. and DUNKELS, A. (1989) 'Stem-and-leaf plots in the primary grades', *Teaching Statistics*, 11, pp. 34–7.

PERNER, J. (1991) *Understanding the Representational Mind*, Cambridge, Massachusetts, MIT Press Bradford Books.

PERRY, W.G. (1968) *Intellectual and Ethical Development*, New York, Holt Reinhardt and Winston Inc.

PIAGET, J. (1927) *La Causalité Physique chez l'enfant*, Paris, Alcan.

PIAGET, J. (1963) 'L'explication en psychologie et le parallélisme psycho-physiologique', in FRAISSE, P. and PIAGET, J. (Eds) *Traité de Psychologie Expérimentale*, Paris, Presses Universitaires de France, pp. 121–52.

PIAGET, J. (1968) *Le Structuralisme*, Paris, Presses Universitaires de France (English translation: *Structuralism* (1971), London, Routledge and Kegan Paul).

PIAGET, J. (1974) *Les Explications Causales*, Paris, Presses Universitaires de France.

PLOETZNER, R., SPADA, H., STUMPF, M. and OPWIS, K. (1990) 'Learning qualitative and quantitative reasoning in a microworld for elastic impacts', *European Journal of Psychology of Education*, Special Issue: 'Psychology of Learning Physics', 5, pp. 501–16.

PRATT, C. and GARTON, A.F. (1993) *Systems of Representation in Children: Development and Use*, Chichester, John Wiley and Sons.

RICH, B. (1993) 'The Effect of the Use of Graphing Calculators on Classroom Presentation', *Proceedings of the International Conference on Technology in Mathematics Teaching (TMT 93)*, Birmingham, University of Birmingham, p. 556.

RICHMOND, B. (1987) *An Academic User's Guide to STELLA*, New Hampshire, High Performance Systems Inc.

ROBERTS, N., ANDERSON, D., DEAL, R., GARET, M. and SHAFFER, W. (1983) *Introduction to Computer Simulation: A System Dynamics Modelling Approach*, New York, Addison Wesley.

ROJANO, T. and SUTHERLAND, R. (1992) *A New Approach to Algebra: Results From a Study with 15 year old Algebra-resistant Pupils*, paper presented at Cuatro Simposio International Sobre Investigacion en Educacion Matematica, Ciudad Juarez Mexico.

ROSEBERRY, A. and RUBIN, A. (1990) 'Teaching statistical reasoning with computers', *Teaching Statistics*, 12, pp. 38–42.

RUTHVEN, K. (1990a) *Personal Technology in the Classroom — the NCET Graphic Calculators in Mathematics Project*, Cambridge, University of Cambridge, Department of Education/NCET.

RUTHVEN, K. (1990b) 'The influence of graphic calculator use on translation from graphic to symbolic forms', *Educational Studies in Mathematics*, 21, pp. 431–50.

RUTHVEN, K. (1992) *Graphic Calculators in Advanced Mathematics*, Coventry, NCET.

RUTKOWSKA, J. and COOK, C. (Eds) (1987) *Computers, Cognition and Development*, Chichester, John Wiley and Sons.

SCHIBECI, R. (1989) 'Computers in the chemistry classroom', *Education in Chemistry*, 26, 1, pp. 16–18.

SHULTZ, T.R. (1982) 'Causal reasoning in the social and non social realms', *Canadian Journal of Behavioural Science*, 14, pp. 307–22.

SIMON, H. (1988) 'Teacher professionalism and the National Curriculum', in LAWTON, D. and CHITTY, C. (Eds) *The National Curriculum*, Bedford Way Papers no. 33, London, Institute of Education, University of London and Kogan Page.

SUTHERLAND, R. and ROJANO, T. (1993) 'A spreadsheet approach to solving algebra problems', *Journal of Mathematical Behaviour*, 12, pp. 353–83.

THORNE, M. (1986) *Call in the expert!*, London, CET.

TOFFOLI, T. and MARGOLIS, N. (1987) *Cellular Automata Machines: A New Environment for Modelling*, Cambridge, Massachusetts, MIT Press.

TUFTE, E.R. (1983) *The Visual Display of Quantitative Information*, Connecticut, Graphics Press.

TUKEY, J.W. (1977) *Exploratory Data Analysis*, New York, Addison Wesley.

TURKLE, S. (1984) *The Second Self: Computers and the Human Spirit*, New York, Simon and Shuster.

TURNER, J. (1990) *From Linx to SuperLinx*, Kingston, Kingston University School of Information Systems working paper.

ULAM, S.M. (1970) 'On some mathematical problems connected with patterns of growth of figures', in BURKS, A.W. *Essays on Cellular Automata*, Chicago, University of Illinois Press, pp. 219–31.

UNEP (1987) *Environmental Data Report*, Oxford, Basil Blackwell.

VON GLASERSFELD, E. (1987) 'Preliminaries to any theory of representation', in JANVIER, C. (Ed) *Problems of Representation in the Teaching and Learning of Mathematics*, Hillsdale, NJ, Lawrence Erlbaum Associates.

VYGOTSKY, L. (1934, edited and translated 1962) *Thought and Language*, Cambridge, Massachusetts, MIT Press.

VYGOTSKY, L. (1981) 'The genesis of higher mental functions', in WERTSCH, J.V. (Ed) *The Concept of Activity in Soviet Psychology*, Armond, New York, M.E. Sharpe.

WATERMAN, D.A. (1986) *A Guide to Expert Systems*, Reading, Addison Wesley.

WATSON, D.M. (1987) *Developing CAL: Computers in the Curriculum*, London, Harper and Row.

WEBB, M. (1987) An Investigation of the Opportunities for and Potential Benefits of Computer Based Modelling in Secondary School Science, Unpublished Dissertation for Associateship in Education, Kings College London.

WEBB, M.F. and HASSELL, D. (1988) 'Opportunities for computer based modelling and simulation in secondary education', in LOVIS, F. and TAGG, E.D. (Eds) *Computers in Education*, North Holland, Elsevier Science Publishers.

WEIR, S. (1987) *Cultivating Minds: A LOGO Casebook*, New York, Harper and Row.

WIDEMAN, H.H. and OWSTON, R.D. (1988) 'Student development of an expert system: a case study', *Journal of Computer Based Instruction*, 15, pp. 88–94.

WONG, D. (1987) 'Teaching A-Level physics through microcomputer dynamic modelling: II. Evaluation of teaching', *Journal of Computer Assisted Learning*, 3, pp. 164–75.

Notes on Contributors

Joan Bliss is Reader in Education at King's College London. She studied and worked with Jean Piaget for ten years and whilst in Geneva worked for the Nuffield Mathematics Project, writing diagnostic tasks based on Piaget's work. On returning to England she worked with the Higher Education Learning Project (physics) which looked at undergraduates' motivation to learn. In 1986 she set up at King's College London, the London Mental Models Group. She directed (with Jon Ogborn) the Tools for Exploratory Learning Programme.

Richard Boohan taught science and chemistry in London comprehensive schools before taking up a research post at the University of London Institute of Education. He worked on the Tools for Exploratory Learning Programme, and was co-author of Making Sense of Data: Nuffield Exploratory Data Skills Project. He designed 'WorldMaker', a new modelling system for schools, funded by DES/NCET. He is currently developing ways of using pictorial representations to teach secondary-school pupils about energy and processes of change.

Tim Brosnan taught in schools in West London, and then at St Mary's College Strawberry Hill before joining the Science Department at the Institute of Education in 1988. His research interests include computational modelling, conceptual and curriculum development in chemistry and issues concerned with the public understanding of science. He co-directed the CHATTS Project which looked at the ways that groups of primary-school teachers made sense of the science behind current media issues.

Sue Burns has been Deputy Director of the Nuffield Advanced Mathematics Project at King's College London since 1990. She first worked as a teacher of secondary mathematics and she ran a modelling group for teachers of A-level mathematics. She did research into the role of a Newtonian microworld in helping students model motion and later worked as project officer on the Computer Based Modelling across the Curriculum Project.

Margaret Cox is Senior Lecturer in Educational Computing at King's College London. She began developing educational software in the 1970s for undergraduate students at Surrey University. She was later Director of the Computers in the Curriculum Project at King's College for ten years, and recently co-directed the

DfE's project evaluating the impact of information technology on children's learning. She is now a co-director of the Modus Project. Her other research interests include the role of computers in schools, and the effects of new technologies in education.

David Hassell is Programme Manager for Software with the National Council for Educational Technology, where his chief interests are in improving the quality of software available to education and improving its availability. Previous to this he taught geography in schools for nine years before becoming programme officer at the Advisory Unit for Microtechnology in Education in Hatfield. He acted as project officer on the Computer Based Modelling across the Curriculum Project.

Harvey Mellar is Senior Lecturer in Educational Computing at the Institute of Education. He worked on both the Tools for Exploratory Learning Programme and the Computer Based Modelling across the Curriculum Project. His other chief research interests are in the area of computer-mediated communications.

Rob Miller began his career as a mathematics teacher in a London comprehensive. After a sabbatical year in which he took a further degree in computer science, he became involved in research in educational computing at Imperial College London working on the Tools for Exploratory Learning Programme. He is currently completing a PhD in AI and temporal reasoning at Imperial College.

Jon Ogborn is Professor of Science Education at the Institute of Education, University of London. He has been responsible for developing a number of computational modelling systems, and (with Joan Bliss) directed the Tools for Exploratory Learning Programme. His other research interests include the nature of common-sense reasoning.

Haralambos Sakonidis is a Lecturer in Mathematics Education at the University of Thrace, Greece. He is a mathematician and mathematics educator who has been involved in research in the language of mathematics and in modelling for educational purposes at King's College London. His particular interests focus on the means of communicating mathematical and especially algebraic ideas to children and the psychological and sociological dimensions of these means.

Ian Stevenson is currently lecturing in mathematics at Edge Hill College of Higher Education. From 1990–2 he was a Development Officer with the Computer-Based Modelling Across the Curriculum Project based at the Institute of Education in London. He spent ten years teaching mathematics in London schools prior to this. His interests include the use of computers in teaching and learning mathematics, computer-based mathematical modelling and the philosophy of mathematics and mathematics education.

Rosamund Sutherland is Senior Lecturer in Mathematics Education at the Institute of Education. Her work is concerned with the use of computers for teaching and learning mathematics, in which area she had directed a number of research projects. Her particular interest is in investigating the ways in which we can identify and take advantage of pupils' informal problem-solving approaches whilst supporting them to make links between these approaches and more formal methods.

Chris Tompsett is Deputy Director for the postgraduate programme of the School of Information Systems at Kingston University. His teaching responsibilities within the area of artificial intelligence include knowledge engineering and qualitative modelling. Previously he taught for ten years in schools, and later set up the Information Technology Development Unit at Kingston College of Further Education, where he coordinated a series of projects, applying knowledge-based techniques to both education and training.

Mary Webb taught science in primary and secondary schools for ten years before moving to the Advisory Unit for Microtechnology in Education in Hertfordshire. She is coordinator of the Modus Project, a joint venture with King's College London, which has undertaken research and developed materials to support computer-based modelling in schools. Current research interests include modelling in science education and the development of computer-based modelling skills.

Peter Wilder taught mathematics in a secondary school in North London for eight years. He is now Senior Lecturer in Mathematics Education at Bedford College of Higher Education and a visiting research fellow at King's College London. He has particular research interests in statistical education in secondary schools and the teaching and learning of probability.

Peter Winbourne works at South Bank University where he is Senior Lecturer in Mathematics Education. He worked as a teacher of mathematics in London schools for fifteen years before becoming an advisory teacher in the London Borough of Sutton. Since then he has worked as mathematics project officer for the National Council for Educational Technology and as a lecturer and research officer at King's College London.

Index